AIR SUPERIORITY
OPERATIONS

Brassey's Air Power: Aircraft,
Weapons Systems and Technology Series

VOLUME 5

Brassey's Air Power:

Aircraft, Weapons Systems and Technology Series

General Editor: AIR VICE MARSHAL R. A. MASON, CB, CBE, MA, RAF

This new series, consisting of eleven volumes, is aimed at the international officer cadet or junior officer and is appropriate to the student, young professional and interested amateur seeking sound basic knowledge of the technology of air forces. Each volume, written by an acknowledged expert, identifies the responsibilities and technical requirements of its subject and illustrates it with British, American, Russian, major European and Third World examples drawn from recent history and current events. The series is similar in approach to the highly successful Sea Power and Land Warfare series. Each volume, excluding the first, has self-test questions and answers.

Brassey's Titles of Related Interest

AIR SUPERIORITY OPERATIONS

Air Vice Marshal John R. Walker, CBE, AFC, RAF

BRASSEY'S (UK)
(a member of the Maxwell Pergamon Publishing Corporation plc)
LONDON · OXFORD · WASHINGTON · NEW YORK · BEIJING
FRANKFURT · SÃO PAULO · SYDNEY · TOKYO · TORONTO

U.K. (Editorial)	Brassey's Defence Publishers Ltd., 24 Gray's Inn Road, London WC1X 8HR, England
(Orders)	Brassey's Defence Publishers Ltd., Headington Hill Hall, Oxford OX3 0BW, England
U.S.A. (Editorial)	Pergamon-Brassey's International Defense Publishers, Inc., 8000 Westpark Drive, Fourth Floor, McLean, Virginia 22102, U.S.A.
(Orders)	Pergamon Press, Inc., Maxwell House, Fairview Park, Elmsford, New York 10523, U.S.A.
PEOPLE'S REPUBLIC OF CHINA	Pergamon Press, Room 4037, Qianmen Hotel, Beijing, People's Republic of China
FEDERAL REPUBLIC OF GERMANY	Pergamon Press GmbH, Hammerweg 6, D-6242 Kronberg, Federal Republic of Germany
BRAZIL	Pergamon Editora Ltda, Rua Eça de Queiros, 346, CEP 04011, Paraiso, São Paulo, Brazil
AUSTRALIA	Pergamon-Brassey's Defence Publishers Pty Ltd., P.O. Box 544, Potts Point, N.S.W. 2011, Australia
JAPAN	Pergamon Press, 5th Floor, Matsuoka Central Building, 1-7-1 Nishishinjuku, Shinjuku-ku, Tokyo 160, Japan
CANADA	Pergamon Press Canada Ltd., Suite No. 271, 253 College Street, Toronto, Ontario, Canada M5T 1R5

First edition 1989

Library of Congress Cataloging in Publication Data

Walker, J. R.
Air superiority/John R. Walker. – 1st ed.
p. cm. – (Brassey's air power; v.5)
Includes index.
1. Fighter plane combat. 2. Fighter planes. I. Title.
II. Series.   UG700.W34 1989   358.4'3 – dc 19
88-39983

British Library Cataloguing in Publication Data

Walker, J. R. (John R.)
Air superiority. – (Brassey's air power: aircraft, weapons
systems and technology series: v5)
1. Air operations   I. Title   358.4'3
ISBN 0-08-035819-5 Hardcover
ISBN 0-08-035818-7 Flexicover

Printed in Great Britain by BPCC Wheatons Ltd., Exeter

Preface

IT IS a privilege to have been asked to write this, my second volume in the Brassey's Air Power series, the first being *Air-to-Ground Operations*. As before, I have attempted to stay within the bounds of my brief as closely as possible and this work is directed at the junior officer starting out on his career and at the interested civilian. I am well conscious that the experienced warrior, or those in the aerospace industry with expert knowledge, may find a more weighty tome to their taste. But their requirements are met elsewhere and more technical books are available; what is less easy to find is the *primer* which attempts to explain in straightforward terms what the three-dimensional air battle is all about and how a *mind-set* can be developed to understand better some of its intricacies. This book attempts to be such a primer.

It is not claimed to be the definitive work; for no better reason than in this field there is no such thing. Certain factors are common to all interpretations of the air combat scene – the physics, for example – but thereafter what makes an *ace* as distinct from a mere also ran is the way those physical laws can be orchestrated in the highly stressful and increasingly lethal air combat battlefield. It will be suggested later that science plays an increasing part in success and failure in air combat, but it is far from a black and white matter and there is still that need for artistry if fame – or better, longevity – is to be achieved.

Some of the techniques outlined here are those which the author has found to be a useful means of visualising the three-dimensional battle from the cockpit. They are by no means exhaustive of the methods available and the fighter pilot will, with experience, develop his own tricks of assessing the dynamics of the battle. Until he does, he should read as widely as possible, for it is a field in which no one source has the monopoly of good ideas and one man's visualisation of a concept or tactic may strike a chord better than another.

Some never will make the ranks of the fighter pilots, for although it is popularly asserted that, given enough training, even the proverbial 'grandmother' can be taught to fly, it does not follow that she, or many others, can be taught the natural affinity for closure speed and angular change, or for projecting the battle forward those few precious seconds, which has to be second nature to the fighter pilot in combat.

The temptation to catalogue all the various fighter manoeuvres has been resisted, albeit with some difficulty, in order to concentrate on the basics on which the variations are played. Similarly, there has been little attempt to follow a combat through turn after twisting turn, not only because it makes for confusing and dull reading but also because the variations are so immense that the exercise would be at best an indulgence. The first manoeuvre in a combat may be pre-planned – if it is indeed the *first* manoeuvre in the combat – but thereafter the very pre-planning could prove to be the downfall and an extemporaneous performance is called for. In some respects an air combat primer must bear some passing resemblance to a like work on chess.

It is hoped that the reader will get a little more from this volume than merely an insight into fighter combat manoeuvres. It may suggest to him that, as the nineties approach, there are some major changes appearing in the traditional air combat scene. As tactical aviation went into decline on the advent of the nuclear age in the fifties and sixties, fighter aircraft lost much of their manoeuvrability. In the late sixties, Vietnam proved that to be a false path and it was in the skies over Hanoi and Haiphong that the current series of highly agile fighters were conceived; fighters with high lift and high thrust, the combination of which being the secret of success in the air combat arena of the seventies, eighties and into the start of the nineties, an arena which sees the tight, high 'G' *furball*. In the last decade of the Century, however, the importance of the Beyond Visual Range (BVR) battle will start to make itself felt and radar range, missile reach and stealth may take on importance exceeding that of high agility. As the lethality of the battlefield increases, the operational advantage may go to he who can stay *disengaged* and fight from *sanctuary*.

If this offering can assist the interested civilian in framing some pertinent questions about the defence scene then it will have served a purpose. Perhaps the reader can look for the pattern of Soviet aircraft development running through the Flogger, Foxbat, Foxhound, Fulcrum and Flanker to . . . what? What will the MiG-2000 look like? What will be its design philosophy? What operational doctrine will it fulfil? How will that compare with the US Advanced Tactical Fighter and Advanced Combat Aircraft? Where do the European Fighter Aircraft, the Rafael, the Swedish Grippen and the Israeli Lavi fit into this doctrine or philosophy?

The civilian should be interested in this, particularly if he is a taxpayer. Military equipment is escalating in cost far faster than can be excused solely by fiscal inflation. Technology is offering greater capabilities and operational requirement staffs the world over are asking for what is on offer, but there is a heavy cost to be paid and difficult choices to be made. An expensive aircraft which has had only a few corners cut in the interests of economy could become easy prey to the super-expensive aircraft which has just that edge on performance which makes all the difference. Where do the cost-effectiveness curves cross? It is an important point to determine for it is from there that judgement has to be applied and that must make some allowance for the fact that in warfare, even of the most modern kind, numbers still count.

An extension of that debate, outside the corridors of power, is a healthy thing in a democracy, not just because the democratic system should remain accountable to those it serves, but also because well-founded and open examination of the arguments, for and against, keep staffs on their toes and decisions more justifiable. That cannot be a bad thing.

1988   JRW

About the Author

Air Vice Marshal John Walker is currently serving as the Deputy Chief of Staff for Operations and Intelligence at Headquarters, Allied Air Forces Central Europe and is internationaly recognised as a leading authority in the field of air power strategy, operations, and tactics.

After tours in fighter, fighter-bomber and reconnaissance squadrons he served as a tactical trials pilot on the Air Fighting Development Squadron of the Central Fighter Establishment. Thereafter he spent two years on exchange duties with the 12th Air Force of the USAF Tactical Air Command.

After commanding the Offensive Support Cell of the Central Tactics and Trials Organisation he was selected to introduce into service the Jaguar aircraft. He commanded the Operational Conversion Unit for its first three years before assuming command of RAF Lossiemouth and, later, RAF Bruggen in Germany. After a tour as Group Captain Offensive Operations in Headquarters RAF Germany he rejoined the Central Tactics and Trials Organisation as its commander.

After attending the Royal College of Defence Studies he was appointed as the Director of Forward Policy (RAF) at the Ministry of Defence. On promotion he was appointed to the dual-hatted post of Senior Air Staff Officer at RAF Strike Command and the Deputy Chief of Staff, Operations and Intelligence, UK Air Forces.

John Walker has been awarded the Queen's Commendation for Valuable Service in the Air for his work at the Central Fighter Establishment, the Air Force Cross for his introduction into service of the Jaguar, and was made CBE after his tour in command at Bruggen. He has twice represented the RAF in international air-gunnery competitions, and has been an aerobatic display pilot on both the Hunter and the Jaguar. He is a regular contributor to professional journals and other publications, and is in demand as a lecturer on air power. His two previous books, *The Future of Air Power* and *Air-to-Ground Operations* have established him amongst the first rank of authors in his speciality.

Contents

List of Figures

List of Plates

1.

Introduction

AIR SUPERIORITY is one of the most widely used, and misused, terms in the airman's vocabulary. It has a ring about it and conjures up pictures of total domination of the skies. It lends itself to the macho image which, despite being proved unnecessary by so many of the really great fighter pilots, is still that to which all budding combatants are expected to aspire. Air Superiority fits the image – the image fits Air Superiority.

The truth of the matter is some way removed from the idealistic view. It is almost impossible in the real world to dominate the skies completely. There is no black or white of the matter, only a wide spectrum of greys, and it is in this less pure area that the debate on, and the practice of, air superiority has to take place.

Airmen are reluctant to concede that it is not only aircraft which contest the freedom of the skies, and popular perceptions interfere with rational argument unless great care, and not a little discipline, is brought to bear on the discussion. Certainly the older generation of airmen, brought up on the heroic exploits of W. E. Johns' character Biggles, found their enjoyment, and perhaps even a little of their inspiration, in his daring deeds against the nation's enemies with the manned aircraft a major player in the drama.

To them it would have been unthinkable, in addition to being dull reading, if that battle had been fought with the switches of an electronic warfare equipment, or with a missile engagement far beyond visual range, or with lasers, or with missiles fired from the ground. Such combat is far more the preserve of the later generation whose early days on science fiction have prepared them much better mentally for the modern perceptions.

Total domination of the skies is not a reality. Air superiority exists when one side can achieve its purpose while frustrating the purpose of the other side. This does not mean that the purpose is achieved without loss. In any modern war, the sky will be a dangerous place and losses will be sustained by both sides; what matters is whether those losses can be kept sufficiently under control to enable the purpose to be achieved before the resources or, as important, the *will* runs out.

The whole business of air superiority has been influenced by the very effectiveness of modern aircraft. Wars start with aircraft on either side numbered in hundreds; in a major war between NATO and the Warsaw Pact, the figure will run into the thousands. In the past, such numbers were essential to achieve the aim but weapon effectiveness was poor then and, of even greater importance, aiming accuracy left much to be desired. Numbers were required for the same reason as the shotgun fires many pellets; the individual accuracy was insufficient to give high probabilities of kill.

Now, however, the last remaining aircraft of a desperate force, penetrating with a

1

nuclear weapon, could cost an opponent his capital city. A single aircraft, armed with a tactical nuclear weapon, can deliver to its target a weight of attack greater than the total delivered by Bomber Command of the RAF throughout the five and a half years of World War Two. What is 'air superiority' if that cannot be prevented?

Some will argue that air power as conceived by the early prophets, and so regularly derided over the years, has only ever been demonstrated twice; once over Hiroshima and the other over Nagasaki. In both cases one aircraft and one weapon closely equated to one city and that, even to the jaundiced, is an impressively high exchange ratio. At a time when the world was used to seeing the aircraft used as the *bludgeon* in forces of hundreds, and occasionally over Germany in thousands, it showed that the aircraft could be a bludgeon as a *singleton*. The awfulness of those nuclear attacks, which brought the Japanese to the peace table, should not be allowed to divert attention completely from the purely *conventional* attack on Rotterdam in 1940 which had exactly that effect upon the Netherlands.

But bludgeon it still needed to be because, although the power of the weapon was being so greatly improved, the accuracy of delivering it was still not impressive. After the Vietnam conflict renewed the interest in accuracy, there has been a steady improvement over the last two decades and accuracies measured in single numbers of metres can now be achieved. With such accuracy, large warheads are unnecessary for all but the largest of targets and the age of air power, using the *rapier* rather than the bludgeon, is close. When that age will dawn will be governed as much, if not more, by the acceptance of new and exciting concepts and doctrine than by any delay in the availability of the technology.

It means, in its turn, that the effectiveness of smaller numbers of aircraft is not restricted solely to those carrying nuclear loads. Even conventional armament delivered to such accuracy can have a great effect on a variety of targets. The Thanh Hoa bridge in North Vietnam, which achieved such notoriety for the losses it caused to aircraft attempting to destroy it with conventional bombs, was finally dropped by a small force using the newly developed laser-guided-bombs for no loss. The cost-effectiveness arguments for modern weaponry could well start with this operation as a benchmark.

The greatly increased effectiveness of small numbers of aircraft makes the achievement of air superiority all the more difficult when considered in its definition as, inter alia, 'frustrating the enemy from achieving his ends' because the smaller the force which can have a great effect the more difficult it is to prevent that effect being achieved. If the enemy is to be frustrated, however, and while accepting that there is no such thing as total air superiority either way, an effort has to be made to impose the *will* upon the other side. Air superiority, such as it may be, has to be contested.

The nature of the means by which it is contested can vary widely. A surface-to-air (SAM) missile defence about a target area may contest air superiority, even if it is over a local and restricted area. It may be far from total air superiority, in that aircraft can still penetrate but can do so safely only if they operate above a certain height, or faster than a certain speed, or by performing some evasive manoeuvre. It can be argued that, as the aircraft had penetrated the target area, the SAM was ineffective, but that may be too pure an assessment. If, by being forced to operate beyond the speed and height ideal for the delivery of the weapons carried, the accuracy of the attack was degraded to such an extent that instead of ten bombs on target only five hit, what is the balance of 'air superiority'?

What if, in a night attack, a modern all-weather aircraft, using its terrain-following and ground mapping radar, experiences ground jamming on its radar frequency which forces the pilot to fly the aircraft at a higher than normal altitude? This puts the aircraft within the acquisition radar of SAM systems, resulting in a higher loss rate for the force. Where is the balance of 'air superiority' in this instance? The offensive aircraft are still penetrating and the bombs, at least some of them, are falling on the target area, but at the cost of increased attrition. Attrition mathematics are an unmerciful discipline and although high attrition may be accepted on the first raid, and conceivably on the second, what about the third? The electronic counter-measures may not have completely defended the target on the first raid but they could have completely defended the target by the third.

Aircraft therefore are not the only weapons in the battle for air superiority, but they undoubtedly feature strongly in the conflict. They do so in two forms which, it has to be admitted, have to be differentiated between with a degree of mental gymnastics. The airman himself will be convinced he knows the difference between the two, but it is not hard to get him to admit after gentle probing that his conviction about the difference springs as much from instinct as from intellect.

The difference is shown in the terms 'air superiority fighter' and 'air defence fighter'. The air defence fighter is generally accepted to be one engaged in the air defence battle against intruders intent on an offensive purpose; in other words, bomber destroyers. The Spitfires intercepting Dorniers and Heinkels in 1940 were 'air defence fighters' and they were engaged in the air intercept mission. Although the Dorniers and Heinkels could, and often did, evade they were not engaging in 'air combat' as such. Indeed, an offensive aircraft full of fuel and armament on its way to the target and its primary purpose is unlikely to be interested in getting into a fight with an aircraft much better placed to distinguish itself. This then seemingly gives a firm starting point; 'air defence fighters' engage in 'air intercept' and shoot down non-combatant 'bombers'. Said in as many words, it sounds fun!

Unfortunately, as the Spitfires found at times to their disquiet, either the blips on the early radar tubes did not turn out to be Dorniers but rather Messerschmitts or, to get at the Dorniers, the escorting Messerschmitts had to be overcome first. The line between air intercept and air combat – or 'superiority' – is therefore a fine one and, making the discussion more difficult, is getting finer.

The reason for this is the popularity of the 'fighter-bomber'. Many modern fighter-bombers are derived from pure fighter designs. The F-16 is a fine air combat machine yet is used extensively in the fighter-bomber role. The F-15, built under the slogan 'not-a-pound-for-air-to-ground', is entering service in the F-15E 'Strike Eagle' version not only as an excellent offensive aircraft but also retaining impressive fighter attributes. Consequently, on the modern battlefield, the air intercept fighter may well engage a fighter-bomber penetrating to the target with a heavy offensive load. In such a circumstance the intercepting fighter, configured for the intercept mission, may have great advantage in terms of weight and speed over the heavily-loaded penetrator, but by a push of the jettison button on the fighter-bomber, the performance comparison could be transformed and the nature of the fight changed immediately from air intercept to air combat.

It is with air combat between fighters, or fighter types, that this volume is concerned – the combat between high performance aircraft where both are seeking dominance of the sky, or 'air superiority'; in a phrase, dog-fighting. Another volume in this series* deals in greater depth with air intercept, which has its own science and techniques. Clearly, there will be some measure of overlap because the beyond-visual-range (BVR) missile features in the armament of both the air intercept fighter and the air combat fighter, and the modern dog-fight starts long before the first visual acquisition of the enemy. As will be shown later, the BVR battle has to be, at the very least, 'survived' before any close-in combat can be engaged.

Other methods of attaining air superiority will not be dealt with. Some have already been mentioned, using SAM and electronic warfare for example, and the most important of the alternative methods of attaining superiority over the opposing air force, the offensive counter air campaign, where the battle is fought over airfields and aircraft on the ground, is dealt with in Volume 2 of this series on Air-to-Ground Operations.† This is not to suggest that they are in any way inferior in the contribution they make to the air battle, for they are a major part of the complete campaign. Indeed, the Israeli attack on the Egyptian Air Force in 1967 was so devastating that, within a day, that force was effectively out of the war. The shock waves from that demonstration of the power of pre-emptive air attack were such that within 18 months hardened aircraft shelters were being constructed in the Warsaw Pact, followed by NATO shortly afterwards. Falling from that, in turn, was a complete reappraisal of the doctrine for attacking airfields and a programme of weapon development to match it was instituted, which is still in full swing today. When a combat aircraft spends less than 2 per cent of its life in the air, and when it is so vulnerable when out of its element and on the ground, it is easy to see why such priority is given to the counter air campaign.

The history of the development of air combat will be looked at first. Although modern technology has offered a range of new options, many of the effects merely offer better ways of doing things which are well established techniques or tactics from the past. There is a tendency for tacticians to search forever for the new technique; surrounded by scientific colleagues regularly crying 'Eureka'. There are those who believe that the airman should emulate them. A considerable amount of nugatory effort can result, for the airman has been blessed in the past with some – although it must be admitted far too few – far-sighted prophets and the general principles of air warfare are well known and straightforward. Further, there have been previously many excellent innovative ideas which have failed, not through any fault in the rationale or the technique, but rather because the technology of the day has been unable to put the right equipment into the hands of the operator. Now that the technologist can provide, it is a waste to invest original thought when the past has lessons to teach and ideas waiting to be exploited. The airman could, in any event, do worse than to take note of the advice tendered by Walter Chrysler when he exhorted his young engineers,

'Let your imagination soar, and then engineer down to reality.'

To understand air combat, it is necessary to have a passing familiarity with the

*Air Defence by Group Captain M. B. Elsam FBIM RAF.
†Air-to-Ground Operations by Air Vice Marshal J. R. Walker CBE AFC RAF

tools of the trade. The aircraft will be examined in the form which is of interest to the fighter pilot, that is, as a performing machine. Air combat is a scientific pursuit and the days of winning combats by the 'seat-of-the pants' is long gone for all but the unnaturally gifted. There was a time, not that long ago, when the winner of a practice dog-fight was the pilot who won the debrief; the man with the extrovert personality, mobile hands – usually equally mobile mouth – and not without a little rank. It was a brave, and not a little foolhardy, Pilot Officer who claimed from the back of the room to have shot his Flight Commander before that experienced gentleman had shot him! Now there are excellent training aids in service which record for posterity every move in a fight, even to the point of indicating weapon shots and assessing their success. Combats can be flown in dome simulators where the fight is decided without leaving the ground, or on the highly instrumental air combat ranges where the battle is recorded as the real aircraft fight in the skies. It has made life much more stressful for the big-mouthed Flight Commander but occasionally highly satisfying for the fledgling fighter pilot!

Weapons and radar will be examined, for they are equally part of the tool kit. In the BVR battle, radar becomes the eyes of the pilot; without it, he is blind and has all the vulnerability of the blind man in a hostile place. It is not without reason that the eyes are man's primary sensor and outside their range radar takes their place. Weapons, on the other hand, are the all-important factor. A fighter pilot's task is to kill other aircraft and no amount of distinguished flying will accomplish that without the killing mechanism itself – the weapon.

The weapon, nevertheless, has to be brought to bear and that is where the fighter manoeuvres apply. They will be examined to show what options are open. Fighter manoeuvres consist of a few basic principles which are then used in an extemporaneous fashion to produce the result against an opponent attempting to do the same. There is a similarity with ballet. There are a number of basic steps and movements which are the preserve of all ballet dancers; the great ones are those who combine the basics to produce a result more perfect and artistic than others. So it is with combat; the better 'artist' wins, but all have, or should have, knowledge of the fundamentals.

Formation tactics are a more complex field and to cover all the variations possible to a number of aircraft would take a volume far larger than this but there are some basic rules and these will be touched upon. What cannot be ignored is that the sky is rarely empty and it is seldom that the aircraft which is in sight is the one which causes grief. Studies of a series of wars have shown that 80 per cent of the aircraft killed in combat have been claimed by aircraft which they had not seen; a study of gunsight film taken during another series of combats has shown that at the moment of strike 70 per cent of the aircraft had less than 30 degrees of bank applied – hardly harsh evasion. This fact will be repeated in this volume – without apology – because it is one of the most important things a budding fighter pilot must realise. Formation tactics are important because the human being is largely restricted to sight in his forward hemisphere and he designs his aircraft to allow him to do so. Even his radar is generally restricted to a forward view, yet, to date, his area of greatest threat has been to the rear where aircraft design and human physiology place him at a disadvantage. While this remains the case, a fighter pilot's life can rest firmly in the hands of his wingman – and vice-versa.

Operations will be looked at because the fighter pilot is not the arbiter of his own fate. If the battle is fought incorrectly by the higher command, and the aircraft used in a way to give advantage to the enemy, then no amount of skill and daring will make up for the disadvantage which accrues. This does not mean necessarily that the higher command needs to interfere with the battle once contact is gained. By holding alert states for too long at too high a state, a small modern force can be worn down before the battle starts. Combat Air Patrol (CAP) positions too far out can reduce a force to exhaustion in a remarkably short time. In the conduct of air operations there is an element of the chess game – or is it poker?

Man and his training will complete the volume. Training is becoming an expensive business; it now costs the Royal Air Force close to £3 million to train a fast-jet pilot to the stage where he reaches his first squadron. He may wait another three to six months thereafter before he is deemed to be combat-ready, depending on the role. The selection process is thorough but choosing the 18-year-old who is going to succeed as a 21-year-old graduate from flight training is difficult and is resistant to any reliable quantification. There will be no attempt here to suggest any archetypal fighter pilot because history has already proved that there is no such thing. It would be difficult even to suggest the base parentage of any future 'clone' because good fighter pilots come in all shapes and sizes. What can be looked for is a few of the common qualities and they will be seen to be not all in accord with the norms in western society at the moment.

Some believe that the first RAF squadrons emerged from the cavalry regiments and that their use in reconnaissance on the early battlefield equated most closely to that arm. The argument is sometimes extended to comparing the relationship between the cavalry officer and his horse to that of the fighter pilot and his aircraft. At this point the argument breaks down. If either aircraft or pilot is proved defective then the combination fails together; the cavalry officer was better protected by an intelligent horse!

PLATE 1. One of the few remaining air worthy *Spitfires* taxies out to engage its old enemy the *Messerschmidt Me-109* at the Bex airshow in Switzerland. The fuel injected engine of the Me-109 gave it an advantage in negative 'G' manoeuvring. The *Spitfire's* beautiful elliptical wing gave it the edge in turning performance. In both aircraft the view to the rear was far from outstanding. *(Photo: Author)*

PLATE 2. Another approach to the problem. The cranked wing *Corsair* was one of the better United States carrier aircraft to see service in World War Two. Unlike the water-cooled in-line engines of the *Spitfire* and the *Me-109*, the large radial engines had their advantage in air-cooling, so doing away with radiators, piping and yet another vulnerable system. The penalty was increased frontal area and the consequent drag raise. Radial engines seemed to know no bounds before they were replaced by the turbine engine. One design had 28 massive cylinders arranged in four banks of seven. It powered the Stratocruiser airliner. (*Photo: Author*)

PLATE 3.   This picture from the United States Air Force Art Collection depicts a duel between an *F-86 Sabre* and a *MiG-15* over the Korean countryside. The design of the *F-86 Sabre* was heavily influenced by the combat experience of World War Two and the bubble canopy was an excellent feature of this aircraft. A well-flown *Sabre* was difficult to 'bounce' because of the excellent visibility from the cockpit. Although, on paper, a superior performing machine, the *MiG* met its match because of the excellent handling qualities of the *Sabre* and because of the greatly superior air combat training of the US pilots. The United States had a twelve-to-one exchange ratio in their favour. (*Courtesy of United States Air Force*)

PLATE 4. Before the Korean war had even started 'studies' had, yet again, suggested that air combat was on the wane and the need was for specialist interceptors in the emerging missile age. Hence the *F-4 Phantom*, designed to a United States Navy specification and arguably one of the most successful fighters ever built. It has distinguished itself in many roles: strike, attack, reconnaissance, anti-SAM, air defence fighter – and still it serves. Notice in this picture of *F-4Ds*, taken against a backdrop of the Californian Sierra Nevadas, how the crew are faired into the fuselage. After all, why does an interceptor want to look backwards?

(Photo: Author)

PLATE 5. The *Phantom* Saga. An RF-4C reconnaissance *Phantom* of the West German Air Force. (*Photo: Author*)

PLATE 6. . . . and a 'Wild Weasel' aircraft of the United States Air Force engaged in SAM Suppression. This model is the *F-4G* and can carry the new *Harm* anti-radiation missile . . . *(Photo: Author)*

PLATE 7. . . . While the United Kingdom version, the *FGR2*, endured the transplant of the Rolls-Royce Spey, afterburned by-pass engines, which required major surgery both at intake and exhaust, yet still the Phantom took all in its stride . . . *(Photo: Author)*

PLATE 8. . . . While the German F-4F, a model with an internal Gatling gun mounted under the nose, is due to receive a radar update which will equip it to acquit itself well up into the next century . . . *(Photo: Author)*

2.
History

Those who do not remember the past are condemned to relive it.
Santayana

IT was not only the military mind which was dubious about the value of the new-fangled aeroplane. At various times scientists, philosophers and politicians alike predicted that the heavier-than-air machine was little but a passing phenomenon. As a group, they were not to be discounted lightly for amongst their number were some important men. Members of government, like Simon Newcombe in the United States, confidently predicted that,

'There are no known substances or forms of force, that can be united in a practical manner by which man shall fly long distances through the air'.

Within the year, the Wright brothers' flight at Kitty Hawk both re-emphasised the dangers of prediction and also showed that history has a sense of humour.

The first acknowledged use of the aircraft as a war machine was as a natural extension to the use to which balloons had been put many years before. Despite standing upright man is still a relatively small animal and, combined with the fact that the world on which he lives is inconveniently round, the distance he can see is severely reduced. He has sought to ease his difficulty and the back of the horse – or even the elephant – has been a favourite perch for commanders throughout the ages. The manoeuvre for high ground, enshrined in land force doctrine even today, is less to do with it being easier to fight going down-hill rather than up, than it is to do with being able to see better. Contemporary prints of the great battles centre on commanders resplendent on the backs of chargers and it is sometimes easy to neglect to note that the chargers are usually standing, patiently, on the top of a hill.

To the armies and navies of the world, the aircraft offered a higher hill and a taller mast and it was in this secondary purpose that the aircraft was accepted. Reconnaissance was the first role for the aircraft in war and it remains an important task today for, despite the best efforts of science and technology, the height factor in reconnaissance systems is still vital. The satellite, well known for its use in reconnaissance and surveillance, shows this in the extreme.

Air combat had to wait for some time before appearing on the scene because bombing was the next role for the aircraft. In the Italian-Turkish war, a crude hand-held device was thrown over the side of an aircraft in Libya in 1912 and the report afterwards talked enthusiastically of the confusion so caused, particularly that it had 'scared the horses'. It was as late as 5 October, 1914, more than a decade after the Wrights' triumph, that the first aircraft was recorded as shot down in an aerial encounter. A French rear-engined Voisin, piloted by Sergeant Joseph Franz was brought alongside a German Aviatix and his observer, Corporal Louis Quinault, shot down the unsuspecting aircraft with his machine gun. The poor German may have been truly 'unsuspecting' as stories from those early days tell of cheery waves exchanged by reconnaissance pilots whose paths crossed as they went about their business, despite that business being for different sides. To have such cameraderie rudely shattered by being shot-down must have been seen if not as a fatal, certainly as a traumatic, change of style.

The impetus for the development of the fighter did not come from any great desire to command the skies *per se*. The Generals on the ground had their own awful problems with which to contend and they could quite do without extending the theatre of war above them. The air combat aircraft emerged because of the effectiveness of the aircraft in the reconnaissance role; reconnaissance in the accepted sense, that is the detection and reporting of the movement of enemy forces, and also in a role which was so to transform the battlefield – that of artillery spotting. The use of aircraft to correct artillery fire allowed the laying of the devastatingly effective barrages for which the Great War became renowned; indeed, it has been called the Great Artillery War and the part aircraft played in that was substantial.

Once the threat of the aircraft, as the spy in the sky, had become recognised, the race was on to perfect the means of countering it. Even at this early stage, there was advice available from some of those far-sighted prophets of air power. The Italian Giulio Douhet had put his mind to the *'Fundamentals of Air Strategy'* as early as 1909, and parts of that work are as applicable today as they were then. He is remembered more for his advocacy of strategic bombing but he had a much wider appreciation of air warfare. Before the first ever bombing raid, and some long time before the first 'air combat', Douhet had this to say about the new medium:

> 'The sky is about to become another battlefield no less important than the battlefields on land and sea. In order to conquer the air, it is necessary to deprive the enemy of all means of flying, by striking him in the air, at his bases of operations, or at his production centres. We had better get accustomed to this idea and prepare ourselves.'

In peace, democracies find such advice unwholesome and Douhet was not alone in being branded as a trouble-maker. As a result, most of the European nations caught up in the Great War went into that conflict naked both in effective air power and in effective thinking about it. But war has always been a means for concentrating men's minds and things soon changed. The change occurred in three areas; men, machines, and tactics.

There was little serious thought in those early days about the qualities required to be an airman. People drifted into aviation because they were as fascinated by flight as man had been throughout the ages. Others arrived almost by accident, and it was to be some time before the selection for aircrew would be put on any sort of formal footing. The result was that in the Great War there was a strange collection of bedfellows; at that time aviation, somehow, tended to attract some odd people.

One could almost be excused for believing that some defect in health or character was a pre-requisite for 'ace' status and that the rule was true regardless of nationality. Edward 'Mick' Mannock was so badly treated in a Turkish jail that his health was permanently affected and he was found unfit for military duty. He found ways of overcoming officialdom and became a renowned ace on the Western Front, despite being blind in one eye, and suffering nausea from fear so badly that at one stage he was accused of cowardice. Raoul Lufbery, another tactician who has left his name in the list of fighter manoeuvres, was so clumsy in his flight training that he was almost rejected. Ernst Udet had always wanted to be an artist and his temperament came to the fore in his initial combats, when he found himself so frightened that he could not fire his guns; once that fear had been overcome, he became a proficient and successful fighter pilot. Rene Ronck, the top Allied ace with 75 victories, had hardly any friends and was known as a brash, unpleasant, braggart; hardly the qualities necessary for commissioning in a peacetime force.

Eddie Rickenbacker was not at ease in polite company either, being described as a 'crude roughneck', the 'most unpopular man alive' and being renowned for his profane vocabulary. It was only the intervention of the high ranking officer for whom he drove, that he managed to overcome the fact that he had too little formal education to qualify for flight school. As the greatest of the American aces, he certainly justified the trust and was one of a long line of fighter pilots who gave lie to the popular theory that academic capability is any judge of combat worth.

Perhaps these characters remain in history's view because they were successful and either survived or, in some cases, at least survived long enough to make their mark. Perhaps all the *normal* people did not survive; or was it that the aces were archetypal of the norm and they were all like that? It is hard to credit it. Certainly it was the fate of many not to survive and the lethality of combat proved to be very high. The French suffered the loss of 77 per cent of their total aircrew over the course of the war. After their entry into the conflict, the United States lost half of all the pilots who were sent to Europe. The mathematical odds were so high against, it was calculated that only one out of every 20 British pilots who left for France on the early squadrons ever saw the shores of the United Kingdom again. At one stage the average life expectancy on joining a British fighter squadron at the western front was between three and six weeks.

Oswald Boelke, one of the most famous of the German fighter pilots and tacticians, in whose honour a squadron of the present German Air Force is still named, was once seriously censured for taking young nurses aloft in his Fokker – his single-seat Fokker! Would such cavalier indiscipline be tolerated today? Max Immelmann, the originator of the tactical turn which bears his name, was reported as having good flying qualities but 'coupled with a truly childish temperament'; probably enough to disqualify him from a modern officer's school. Georges Guynemer, the French ace, was turned down as 'too frail' for the infantry or the cavalry, suffered symptoms of tuberculosis and was known to be so delicate that he fainted on parades. Erich Lowenhardt was also declared unfit for the infantry and it was a pity for the 53 allied pilots he shot down thereafter that, at the time, that did not seem to rule him out of flying fighters.

William Bishop, on the other hand, was saved by the outbreak of the war from being sent down from the Canadian Royal Military College with a report which spoke of him being 'the worst cadet ever' and being 'a rebellious brawler and a hopeless scholar'. It is amusing to ponder whether the author of that unfavourable report would ever, later in life, have had to pay his respects to Air Marshal William Bishop, VC, CB, DSO and Bar, MC, DFC, Chevalier of the Legion of Honour, Croix de Guerre with Palm. A cautionary tale for modern Staff College directing staff!

But what modern flying training system would tolerate a student who not only failed his first examination through lack of application but also crashed his machine on his first solo? There would be little discussion needed; Manfred von Richthofen, the future Red Baron, would have to go – and 80 allied pilots would have been given a second chance!

Many of the deaths were caused by accidents rather than by combat. Flight tuition was not a highly developed art, let alone a science. Dual controlled aircraft were a rarity and it was customary for the student to sit behind the instructor and to reach around him for the odd feel of the controls before being sent solo. Nor were there extensive syllabi; 'Boom' Trenchard, the father of the modern Royal Air Force, qualified as a pilot after only one hour and four minutes flight time, and that spread over 13 days. Early in the war, young pilots were appearing at the front to join their operational squadrons with a total of only eight hours in their log books.

Even then the instruction left much to be desired, not through any lack of dedication or application on the part of the instructors, but more because, in many instances, the blind were leading the blind and the knowledge of the principles of flight and of rudimentary aerodynamics was far from extensive. An example of the situation at the time can be gleaned from the findings of an early Royal Flying Corps accident inquiry. The pilot had failed to take-off from a field and had ended up firmly embedded in the hedge, damaging the machine beyond repair. As little was known about the advantages of taking-off into wind, and the *operating data manual* was to replace folklore only in the distant future, the pilot was exonerated from blame on the basis that he had been ordered to take-off before sunrise and:

'. . . it was well known that there was no lift in the air before the sun was up.'

Structural problems also took their toll. The early aircraft were frail machines well described as *stringbags* and many of the aerodynamic interactions were still to be fully understood. The engines of the day did not produce sufficient power to enable pilots to use high 'G' forces in any sustained way but the snatch pull could overstress the wood-and-canvas designs very easily. Once damaged, the canvas covering could detach, increasing drag and interfering with flying qualities which were far from tolerant to start with. Instrumentation, if it existed at all in some of the designs, was crude and unreliable and it was some time before blind flying instruments were to be developed. Flight through cloud was therefore hazardous and, although it was not regularly practised, cloud was used as a means of escape when out-numbered or out-classed in combat. At times the cure was worse than the disease.

The early designs to see combat at the front were flying machines rather than combat aircraft. For the accepted primary role of reconnaissance there was no reason for them to be much else and it was only when the requirement to engage other aircraft in combat became clear that the inadequacies of the designs became apparent. Initially this centred on the provision of armament which, over a short time, covered a wide spectrum. Experiments were made at dropping rocks on the enemy from above; another method was to tow an anchor on a long rope and try to snare the opposing aircraft, pulling the canvas from the machine and shattering the wooden propeller. The advantages of the more conventional service revolver, and later the rifle and machine gun, were obvious. However, even guns had their difficulties and taking aim from the open and cramped cockpits, sometimes against a crossing target and over the side of the machine, gave a low probability of success. With a revolver it was bad enough, with a long service rifle it was almost impossible without an observer.

It soon became clear, with the restricted power available from the engines of the day, that there was a heavy penalty for flying a two-seater rather than a single-seater. The weight of the additional man was a finite part of the all-up-weight of the machines and severely constrained the performance. The debate still rages today on the performance penalty to be paid for a two-place aircraft, even with modern design and at a time when engines are producing very high power-to-weight ratios. There are few fighter pilots who would admit to having enough power; there are always things to be done with more, and Bleriot's first words on stepping from his craft after the first cross-channel flight still form a popular cry about the world's crewrooms,

'More power – I must have more power'.

With a single pilot there was the problem of servicing and aiming the gun. Soon, hand-held armament was abandoned and the gun was fixed to the fore and aft axis of the aircraft. The gun had to be attached above the pilot on the top wing so that the rounds would clear the propeller. This made the problem of clearing stoppages difficult and did nothing to improve the aim. Practical development of the art of aerial gunnery had to be undertaken in the traumatic days of war because of lack of foresight in peace, or at least, lack of perseverance. In 1912 a machine gun was fired from an aircraft on trials in the United States and hits were scored on a target. The Army were not impressed and, explaining why experiments in aerial gunnery were to be stopped, a spokesman said:

'The continuance of such schemes can serve no practical purpose whatever'.

That opinion was not shared by all. As early as 1913 Raymond Saulnier was experimenting with a synchronising device which would allow bullets to pass safely through the spinning disc of a propeller. His idea was paralleled by a Swiss, Franz Schneider, working in a small workshop in Berlin. By connecting the position of the propeller to a device which fired the machine-gun electrically it could be arranged for the gun to fire only at those times when the bullet would pass harmlessly between the blades. It allowed guns to be mounted in the sight line of the pilot, much improving his gunnery accuracy, and was one of the major stepping stones in the development of warplanes.

Such developments, together with the production of better performance with the introduction of more powerful engines and more advanced aerodynamics, soon started to show over the battlefield. Reconnaissance became more problematical and losses started to rise. It became clear that to achieve any purpose, be that reconnaissance or the early forays into bombing, the aircraft had first to look to its own survival. When these two requirements became incompatible, the first experiments were made in escort, with one group of aircraft protecting another. The losses of reconnaissance aircraft were so concerning to the Royal Flying Corps in 1916 that in the January of that year an RFC flying order was issued:

'Until the RFC are in possession of a machine as good as or better than the German Fokker, it must be laid down as a hard and fast rule that a machine proceeding on reconnaissance must be escorted by at least three fighting machines'.

The sentiment behind that order gives a good insight into the discipline of air combat and how it is affected so fundamentally by performance. No matter how expert and proficient the pilot, there is a limit to how much of a performance deficiency can be taken out of the equation on skill alone. In the case at the time it was true that the German Fokker had a real advantage over most of the allied aircraft which it maintained for a large part of the conflict. A year later Trenchard, in command of the British air force in France, was exhorting the Ministers in London to hasten the supply of comparable aircraft:

> 'You are asking me to fight the battle this year with the same machines as I fought it last year. We shall be hopelessly outclassed, and something must be done about it. All I can say is that there will be an outcry from the pilots out there if we do not have at least these few squadrons of fast machines and what I have asked for is absolutely necessary.'

In the meantime it was becoming clear that shooting down an evading aircraft was no easy task; it was an elusive and, at times, remarkably resilient target, notwithstanding the fact that it was so lightly built. Unlike the modern aircraft, where every space is gainfully employed and filled with fuel or electronics or whatever, the early aircraft were mostly filled with fresh air. The engine was vulnerable, but only certain components of it. The fuel tank was a different matter and fire was an ever present hazard which claimed so many lives. The reluctance of the RFC to sanction the use of parachutes, despite the successful experiments in 1916, because it was thought that they would encourage cowardice amongst the crews, has been estimated to have cost as many as one in three of the combat casualties in the air war; the American Lufberry jumped to his death rather than stay with his burning aircraft. But it was the pilot himself who was probably the most vulnerable *target system*. The weight of the aircraft was too critical to allow much in the form of armoured protection and, in any case, the open cockpits left a good deal of the pilot exposed to view. There are stories nevertheless which tell of the use to which cast-iron stove tops were put – they gave an uncomfortable seat but tremendous reassurance.

Because the aircraft was an elusive target it was important to make the most of any firing opportunity and the rate of fire of the guns became an important factor. Aircraft guns at the time were modified army weapons and a rate of fire of some 600 rounds per minute was about the norm. It may sound a lot, but not when a fast crossing target may give only a fraction of a second during which a killing burst can be laid. Modern air-to-air guns, with the same problem to solve, regularly operate at cyclic rates closer to 6,000 rounds per minute. Before guns were developed with higher rates of fire, the only answer was to increase the number of guns. Immelmann pursuaded Fokker that this was the path to the future and he had him build a model with three guns, greatly expanding his fire-power. Although the extra weight adversely affected the handling of the excellent machine, Immelmann's skill and the additional lethality of his bursts made up for the disadvantage and he was rewarded by success. Unfortunately, the three guns, all firing with the use of interrupter mechanisms through the propeller, increased the chance of a technical failure and on 18 June 1916 it happened; the synchronising device malfunctioned causing Immelmann to shoot his propeller to pieces and this, together with the nose heavy design, caused by the additional guns, was the reason for his death.

The development of tactics at this time was unstructured. The protagonists were *artists* and all had their preferred acts. As has been seen, some were not of a nature to

BOELCKE'S DICTA

1. Try to secure advantages before attacking. If possible keep the sun behind you.
2. Always carry through an attack once you have started it.
3. Fire only at close range and only when your opponent is properly in your sights.
4. Always keep your eye on your opponent and never let yourself be deceived by ruses.
5. In any form of attack it is essential to assail your opponent from behind.
6. If your opponent dives on you, do not try to evade his onslaught, but fly to meet it.
7. When over the enemy's lines never forget your own line of retreat.
8. Attack on principle in groups of four or six. When the fight breaks up into a series of single combats, take care that several do not go for one opponent.

share their tricks and techniques, while others hardly survived long enough to develop any. Such development as there was during the period owed much to conscientious squadron commanders who, appalled by the casualty rate, tried to teach the junior pilots at least the rudiments of survival. It was along these lines that Boelcke became the tutor to one of his new pilots, Manfred von Richthofen and not that long afterwards von Richthofen, in command of his own squadron, was following the pattern and teaching his young pilots the basics.

Basics they were, and developed without the scientific support and analysis so common now. Yet amazingly, the ground-rules which emerged from those early days have survived the passage of time and many are as applicable to the modern combat of today as they were then. It says much for the professionalism which developed in the hot crucible of war. BOELCKE's DICTA is perhaps the best known of the tactical doctrines although there were others less formally recorded. Common to all of the doctrines of the day were three which could be looked at as the primary tenants emerging from the Great War:

'He who has the height controls the battle.'
'He who has the sun achieves surprise.'
'He who gets in close shoots them down.'

Gunnery was conducted at very close range. Some of the aces claimed that fire should be held until the range was well below 300 feet and some even advocated firing from a few tens of feet. Without the assistance of lead computing gunsights, and at a time when deflection shooting was still somewhat of a mystery in air combat, it was clearly a wise policy. Even with the much greater assistance available now, and with armament possessing much greater reach, the ranges at which the modern aces have achieved their gun kills remain remarkably modest. In South East Asia, for example, only 25 per cent of all the gun kills occurred outside 2,000 feet and the majority were achieved between 400 and 1,200 feet. Gunsight film from modern combats frequently show target aircraft filling the screen because they are so close.

At the mid-point of the Great War, or thereabouts, the battle had become one of air superiority in the true sense; a battle for the control of the skies, so that the overall purpose could be achieved and that the enemy could be denied the same liberty. It was a battle of fighters against fighters and tactical and technical development began to reflect this. At about this time, however, the introduction of the bomber, with all its emotional impact, caused the fighter task to be reviewed and started a trend which had far-reaching implications.

The attacks against the United Kingdom by the giant airships caught the imagination but the raid on London on 13 June 1917 by the Gotha bombers had a greater effect. Some sources suggest that the purpose of conducting this operation was deliberately to draw fighters away from the Western Front; if that was the intention it worked and Trenchard was soon complaining about the depletion of his front-line forces as squadrons were pulled back to defend the homeland from air attack. It was a considerable psychological shock to the British to realise that the Channel, the protector for hundreds of years, was now irrelevant in the face of the new weapon system. Was it this unpleasant realisation which stayed firmly in mind at the beginning of the next war when Dowding so steadfastly argued against sending the bulk of his fighter forces forward and harboured them for the task of home defence?

It certainly seemed to have an effect on Trenchard who had his views reinforced on the essentially offensive nature of air power and the effect that it had on an enemy.

'The aeroplane is the most offensive weapon that has ever been invented. It is a shockingly bad weapon of defence'.

The squadrons sent home to defend against the bombers demonstrated the first split between '*air defence*' fighters at home and the '*air superiority*' fighters on the Western Front. That split exists to this day. In terms of technology and design it meant little; the aircraft were effectively the same, but the difference in doctrine, even perhaps in the sub-conscious, may have been under-estimated. More so when the bomber debate proceeded on its stately way, untested by reasoned argument and certainly not by any form of tactical development flying.

The United Kingdom finished the First World War with bomber designs capable of reaching Berlin from East Anglia. The shock and horror of the raids on London were still uppermost in mind and there were some influential advocates of strategic bombing, not least Trenchard and Douhet. They were supported in some powerful quarters and it was none less than Prime Minister Stanley Baldwin himself who coined the phrase,

'the bomber will always get through'.

This concentration on the threat from, and capability of, the strategic bomber, combined with the fact that the German fighters were now well removed and far out of range of the British fighters of the time, caused the impetus, such as it was, to move away from the tactical development of fighters in the inter-war years. The bomber became the great threat and all thoughts turned towards its counter. What plans there were for modest expansion at that time were inspired more by the fear of France rather than Germany when it was realised that France had not disarmed to anywhere near the extent of the United Kingdom and was consequently far superior in numbers of aircraft. It did not go without note either that the French were receptive to the theories of strategic bombing and the combination of these two facts left the British uneasy.

There were, of course, other influences. The infamous *ten-year-rule* assumed that another major European war would not occur without a ten-year warning and did nothing to engender the spirit, or the urgency, needed for the innovative development of aircraft or tactics. In Whitehall, the battle over the independence of the Royal Air Force must have been as sapping to rational doctrinal and force development then as the tribal warfare in that place is today. The Army had seen the effect of air power on the battlefield, particularly its effect on reconnaissance and on the artillery dual, and might have been expected to push for its development. But, in the manner of British armies before them and thankfully rid of the mud of Flanders, they reverted physically and mentally to the more enjoyable soldiering in the Empire, where the aircraft was not the necessary tool it was on the continent. In all, for a young air force, they were difficult times and perhaps there is a reason, if not an excuse, for the introverted thinking at that time.

In the wider canvas, the trend fitted well and the British psyche continued to pursuade itself that the Great War had been that final one to end all wars, conveniently neglecting human nature and past history. Squandering peace had

SCHNEIDER TROPHY

The Schneider Trophy was initiated during the early days of powered flight to encourage the development of seaplanes and flying boats. It took the form of a race over a closed circuit and the Royal Air Force won the event for the first time in 1914.

In 1927 the RAF formed the High Speed Flight to compete in the Schneider Trophy and to conduct research into the then unknown aerodynamics of high speed flight. A specially built seaplane was produced and entered into the event held in Venice in 1927; it was the Supermarine S.5 powered by a Napier engine and it won with a speed of 281.65 mph,

In 1929, in competition with the Italian Air Force, Flying Officer Waghorne won for the RAF in a Supermarine S.6A powered by a Rolls-Royce 'R' engine of 1,900 HP at a speed of 328.63 mph. On 12 Sep 1929, Squadron Leader Orlebar set the world absolute air speed record in this modified machine with a speed of 357.7 mph.

By 1931 the government had lost interest in the event and RAF participation was made possible only by the generosity of Lady Houston. Her enthusiasm was well repaid and the trophy was won by Flight Lieutenant Boothman, flying a Supermarine S.6B at a speed of 340.6 mph, but this was exceeded handsomely by Flight Lieutenant Stainforth in the September of that year when he achieved the world absolute speed record of 407.5 mph in a Supermarine S.6B fitted with a 2,600 HP Rolls-Royce engine.

After such a run of success, amazingly, the High Speed Flight was then disbanded.

In the short period between 1927 and 1931 the speed achieved by these high-drag float-planes had been pushed from 281 to 407 mph. A truly impressive advance by any standard and more particularly so when judged against the performance of the new fighters in front line service at the outbreak of war, eight years later.

become ingrained and was far from limited to the air arm. Despite the best efforts of that far-sighted weaponeer, Admiral Sir Percy Scott of the Royal Navy, too few ships had gone into action at Jutland with director firing equipment. Gunnery just was not popular – it dirtied the paintwork of ships kept pristine for their ceremonial duties – and the ability of the British to excuse inefficiency, even to exalt it, came to the fore in an official correspondence from the Admiralty on the matter of accurate gunnery:

> 'What use are more accurate guns? The enemy would merely dodge them. With our present pieces they are in danger everywhere.'

A similar story was to be found in the development of the shells themselves. After Jutland the Admiral Hipper of the German Navy went on record to state:

> 'It was only the poor quality of the British bursting charges which saved us from disaster.'

It was no better on land. The nation which had given the world the tank, and introduced it to battle at Cambrai, entered the following war out-numbered, out-classed and out-thought by an enemy which had better taken to heart the writings of Liddell-Hart and Fuller at a time when their message sat uncomfortably with their fellow countrymen. The Royal Air Force was not alone in its suffering therefore; it was, rather, sharing in the general malaise.

It was necessary to look towards the civil field to find innovation and daring between the wars and it existed in profusion.

Long-range flying caught the imagination and there were records to be had for the asking. Many were those set by the great airships and would prove difficult to beat but there were enough to try their hand.

Those attracted to the challenge were the same strange amalgam that had been seen amongst the war aces. Alcock, of the duo Alcock and Brown, conquerors of the Atlantic in June 1919, walked only with the aid of a stick after his leg had been badly smashed in an air accident. The irrepressible Wiley Post, the first man to fly solo around the world, dropped out of school in the eighth grade and, following an injury with a sliver of steel, pursued his flying career with only one eye. In his Lockheed Vega, *Winnie Mae*, he completed the round the world trip in eight days, 15 hours and 51 minutes and bettered the previous record set by *Graf Zeppelin*.

One of the first attempts by the military to enter the record books was led by the United States Army Air Service. Four Douglas seaplanes, powered by modest 400 HP engines, left Seattle on 6 April 1924 and returned 175 days and 72 stops later from their circumnavigation. In 1929 the Royal Air Force sent Squadron Leader Jones-Williams and Flight Lieutenant N. H. Jenkins the 4,130 miles from Cranwell to Kharachi non-stop. In doing so they took the record off another ex-RAF man, Charles Kingsford-Smith who had flown the 3,200 miles from Hawaii to Suva only a year before. Such was the pace that the servicemen held the record for only a short time and were beaten by Dieredonne Costes flying the 5,000 miles from Paris to Manchuria. He, in turn, must have been galled to be beaten by only 12 miles by Russell Boardman and John Polando flying a Bellanca from New York to Turkey.

A new word entered the aviation language when in 1933 the Italian Minister for Air, Italo Balbo, was instrumental in organising a formation flight of 25 Savoia-Marchetti SM-55X flying-boats from Italy to the World Fair in Chicago. Considering the difficulties, the mission was a great success and the aircraft performed at the Fair on time. The round trip took six weeks and only two aircraft were lost; one outbound at Amsterdam, the other inbound at Lisbon, but this did little to dull the achievement. To this day large formations of aircraft are popularly referred to as *Balbos*.

While the thirst for distance records continued, there were moves at the performance end of the spectrum. The Schneider Trophy events probably did more than anything else in those mid-war years to enhance fighter design. Reginald Mitchell's famous Spitfire owed much of its lineage to the designs of the seaplanes for the Schneider Trophy. And for the time, performance it was; the competition was being won at the end with speeds around 400 mph and this despite the large drag-inducing floats. It was in this event that competition pilots first reported the effect of 'G' as they had difficulty in focussing and concentrating as they pulled steeply around the pylons.

Engines were getting more powerful and there was a limit to how far the lath and canvas airframes could accept the new demands made upon them. The advent of the metal airframe, utilising aluminium opened up the way for strong and light aircraft designs. Using metal rather than canvas, stress could be taken partially on the skin, so allowing weight to be saved on the internal primary structure. The use of metal and the cantilever principle gave rise in turn to the monoplane with all its drag-reducing advantages. Sometimes not acknowledged is the improvement to lookout from the new fighters when the obstruction of the top wing was removed.

Such developments gave rise to the Spitfire and the Messerschmitt Me-109, aircraft much of a type with only small differences in advantage and disadvantage. The Spitfire's elliptical wing gave it the edge on manoeuvrability at the price of being more difficult to manufacture, an important quality for a warplane; the Me-109's Daimler-Benz engine, on the other hand, was fuel injected, rather than being normally aspirated, as was the Spitfire's Merlin. This prevented the engine cutting out when under negative 'G'. Swings and roundabouts. They were both excellent products.

Technical development throughout the 1939–45 war occurred in two ways; the first in the incremental development of basically sound designs, and the second in the technological breakthroughs such as the fielding of the first jet fighters. The Spitfire is a good example of incremental development. Originally a 6,200 lb, 350 mph aircraft with a 1,030 hp engine driving a two-bladed propeller and armed with eight 0.303 inch machine guns. Within a period of a decade it had developed into a 9,900 lb, 450 mph machine, needing a five-bladed propeller to absorb the 2,050 hp of its Griffon engine and armed with 20 mm cannon. Before taken out of production, 24 marks of the Spitfire were produced and both it, and the Me-109, served throughout the duration of the 1939–45 war.

The Meteors and the Messerschmitt Me-262 were the best of the jet fighters to see service at that time. They were not fielded sufficiently early to influence affairs greatly and engines, uncertain aerodynamics and short range, limited the opportunity to exploit the performance in new tactical doctrine. At the latter stages of the war, however, when Adolf Galland was commanding Jaqdgeschwäder (JG) 44, the use of the fast slashing attack in the Me-262, to avoid the turning combat, started to be preached. It was similar to the doctrine practiced by at least two of the world's air forces today. The Me-262 pilot had soon found that care had to be taken in combat, despite his speed advantage, because the conventional piston-engined fighters were reaching a high state of development and, in the turning battle, there was not much performance differential.

Strangely, the development of new tactics was not a marked feature of the 1939–45 period. Old tactics were refined and the new performance was used in different areas of the tactical spectrum but it was in the period before then that most of the new thinking took place. The newly emerged Luftwaffe had the advantage of using the Spanish Civil War as a training ground and as an arena for the development of new tactics. Werner Molders was one of the first to see that the higher speeds available from the new fighters made the old ideas of formation flying outdated. Formations developed in the Great War were still popular; *vics* and *finger-fours* were flown a few spans apart and demanded that much of the pilot's attention should be directed towards collision avoidance, to the detriment of lookout. Yet, at the new high speeds, lookout was all important as hostile aircraft could close from being a small dot in the sky to being in a killing position very quickly.

Molders developed the widespread formation with aircraft some hundreds of metres apart; the *rotte* of two aircraft and the *schwarm* of two or more *rottes*. It is still the basis of many battle-formations today and he surely earned his place in the history of air combat. Lacking the benefit of the Spanish training ground, it was to be at the end of the Battle of Britain that the RAF acknowledged the flaw in its own doctrine and emulated the Molders formations. Was it only good organisation and the splendid Me-109 which earned the Luftwaffe its reputation for invincibility during the early days of the 1939–45 war, or was it more to do with their advanced tactics? Certainly, at that time, no other air force was taking the matter as seriously as the Luftwaffe.

It was necessary to wait for the Korean war before any further development of any note went on in the field of tactics. The Korean war saw the first widespread use of jet fighters and the first jet fighter combats. The two principal players on the field where the F-86 Sabre and the MiG-15. Like the Spitfire and Me-109 before them, they were evenly matched in many respects and requiring their pilots to seek those fine areas of advantage if they were to succeed – or survive. The higher speeds were immediately seen to cause the dimensions of the fight to expand and a jet fighter dog-fight covered a great deal of airspace. Because of that, it was easy to lose sight of aircraft which were engaged and to be shot at by aircraft which had crept up unseen. The premium on good teamwork and formation discipline was raised.

Although the Sabre and the MiG-15 were capable of flying supersonic in a shallow dive, the combats were soon seen to degenerate into a slow speed combat, unless steps were taken to deliberately prevent this happening. Often, combat reports spoke of fights taking place a few knots above the stall in the classic *scissors* manoeuvres. Occasionally, this may have been the intention of the Sabre pilots, who felt that their hydraulically assisted power controls gave them an advantage over the manual controls of the MiG. They may have been lucky if this was so because the MiG had a better power-to-weight ratio and had a lighter wing loading than the Sabre. Yet another of the examples of playing one advantage off against the other; some advantages in quite different areas.

The wars in the Middle East, on the other hand, have tended to show a number of lessons, many of which have not occasioned the comment they might have done. Primary amongst these must be the fact that a small nation the size of Israel has not only survived but also seemingly prospered while remaining surrounded by hostile nations collectively many times its size. Israel has little strategic depth – amounting to only a few kilometres at one point before the capture of the West Bank territory – is effectively surrounded on land, and vulnerable along a lengthy frontier at sea. Yet, in the wars that have occurred, they have won – in most cases, convincingly.

Some explanation for this can be found in their exploitation of tactical mobility; on land, using armour with all the skill and initiative of a Rommel or Guderian, but principally in the air, using their well equipped and superbly trained air force. The ability of air forces to react quickly to a surprise situation has more than once helped them survive the unexpected and, in the famous pre-emptive attack against the Egyptian Air Force in 1967, they used surprise in the offensive with as devastating an effect as the Japanese had at Pearl Harbor in 1941.

They have also used their air power in an innovative and daring way to extend their purpose over ranges quite impossible for them to do so in any other way. The use of air power to avenge terrorist raids is a frequent occurrence and these are usually short range affairs across the border into the Lebanon. It is from the longer range attacks that there are lessons to be drawn; the Entebbe raid, where daring and surprise paid a handsome dividend; in the attack on the Iraqi nuclear facility, where those qualities were combined with not a little cunning; and the long-range raid, using tanking, into the far Mediterranean to prove yet again that their reach would be used against terrorist targets.

Why are they so well trained? It has been said that being hung on the morrow greatly concentrates the mind, and although living in such a state of constant tension cannot be a pleasant experience for the Israeli people, it certainly helps to keep a military force on the top line. It would be interesting to know how many aircraft noise complaints are received by the Israeli Air Force compared with their Western European counterparts. Their reserve system, which encompasses most of the able bodied men and many of the women too, also means that the population as a whole are orientated to the military cause. Those European nations not having compulsory military service, and without extensive reserve commitments, may lack some of this common feeling of identity and purpose.

The lesson which this teaches is that for a modern military force to prepare convincingly for war, it needs the good will of its populace and, in those societies where that does not come automatically by force of circumstance, then it needs to be worked at with the same dedication, and maybe using some of the same techniques, as used so successfully in selling wash powder. A further lesson is that air power used correctly, and with the right philosophy and doctrine, can give quite small nations an influence far beyond their apparent strategic worth.

On the tactical level, the Israelis are ever conscious, more than most, of the need to conserve forces, to minimise losses and to strive for high exchange ratios. This drives their doctrine and, on achieved results, seems to drive it in the right way. The exchange ratios in most of their conflicts are heavily in their favour; in the case of the Bekaar Valley in the region of 80-to-one. At least some of this can be put down to their caution over engaging in the turning fight. Despite having aircraft which are built for just this sort of combat, the Israeli Air Force prefer to use the performance for the fast slashing attacks first seen with the Me-262 and reserve their turning performance to be used only to achieve the kill offensively, or to foil the weapons solution defensively. Results say that they cannot be far wrong in this doctrine and, with the increasing lethality of the modern combat environment, it must be true that the least time spent achieving the kill the better. Is this successful modern tactical doctrine that different from that propounded so long ago by von Richthofen?

Vietnam taught a variety of lessons; some by commission and others by omission. Both can be equally useful to the observer if the lessons are correctly distilled. It showed above all what air power is not very good at doing. It is not very good at interdicting a supply route through impenetrable forest consisting of thousands of men carrying small amounts of freight on 'A'-frames strapped to their back. The Americans should not feel badly about learning this lesson in Vietnam; but the Soviets should feel badly about not learning from them and having to find out for themselves in Afghanistan. Bombing was also not very good at breaking the morale of a populace unless used to the extreme; another lesson learned in the Second World War and forgotten. The more undeveloped the country, and the more undemocratic the government, the more difficult is it to get a morale effect by bombing.

It also showed that graduated response has to be used with great care. If the response is spread over too long a period then the population adapt to the threat and it consequently becomes less effective. Talk of the Londoners' spirit in the blitz was a case in point; they had the opportunity to orientate to an increasing threat whereas, in comparison, the much smaller raid on Rotterdam was sudden, unexpected and unaccustomed and broke the will of the Dutch government.

In the air war there was almost a replay of the Great War situation in which air combat, such as it was, resulted from that which was forced on the penetrating formations. The North Vietnamese Air Force was used primarily in the air intercept mode, attempting to frustrate the offensive missions over the north. It was as a result of their success against such heavily laden aircraft as the F-4, F-105 and the A-6 that the specifications were laid down for a series of air superiority fighters which turned out eventually to be the F-14, F-15 and the F-16.

By far the greatest lesson to be learned from the conflict from a purely professional viewpoint was that of training. The United States is the world's greatest democracy and it was therefore to be expected that, when embroiled in a long and unpopular war, every attempt would be made to spread the misery fairly. As a result, it was decreed that before any aircrew should be ordered to Vietnam for the second tour, everyone should have completed the first. Unfortunately, the rate of using the fighter-bomber missions was much higher than that in other roles with the result that the experienced fighter-bomber pilots soon exhausted their first tours and had to be replaced by pilots who had been cross-trained into the fighter-bomber role. The result was a lowering of role experience and, it has to be said, of standards. Whatever lessons are drawn from Vietnam, they should be measured against that situation.

The favourable exchange ratios which had been the accepted norm at the end of the 1939–45 war and, particularly, in Korea, did not result from the initial combats over the North. In part, this was because of the interception of heavily-laden aircraft by lightly loaded and high performance air defence fighters, and partly because of the lowering experience levels. This was, however, only part of the story; it was also due to poor air combat tuition, insufficient analysis of the new factors applying to combat, and, manifestly, too few instructors able to teach the rudiments. All these factors were energetically grasped over the period of the conflict and resulted in the formation of fighter leader courses, better doctrine and, in the new generation of fighters, better aircraft. It was during this period that the theories of energy manoeuvrability were forwarded and which have become an accepted part of the air combat discussion since.

In the last three decades, air combat training in the Royal Air Force has either been stopped or severely discouraged on three separate occasions. At one stage, guns were even removed from fighter aircraft. The arguments have varied; the old favourite about speeds being too high for combat to be engaged in practically – a variation on the red flags once compulsory in front of horseless carriages; and that air combat was so dangerous that the advantage in war did not warrant the cost in peace – neglecting that the loss rate in air display flying was greater than in air combat training – have both had their day. Yet, while man remains much the same aggressive self, there will always be air combat, no matter what the speeds or the conditions. When space craft can *straffe* space craft then they will – it is in the nature of things. Man is wonderfully adaptable as a creature for both good and evil and, while this remains the truth, air combat will be a part of the military scene and will have to be trained for, if for no other reason that history has proved enough times that:

'You bleed in peace, or you bleed in war.'

Which is little more than the modern interpretation of the older maxim which has survived for so many centuries before the advent of the powered aircraft:

'*Qui desiderat pacem, praeparet bellum.*'

3.

Performance

NOT all fighter pilots are mathematicians. As has already been shown, some distinguished and successful fighter pilots in the past have been of an artistic rather than a scientific bent. It could be argued that, in modern combat conditions when science and technology so dominate the battle, their artistry would not have proved so effective but that is a matter of opinion. Whether the budding fighter pilot is scientist, mathematician or artist, today there is the same requirement to know the fundamentals of modern aircraft performance, how they relate to each other, and how to make performance comparisons with the likely opposition. Seventy years ago, a good pilot could triumph over a bad pilot, regardless of the merit of his machine, but that situation is far more tenuous now when so much of the battle is fought with equipment rather than skill alone. These days, the skill is to be found in exploiting to the full the performance advantages of one design over the performance disadvantages of another. It is, however, important to know how to determine the difference between the two.

This does not necessarily entail any deep study of aerodynamics or the more abstract areas of thermodynamics, even though many pilots take more than a passing interest in these disciplines. What needs to be known about fighter aircraft performance is quite capable of being understood with the mathematics capable of resolution on a simple calculator. It is more important to understand the *story* a number is telling rather than spending valuable time justifying the number itself. Approximations are in order; there seems little purpose in worrying about the third place of decimals when individual skill only allows the aircraft to be operated to the nearest hundred of whole units. In this respect, performance mathematics need to be kept in perspective; it is *patterns* which count more than the pure performance itself, particularly as one aircraft's pattern needs to relate to those of other aircraft.

Performance assessment falls into two convenient parts; the first is that which governs the aircraft as an object obeying the laws of motion. These laws apply as much to an aircraft as they do to any other object; a stone being swung about the head is obeying the same laws of motion as is the aircraft in a turn. That the aircraft has lift, and drag, and has a cockpit, and is painted green, is quite irrelevant because it is merely an object travelling in a certain way and obeying all the physical laws that that entails.

The second part is where aircraft design comes to the fore. It is aircraft design which allows the basic flight conditions to obtain and which form the raw material against which the physical laws are applied. Given a certain 'G' loading and speed, the radius of turn is derived from basic physical laws; that any given aircraft can actually pull that level of 'G', or attain that speed, is where aerodynamics and thermodynamics come in.

It is necessary to remember which factors are governed by physics and which by design.

PERFORMANCE PARAMETERS

There are five main measures of performance falling from the physical laws:

'v'   True Air Speed – (TAS) (ft/sec)
'n'   The force of acceleration as sensed in the cockpit
'R'   Radius of turn (ft)
'g'   Factor to convert into gravitational units – 32.174
'w'   Rate of Turn (radians/sec – converted to degs/sec by multiplying by 57.3)
(and 'x' Angle of Bank (degs))

For manoeuvre in the horizontal plane these five elements of performance are related according to the following:

$$v.w = \frac{V^2}{R} = g \tan x = g(n^2 - 1)^{\frac{1}{2}} \ldots \qquad (1)$$

ANGLE OF BANK

It can be seen that angle of bank can be derived from part of the total relationship (1):

$$g \tan x = g (n^2 - 1)^{\frac{1}{2}}$$

By removing 'g' from both sides:

$$\tan x = (n^2 - 1)^{\frac{1}{2}}$$

or, putting an example to the formulae, say, 'n' = 2, that is, the pilot sees a figure of 2 'G' on his cockpit indicator:

$$\tan x = (4 - 1)$$
$$= (3)^{\frac{1}{2}}$$

therefore: x = 60 degs.

It might be thought strange that 60 degrees of the available 90 degrees of bank is used to produce such modest 'g' levels but, as Figure 3.1 shows it has much to do with *Pythagoras* and the curve is far from being a straight line. It can also be seen why it is not possible to hold 90 degrees of bank without descending. Aerobatic pilots will be the first to qualify that statement by pointing out that *top rudder* can produce the necessary lift required to achieve level flight – and they have half a point, depending on the machine – but this volume is addressed to budding fighter pilots striving for their first Distinguished Flying Cross rather than to display pilots competing for competition rosettes.

The diagram also shows why aircraft wishing to maintain level flight while pulling high 'n' levels need the aerodynamics to develop the very high lift vectors involved. The *lift vector* is the hypotenuse of a right angled triangle and as the triangle gets

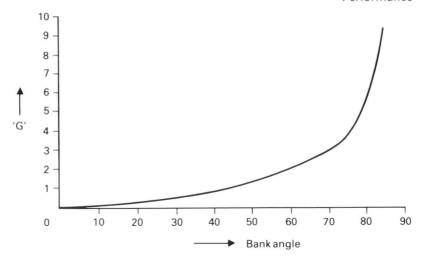

Fig 3.1.   Bank angle vs 'G'

longer and thinner as the bank is increased, the hypotenuse very quickly assumes lengthy proportions. This does not imply that an aircraft unable to generate that amount of lift cannot use the higher angles of attack, of course it can, but it cannot maintain level flight at the same time.

Instrument Rating Examiners – a dedicated group of men who in medieval days would have 'put the question' – are more than usually aware of the relationship between angle of bank and 'G' loading and use it to test to progressively high standards. A fledgling may have to conduct a turn and stay within a certain height band at, perhaps, 30 degrees of bank, and it can be seen that he could make quite large excursions about the par before any violent height change would accrue. The more experienced pilot might be expected to stay within the height bracket at a higher 'G', or angle of bank, and stay within closer tolerances, to prove his greater worth. To conduct a level turn on instruments at bank levels much above 60 degrees is a worthy test of skill and perseverance and the Figure shows why.

RADIUS OF TURN

Very few combats, even in the missile age, are conducted without some form of manoeuvre and, in any turning fight, the ability to turn quickly, or to turn on the minimum radius – by no means the same thing – can be vital.

Transposing from the basic formulae (1) the following relationship occurs:

$$R = \frac{v^2}{g(n^2 - 1)^{\frac{1}{2}}}$$

or, as more commonly referred to: *V-squared-over-G*

The point to note from this formulae is that radius of turn is proportional to the squared function of speed, therefore, if speed is doubled, radius of turn is quadrupled. This can have a major impact on the planning of a combat. In the past, when performance was always at a premium, pilots tried to engage as fast as possible, always conscious of how fast energy could be lost, but there comes a point, when very high speed performance is available and the armament consists of high ability and agility missiles, that engaging with a surplus of speed can result in radii of turn that are too large for the combat. It may be necessary even, for the modern fighter pilot to throttle back as he enters the fight, rather than urging the most out of his machine, because of the excessive turning radius which could result from the very high speeds available; something which his early predecessors would have had difficulty in crediting.

Figure 3.2 illustrates the effect on radius of turn of an aircraft pulling a constant 'G' loading but varying its speed. Figure 3.3 shows the alternative case where the speed is kept constant and the 'G' loading varied. The V-squared-over-G factor is clearly seen.

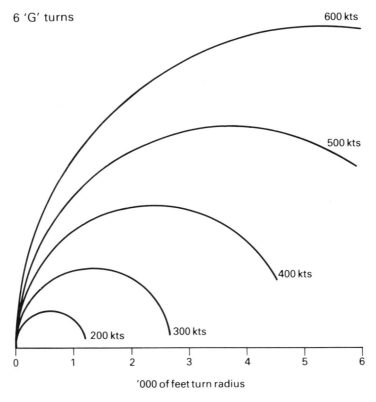

6 'G' turns

600 kts

500 kts

400 kts

200 kts   300 kts

0   1   2   3   4   5   6

'000 of feet turn radius

FIG 3.2.   Radius of turn at varying speeds

RATE OF TURN

As its name suggests, *rate of turn* is that rate at which the nose of the aircraft traverses through the horizon during a turning manoeuvre. It is measured either in radians/second or, more usually, in degrees/second. There is a popular confusion between the merits of *minimum-radius-of-turn* and *maximum-rate-of-turn* with a common

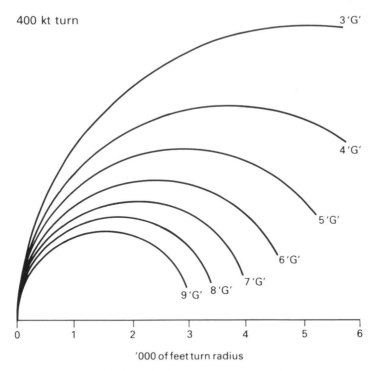

400 kt turn

3 'G'

4 'G'

5 'G'

6 'G'

7 'G'

9 'G'   8 'G'

| 0 | 1 | 2 | 3 | 4 | 5 | 6 |

'000 of feet turn radius

FIG 3.3.   Radius of turn at varying 'G'

misapprehension that the two are synonymous. Rarely is that the case. Figure 3.4 shows that a slow aircraft pulling modest 'G' and a fast aircraft pulling much higher 'G' have similar radii of turn, but the slower aircraft is flying round the flight path at a slower speed and the *rate* of turn is therefore quite different. In the example illustrated, the 'G' being pulled is different, the radius of turn is the same, and the time needed to traverse the similar circumference is half as much again for the slower than the faster aircraft, as the difference in speeds would logically suggest.

Conversely, Figure 3.5 shows two aircraft starting their turn at the same time with both using different speeds and pulling different 'G's but, as both return to the original start point at the same time, their *rate-of-turn* has been identical. The flight paths can be seen, however, to be quite dissimilar.

When to use *maximum rate* or *minimum radius* in a combat situation will depend on the circumstance. An example of the need to use *maximum rate* would be if it was required to turn onto the reciprocal heading to fire a missile at a target which had passed through the 12 o'clock position and was rapidly departing at the 6 o'clock. The radius of turn in this case would be largely irrelevant; what would matter would be how fast the turn could be completed to enable the missile heads to be brought to bear.

Conversely, *minimum radius* might be necessary when the *geometry* of the situation was critical, for example, in the evasion of a missile. In this case the high speed missile may have a large radius of turn because, although pulling many times the 'G' possible with a manned aircraft, its great speed, and the *V-squared-over-G*

Radius 2500 ft.

Aircraft A	200 kts.	Aircraft B	400 kts.
	1.73 'G'		5.76 'G'
	7.74 deg/sec		15.49 deg/sec
	55 degs bank		80 degs bank

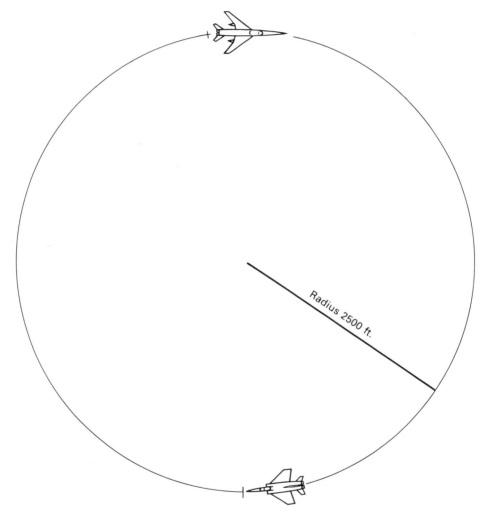

Aircraft A turn complete in 23.24 sec

Aircraft B completed 180 degs of turn

FIG 3.4.   'Rate' and 'Radius' of turn – 1

factor, means that its manoeuvrability in terms of turn radius could be very large. If the aircraft could manoeuvre outside the fusing range of the missile, by utilising a small turn radius, the missile would be rendered ineffective.

Whereas such techniques were quite effective against the earlier missiles, the

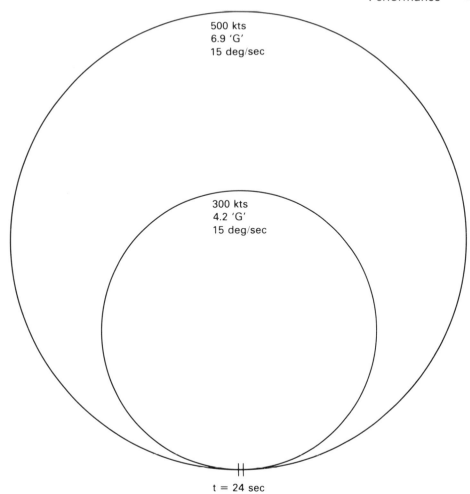

500 kts
6.9 'G'
15 deg/sec

300 kts
4.2 'G'
15 deg/sec

t = 24 sec

FIG 3.5.   'Rate' and 'Radius' of turn – 2

increased speed of modern missiles, and the more sophisticated guidance laws, make the out-manoeuvring of a missile more problematical. The use of manoeuvre, in combination with other counter-measures to break the lock of a missile guidance head, is still a valid tactic, indeed it is growing in importance, and the minimum radius turn must remain firmly in the repertoire.

THE 'G' FACTOR

It is sometimes confusing when discussing 'G' if terms are not well defined. As has been seen in the mathematical notation there is the 'g' which is the factor to convert to gravitational units – 32.174 for those letting a calculator do the hard work, 32.2 being quite satisfactory for those who are not – and there is 'n' which is taken to refer to the 'G' indicated in the cockpit. Some difficulty will arise if it is forgotten that in straight and level flight the aircraft is under a load of one 'G' – not zero 'G', which is a condition of weightlessness and the cause of the peculiar gyrations so familiar to spacemen. The reason that the aircraft does not dive or climb under this one 'G' load is that it merely balances the earth's gravitational pull and, in effect, cancels it out.

Everything in the aircraft is affected by the 'G' loading. The wings of a 10-tonne aircraft will be supporting this weight in straight and level flight but will be carrying a load of 90 tonnes under nine 'G'. Every component in the aircraft will similarly weigh nine times its normal weight at rest. It can be seen therefore, why high 'G' aircraft have to be built so strongly to withstand such stresses and why, to achieve a high 'G' capability while at the same time keeping the structural weight under control, the designer is presented with a difficult problem. Not only the inanimate suffers this weight growth; the human frame is similarly affected and it is the pull of the 'G' making the blood column between heart and head so heavy, and reducing the flow of blood to the brain, which causes the *grey-out, black-out* and eventual unconsciousness, which increasingly concerns the modern combat pilot.

UNIVERSAL TURN DIAGRAM

Because the relationship between the major performance parameters is derived from physics and is independent of specific aircraft characteristics, it can be displayed in a universal turn diagram, applicable to all aircraft, an example of which is at Figure 3.6. This refers to the relationships in horizontal flight. The *flat earth* is, however, the arena of the sailor and soldier rather than the airman, who is a three-dimensional creature, and it is this third dimension which adds complexity, and interest, to the airman's scene.

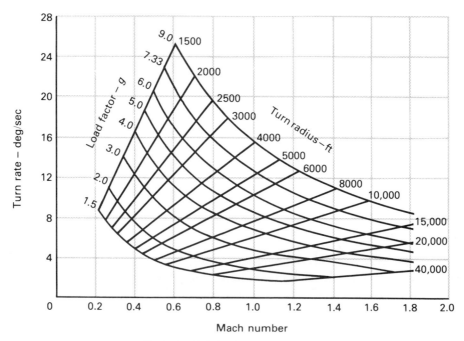

FIG 3.6.   Universal turn rate diagram

Before looking at the third dimension, however, it is useful to spend a moment examining the universal turn rate diagram and memorising some simple points which fall from it. It can be seen that the horizontal axis is Mach Number. The diagram is therefore applicable to all heights, providing the airspeed – either True Air Speed or Calibrated (Indicated) Airspeed – is converted into Mach. The lines of equal turn radius all run from the origin – this will be important when minimum radius turn speeds are calculated from the individual aircraft performance plots. The lines of equal 'G' run in a curve, with that curve rapidly going near vertical at the lower speed end. A few moments thought about why – with the previous formulae in mind – will be profitable. The slope of the turn radius curves at the higher speed part of the diagram suggests that very high 'G' loadings are required if tight turns are to be made at the higher Mach numbers. It should be remembered that missiles operate at speeds even higher than those covered in this diagram.

THE THREE-DIMENSIONAL *EGG*

It has been seen that when in straight and level flight, the cockpit 'G' meter shows one 'G'. The aircraft maintains equilibrium because the force of gravity is balanced. Looked at another way, the aircraft needs to pull one 'G' to cancel out gravity and therefore, as gravity has no effect, as far as the physics of turning is concerned, there is effectively no 'G' being applied.

If, however, the aircraft commences a pull-up into a looping manoeuvre, say with an indicated cockpit 'G' of four, then, as the aircraft started under one 'G', there will only be effectively three 'G' providing the turn in the vertical plane.

Consider the reverse situation, where the aircraft is at the top of the looping manoeuvre and inverted. If it were to maintain straight and level flight in the inverted state it would show minus one 'G' on the cockpit indicator but, if it continued the steady pull, instead of the gravitational force being subtractive, as was the case in the upright condition, this time it would be additive. The four 'G' pull would be effectively five 'G' as far as the physics of turning was concerned.

Not surprisingly, at the mid-point in the loop, when the aircraft was pointing either vertically upwards or vertically downwards, the gravitational 'G' does not help or hinder the turning equation and the four 'G' pull is applied to the physics without amendment.

For the sake of illustration, consider an aircraft conducting a loop under the unusual conditions of constant speed and constant 'G'; assume a speed of 400 knots and a 'G' of three.

The formulae for calculating radius of turn in the vertical plane is:

$$R = \frac{v^2}{g} \, \frac{1}{(n - \cos y)}$$

where:

R = radius of turn (ft)
v = speed (TAS) (ft/sec)
n = 'G' on meter
y = angle of climb/dive (0 degrees = upright)
g = 32.174 ft per sec^2

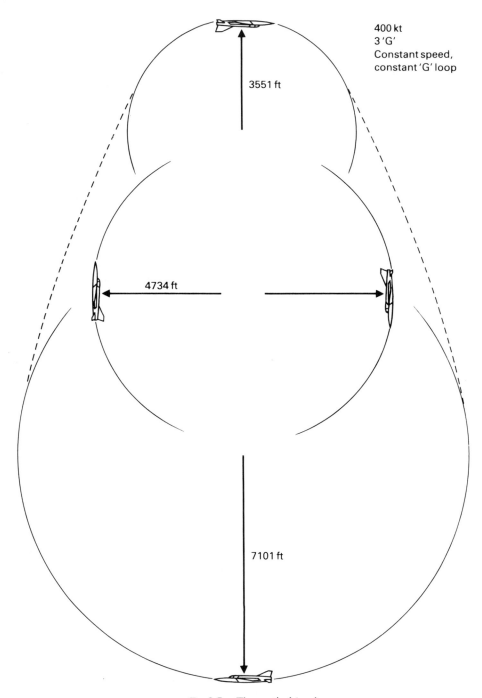

400 kt
3 'G'
Constant speed,
constant 'G' loop

3551 ft

4734 ft

7101 ft

Fig 3.7.   The vertical 'egg'

It can be calculated therefore that the radius of turn at the bottom of the loop is 7,101 feet, at the vertical it is 4,734 feet, and at the inverted position it is 3,551 feet. In other words, as the gravitational effect moves gradually from being subtractive to being additive, so the radius of turn tightens. The effect of this is that the loop flown under such conditions would not resemble a perfect circle but rather would resemble an egg as shown in Figure 3.7. Indeed, this phenomenon is commonly referred to as *the vertical egg* effect.

Few if any would wish to, or be able to, fly such a contrived manoeuvre as a constant speed, constant 'G' loop, but the example does bring out a useful combat lesson. If the best turn performance is required to avoid a particularly hostile threat, the inverted pull-through has much to commend it. This was found true in Vietnam when it was used by many pilots to spoil the attack from the SA-2 surface-to-air missile (SAM). Used against an attack which was less predictable and which may not provide the same level of warning as a SAM launch against a medium level target, the time delay in translating from the upright to the inverted would have to be taken into account. It is unlikely that such fine judgements could be made in the heat of battle and this demonstrates why many of the immediate counter tactical moves need to be pre-judged in the calm of the crew room were the necessary data is available and sensible comparisons of options can be made.

AIRCRAFT PERFORMANCE PARAMETERS

The Universal Turn Diagram shows the relationships determined by physics. It is necessary to consider how the individual aircraft parameters can be applied to the universal laws.

The *V-N* diagram is one of the first sources to consult when examining the performance capability of an aircraft. As its name suggests it plots speed on the x-axis against 'G', or in the accepted notation, 'n', on the y-axis. The characteristic shape of the graph is shown at Figure 3.8 and although straightforward as graphs go it tells a lot about the aircraft. The straight lines show *limits*. In this case there are two limits; the cut-off on the y-axis representing the maximum amount of 'G' that the airframe will stand in terms of its structural integrity – this figure is usually factored by about 1.5 on the ultimate structural strength, that is, where the structure would fail – and the straight line on the x-axis indicates the speed at which the aircraft is limited – this may be matter of the amount of available power or be caused by the inability of the airframe to accept greater dynamic force from the airflow. In this case the line can be referred to as the 'Q' limit. In some designs it can be a limit derived from aerodynamic problems and some of the earlier aircraft had limits set by the handling difficulties caused by the shock-wave movement as they approached the transonic region. Occasionally, very high speed aircraft can be set limits determined by the temperature of the air as it impacts the front face of the engine although better intake design is making this less of a problem on modern aircraft.

The curved line shows how lift – which determines the ability to pull the 'G' – builds up with increasing speed according to the formulae:

$$L = C_L \cdot \tfrac{1}{2} \cdot p \cdot v^2 \cdot s$$

where:

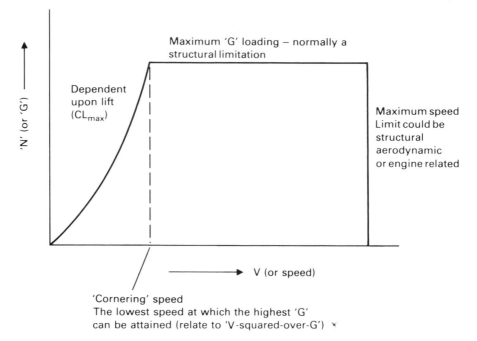

Fɪɢ 3.8.   The V-N diagram

L   = Lift
C_L = Lift Coefficient of the Wing
p   = density of air
v   = Speed (TAS)
S   = Wing area

The *v-squared* factor can be seen in this formula and it could be expected that the curved line would project further according to a normal squared-law if it were not artificially constrained by the structural limit line. In practice, the effects of compressibility would modify the shape at the higher speeds.

The point at which the lift-limit line intersects with the structural limit line gives the speed at which the maximum amount of 'G' can be pulled at the lowest speed. At this point *V-squared-over-G* is optimised and the speed indicated becomes that for the best rate of turn, and is known as the *cornering speed*.

There is an important qualification to be made. This form of diagram merely indicates that the aircraft can pull a certain amount of 'G' at a given speed. It does not indicate that it can maintain that condition. This highlights the difference between *sustained* turn rate and *instantaneous* turn rate. As the names suggests, sustained turn rate is that which the aircraft can sustain continuously and this steady state condition depends on the ability of the aircraft to overcome the drag rise due to the increased lift developed. Drag rise can be very large and the induced drag – that caused by the increased incidence of the wing necessary to develop the lift – can increase to figures as high as 300 per cent over the base case, with only 60 degrees of bank, and increases very rapidly after that. Sustained turn rate is dependent, therefore, on the ability of the thrust to overcome the increased drag. Consequently, *sustained turn rate is thrust, or power, dependent.*

Instantaneous turn rate, on the other hand, is not a continuous state and, as its name suggests, is a transitory condition. It exists beyond the point at which the power can balance the drag rise and is dependent on the maximum lift that can be developed within the constraints of the structural limit. The tactical value of this instantaneous condition is in the circumstances of a *break*, or a tight turn, either for survival or to bring weapons to bear to obtain a killing shot. *Instantaneous turn rate is lift dependent.*

With access to even this simple graph, applicable to an enemy aircraft, a comparison with the friendly type will show whether the advantage lies in speed, in 'G', or where turn advantages, or disadvantages, may lie. At Figure 3.9 is shown a typical plot of speed against sustained 'G' and the difference between the two conditions, *instantaneous* and *sustained*, can be clearly seen by comparison with the previous diagram.

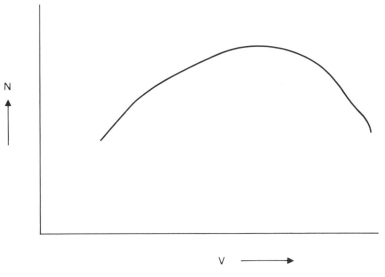

Fig 3.9.   Sustained 'G'

TURN RATE DIAGRAMS

Although the V-N diagram is a useful first step to performance comparison, more information is derived from the turn-rate-diagram where turn-rate on the y-axis is plotted against speed on the x-axis. The diagram is derived from the physical laws and is the universal turn rate diagram described earlier. The value to the combat pilot becomes apparent when individual aircraft performance envelopes are superimposed on the base diagram. An example of this is seen at Figure 3.10.

The shape of the superimposed pattern of individual aircraft performance, while differing in detail between types, follows a similar pattern. Because, with a fertile

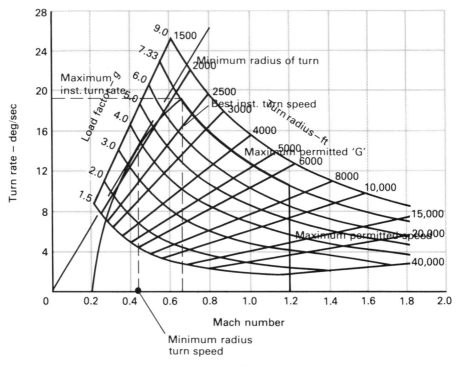

FIG 3.10.   'Doghouse' plot

imagination, it can be likened to the shape of a kennel this particular plot is popularly referred to as the *doghouse* plot.

The speed limit line still runs in a straight line, as with the V-N diagram, but the other main boundaries take a different form because of the turn-rate basis of the y-axis. The maximum 'G' line is seen to be curved and descending rather than horizontal and the lift line becomes more complex than the *square-law* shape of the previous diagram. It is the shape of this line, or more correctly the specific parameters of the individual aircraft, which cause general conclusions drawn from this diagram to be caveated.

The point where the maximum 'G' line intersects the lift line still represents the corner point speed, that is, the minimum speed at which maximum 'G' can be obtained. Minimum radius turn, however, is to be found where the relationship between speed and 'G' are optimised. That point may be found somewhere along the lift line which, by examination, can be seen to be the point at which the aircraft is being flown as slowly as is possible at the highest possible G. It is for this reason that, in the combat environment, the *sustained* minimum radius turn, as distinct from the instantaneous break type manoeuvre, is rarely used – because of the vulnerability of being in a multi-aircraft combat with so little energy. An example of where it is used is in the scissors manoeuvre – but more of that later.

ENERGY MEASUREMENT AND MANAGEMENT

The five primary factors in combat mathematics have been examined, the universal turn rate graph has been introduced, and the particular aircraft parameters have been superimposed. It is now necessary to consider how *thermodynamics*, or thrust and power, is applied to what has, so far, been aerodynamically based.

The study of energy relationships and the application of energy conditions to performance measurement is not new. The application of potential energy to performance estimation was used by the German designers in the inter-war years. It was the disappointment with the combat results in the opening stages of the air war in Vietnam which caused a renewed interest in the subject. In those early days, the combat exchange ratio was much lower than that which the USAF and USN thought it should have been and to which they had become used as the norm from such experiences as Korea. Consequently, in the mid-sixties, the concept of *energy manoeuvrability* was conceived by Boyd and Christie to enable better comparisons to be made between the MiG-21F and the Phantom F-4C. Whereas the German approach had been limited to the consideration of potential energy – that derived from the height of an object – Boyd and Christie extended the theory to include kinetic energy – that derived from the state of movement – and argued that, within the total energy state, the flight condition could be changed; speed, height, acceleration and load factor – or 'G' – could be traded and exchanged. From this theory came the term *specific energy* and *specific excess power*, part of the theory of energy manoeuvrability and energy management.

SPECIFIC ENERGY

Specific Energy is defined as the sum of the potential and kinetic energy of an aircraft, per unit weight.

Total Energy = Potential Energy + Kinetic Energy

$$= W \cdot H + \tfrac{1}{2} mv^2$$

$$= W \cdot H + \frac{Wv^2}{2G}$$

Specific Energy (Es) = $\dfrac{\text{Total Energy}}{W}$

$$Es = H + \frac{v^2}{2G}$$

where:

W = weight
H = height
m = mass
G = 32.174
v = Speed (TAS)

SPECIFIC POWER

Specific power (Ps) is the rate of change of specific energy and becomes the measure of the ability of an aircraft to change its state.

Specific Power (Ps) $= V \dfrac{(T-D)}{W}$

where:

T = thrust
D = Drag

At any given speed specific power is a function of the degree to which net thrust exceeds total drag. It is a point condition and is true for only a specified airspeed, altitude, power setting and weight. By calculating a series of *point* conditions, a set of specific power curves can be produced and these can be applied to the turn-rate diagram which has the doghouse plot already overlaid. Figure 3.11 shows an example of this but note that the height at which it applies, and the weight of the aircraft, have to be clearly specified. While the value inherent in these plots for valid comparisons between aircraft goes without question, it is important to compare like with like and to remember that to plan a battle on the data relating to one weight may catch out those who forget that the modern combat aircraft in afterburner at low level is changing its weight at the rate of some half-a-tonne or more a minute, even before firing off missiles which may weigh a quarter of a tonne each. Also, that modern fighters combating in the vertical plane can be regularly transiting through tens of thousands of feet in very short timescales.

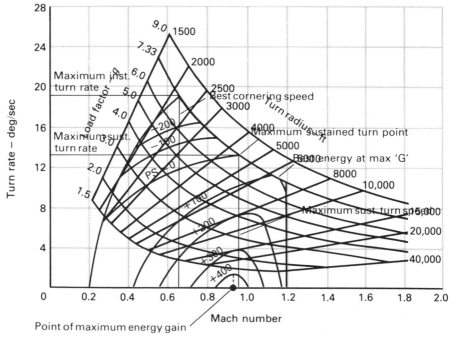

Fig 3.11.   Doghouse chart with energy overlay

In examining the graph with the specific power lines superimposed, the most significant line is where Ps=O. This specifies the state when thrust is balanced perfectly by drag and is the condition where the aircraft can sustain any condition represented by the line. If the aircraft is being flown *on the line* and the pilot wishes to accelerate, to do so he must dive to utilise a component of weight as thrust to help balance the added drag which the increased speed implies. Equally, if the pilot wishes to climb, he may do so but will have to convert kinetic energy into potential energy; he will have to slow up or he will have to execute a *zoom* climb. Once at the desired increased altitude, however, he will find himself on a Ps line of negative value indicating that he will not be able to stay there – it is not *sustainable*. A trade will have to be made; height for speed.

In any condition represented in the negative area of the Ps plots, something has to change; in the positive area there is scope for improvement in one or more ways. When conducting performance comparisons, by looking for the flight conditions where the difference in specific power between the two aircraft most favours the friendly aircraft, the best potential area of combat is to be found and tactics can be derived which force the enemy into that part of the flight regime.

It cannot be stressed too much that the condition shown in any of the plots is specific only for the condition laid down; that of height, and weight. Having said that, it can be seen that any reading taken off the plot is relevant to a *point* condition. It may be that at a given situation the aircraft is at a point where, at that given height and weight, it has a Ps=300. This would indicate that, at that moment, it has the potential for initiating a climb rate of:

$$300 \times 60 = 18,000 \text{ ft/min}$$

As soon as such a climb was instituted, however, the aircraft would climb into a higher altitude band and would be subject to another plot of Ps which would show a lower Ps value. Hence, as the aircraft climbed, the Ps value would lower and eventually the climb would cease – because the Ps=0, which would represent the combat ceiling of the aircraft.

Alternatively, the Ps value can be converted into a measure of acceleration. The instantaneous acceleration available from any given Ps is given by:

$$\text{Inst accel} = \frac{\text{Ps . G}}{\text{V}}$$

By inspection it can be seen that, for example, that with a Ps=300, the instantaneous acceleration available is 10.1 ft/sec/sec. But, as soon as the acceleration starts to take effect the 'V' factor beneath the line increases, so reducing the available acceleration as the speed builds up. Eventually, the 'V' would build up to the point where there was no more instantaneous acceleration available and that condition would be reached where the Ps=0.

PERFORMANCE COMPARISONS

When making performance comparisons based on the overlays of Ps diagrams, and conscious that the result may determine the tactics to be used in one of the most lethal competitions known to man, it is important not only to be aware of the provisos made above in relation to the point relevance of the data, but also that the charts relating to the opposition would not have been readily conceded by them. The source of the enemy data needs to be enquired into; is it from test flights of a captured version of the enemy machine? Is it from the technical assessment of photographic analysis? Is it from some defectors report? Or is it from an enemy data manual slipped from under some somnulent General's pillow by a latter-day Mata Hari? Before the pilot puts his life at risk on the results of a performance comparison he has the right to know what reliance he can place on the data. It is, after all, something like putting the head in the lion's mouth without first enquiring whether it has been fed. Further, what may be a very fair risk to take as assessed by the intelligence officer – who remains in the deep bunker throughout the war – may not appear to be such to the pilot who is going into the jousting ring.

With such reservations to the fore, consider some comparisons. Take two aircraft which, in a stylised form – to avoid infringing security – represent two typical modern fighters and are represented as an overlay at Figure 3.12.

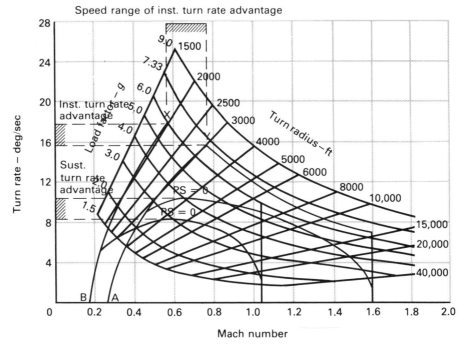

FIG 3.12.   Doghouse peformance comparison

Notice first that aircraft A shows itself as the faster machine which can pull the higher 'G'. Aircraft B is slower in terms of top speed and can pull less 'G', it can, however, fly slower at the low speed end of the range. Further, its lift line profile is such that although it is one 'G' deficient on aircraft A, the combination of the lower 'G' offset by the lower speed combines to give it an overall higher instantaneous turn rate – point X compared to point Y. It can also be seen that this advantage, in the example used for illustration, is held over a quite large speed range in the lower speed regime.

Examining the Ps=0 lines for the two aircraft, it can be seen that aircraft A has a sustained turn rate advantage over most of the mid range of speeds over aircraft B and while aircraft B is turning at his best sustained rate, aircraft A could match him in turn and have excess energy available to climb.

Aircraft B would therefore try to tempt Aircraft A into a horizontal, low-speed flight where Aircraft A's speed advantage is nullified and B could use his instantaneous turn advantage to get snap shooting opportunities or, alternatively, use the turn capability for evasive of defensive manoeuvres.

Aircraft A, on the other hand, would try to keep the fight fast and use his power advantage to good effect in the vertical plane. He would be expected to conduct a series of high-speed slashing attacks, zooming to height following each unsuccessful pass to *sanctuary* where B could not follow.

So much for the simplistic conclusions to be drawn in the first instance from these performance comparisons. Whether they could form a basis of a tactical plan would depend critically on the armament. If both aircraft were gun-armed then there is no doubt that the conclusions enumerated above would be sound, but if aircraft B was equipped with an effective infra-red missile and this was used skilfully in combination with the instantaneous turn advantage, then the higher speed aircraft zooming to its sanctuary, more than probably utilising its afterburner to do so, could conceivably arrive there as debris.

It is not straightforward performance comparison which determines the outcome of a combat. It is the way that performance is applied compared to the performance of the opposition. Weapons and individual skills weigh heavily on the outcome because, even in the scenario painted here, a mistake by the pilot of either aircraft would allow the other to capitalise on the error and to obtain the killing shot. The presence of high performance missiles in the equation makes the accuracy of the assessment more important and the ability to exploit the error that much easier and more lethal.

A proposal which emerges every so often involves the proposition that, instead of buying a few sophisticated, high performance aircraft, a larger number of more simple designs should be procured and numbers should be relied upon to overcome the technology of the more complex, and expensive, designs. There is some merit in the suggestion. Studies have shown that some 80 per cent of aircraft shot down in combat were claimed by aircraft which they had not seen. Even in modern training exercises such as the United States Air Force *Red Flag* exercises, aircraft of the outstanding performance of the McDonnell Douglas F-15 fall to the camera-guns of the humble Northrop F-5s because the smaller, *difficult-to-see* aircraft, are present in the fight in greater numbers and close for the kill unobserved.

How would peformance comparisons look therefore, if a fighter similar to those used in World War Two was compared to a modern design? What would happen if the *many/cheap* versus the *few/expensive* theory was taken to the extreme?

Examine the comparative plots of a mass produced piston engined fighter, something like, say, a P-51 Mustang, with a modern high performance fighter. The plots would look something like those depicted in Figure 3.13. Looking at this comparison between aircraft A and B, it can be seen that the piston engined World War Two fighter, Aircraft A, has higher instantaneous rates of turn and has a higher sustained rate of turn than the more modern aircraft. In a combat in which all other

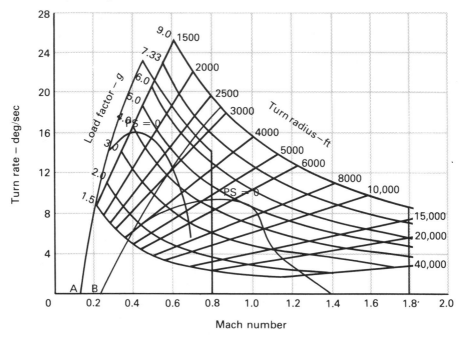

Fig 3.13.   Many/cheap or few/expensive?

things were equal, the piston engined aircraft would triumph because, in any prolonged turning fight, the better sustained turn rate would finally pay dividends and the aircraft would end up in the six o'clock position on the opposition. Further, if it is assumed that the older design was, nevertheless, equipped with modern weaponry, particularly an air-to-air missile, then the superior instantaneous turn rate, allowing nose and missile pointing albeit temporarily, would allow greater opportunity to deliver missile attacks than would the characteristics of the modern fighter. The answer is therefore straightforward; the many/cheap option is proved to be the superior choice.

Would it ever be so simple! Indeed the many/cheap solution would triumph over the conditions outlined above but the pilot of the *few/expensive* aircraft would need to be exceedingly ill-trained to engage in a fight played on such unfavourable terms when his performance allowed him to dictate the conduct of the battle. The World War Two design would have a maximum 'G' specific excess power capability below 100; the modern fighter could have specific excess power capability closer to 1000, certainly in the area of 700 to 800 ft/sec. Consequently, after due study of the performance comparisons, the pilot of the more modern design could engage at will, retaining his energy, and, when the older design began to obtain a turn advantage, the modern design would be put into the vertical plane and the, say, 700 ft/sec specific excess energy capability would be used in the vertical plane as an instantaneous climb rate in excess of 40,000 feet/minute.

The modern fighter would always retain the ability to escape and to re-engage on its own terms. It would be able to *stand-off* in *sanctuary* and to conduct a series of *slashing* attacks until either the geometry was in its favour or, more likely, the opponent had the momentary lapse of concentration which allowed the killing shot to be obtained, by missile or gun.

A new concept? A revolutionary doctrine? No, exactly the tactic developed by JG 44 using the superior speed and energy of the early Messerschmitt 262s against the inferior piston engined designs of the period. The performance differential between the Me-262 and the Mustangs and Spitfires was not so great as that between World War Two designs and the modern fighter used here to illustrate the point by use of the extreme, but the principles involved, and used, resulted in the same tactical doctrine – the superior performance machine tends to use the vertical while the superior manoeuvring machine tends to use the horizontal.

It is interesting to note that the combat scene is going through something of a period of change as the first generation of the high energy fighters enter the front-line inventories. Because their performance is so far superior to those fighters produced only a few years previously, the myth has grown that some fundamental tactical doctrines have changed and that the new generation fighters can play the horizontal and the vertical as one. This is so only in the case of combat against the older generation designs. The present situation is a temporary aberration. When modern fighters are the norm then the necessity to compare designs, plot against plot, will be as necessary as ever because it is not the *absolute* performance figures which determine the measure of advantage but the *relative* performance advantage. The difference used to be measured between 2 and 3 'G'; now it is between 8 and 9 'G' but the tactical doctrine involved has not changed substantially because it is so governed by the relative values. What has changed the combat scene so massively is, of course, the development of air-to-air weapons.

4.

Weapons

WHATEVER the qualities of the aircraft or the skill and perseverance of the pilot, in air combat it is the weapon alone which gets the kill. If the weapon is ineffective then the whole purpose of the combat, indeed the aircraft itself, is thwarted. As the cost of weapons increases, stock levels themselves come under review; it is a relationship which is well borne in mind because, once stocks exhaust, it matters not how many aircraft remain, or their performance in the air, or their value on paper, they are irrelevant to the battle.

This is an important, if simple, point to bear in mind at a time when more people are posing the question about the relationship between aircraft, as vehicles or platforms, and the weapons that are carried. The relationship between aircraft, as vehicles, and the weapons, as the means of achieving the aim, has not changed since weapons were first fitted to aircraft, but before the advent of *smart* weaponry the relationship was more muted. It was much easier to see the eight Browning 0.303 machine guns firmly fixed in the wings of the Spitfire as part of the aircraft as a whole than it is to see a Maverick or an Exocet missile as a part of the launch aircraft. Normal conversation demonstrates the perception; Spitfires are said to have shot down Messerschmitts, not '0.303 Brownings', yet few people do not refer to the Exocet which killed HMS Sheffield rather than the Étendard aircraft which launched it. Similarly, years before, the popular image was of the *Styx* missile which sank the Israeli destroyer *Eilat* rather than the *Osa* fast patrol boat which launched it.

In this chapter, the three main forms of aircraft armament will be covered: guns, short-range missiles and long-ranged missiles. Of the missiles, the first are those usually associated with the air combat environment and are normally infra-red homers, and the later are the radar guided missiles associated with Beyond Visual Range (BVR) engagements but which cannot be divorced from the air combat scene.

RAMMING

It is being entirely realistic and practical, rather than in any way being emotional, to consider ramming as part of the inventory of options open to the fighter pilot. If weapons have been expended and the penetrating aircraft, be that bomber or fighter bomber, still proceeds towards the target, the fighter pilot has to consider what the chances are that the enemy is carrying a nuclear weapon. If that chance appears to be high, and the circumstances of the overall campaign scenario and the intercept itself may provide clues to this, then the challenge has to be accepted and the target destroyed at all cost. The words of General Pétain to the French defenders at Verdun in the Great War would be equally applicable to the young fighter pilot in any future major conflict:

Ils ne passeront pas

Those who feel that such methods of war are suitable only to the Eastern mentality, should ponder on the thought that a single tactical nuclear weapon on a target which entailed high collateral damage to the civilian infrastructure, could cause more deaths than the French suffered at Verdun – and that was enough to have scarred itself not only into French history but also the French psyche.

Ramming may sound easy but could prove difficult when high speed aircraft are concerned. Obtaining the geometry for a head-on ram could be problematical and the merest tweak of either control column at the later stages would be sufficient to guarantee a miss with the speeds involved. Very high performance advantage is required to obtain reliable quarter attack angles from a beam approach and are difficult to arrange against a high speed target which may not be readily identifiable at low level with terrain masking and camouflage to contend with. The larger aircraft, at high level, could have tail armament and the approach to physical contact in the face of such weapons would be unlikely to succeed. This is not to suggest that it is impossible to ram – only more difficult than at first appears, difficult enough for there to be the chance of a few volumes of the *Memoirs of a Kamikaze Pilot* at the end of the war.

GUNS AND CANNONS

Despite the onward march of technology, there is still a place in the modern fighter aircraft for the gun or the cannon. The confusion which exists in the terms should be clarified. A gun is generally taken to be a weapon which fires a solid shot round – the Browning 0.303 of Spitfire fame was therefore a *gun*. A cannon fires rounds which contain a charge – the 20 mm Hispano weapon which followed the Browning into a number of Royal Air Force aircraft was therefore a *cannon* because the 20 mm round had a fused high explosive filling which detonated on contact with the target.

Another reason for maintaining the gun (hereafter used for convenience to cover guns and cannons) is that, ideally, the fighter pilot wants the whole spectrum, from the nose of his aircraft to the furthest reach of his longest range weapon, covered by useable fire. Missiles have to be launched with their control surfaces locked to ensure that immediate hard-overs do not cause the weapon to strike the aircraft, or an inadvertent warhead detonation cause self-damage, and this entails the missiles flying *ballistic* for the distance equivalent to the safety and arming time. In modern missiles this may be as much as 300 metres and within this range in the close combat environment shots against adversaries are to be obtained (Figure 4.1).

An equally powerful reason for retaining gun armament is that the field of radar and infra-red countermeasures is starting to attract the attention it has so long deserved and the effectiveness of air-to-air missile systems is going to be confirmed only on the first day of the war, when nations use their secret and as yet unrevealed countermeasures. Once fired, however, the round from the gun obeys only the laws

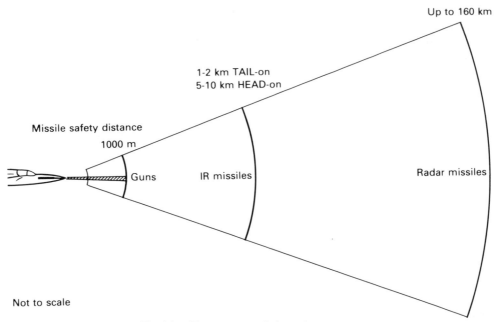

FIG 4.1.   The spectrum of air-to-air armament

of physics and they are notoriously difficult to jam or bend. There is therefore conferred a certain reassurance – or insurance – by fitting guns.

The development of aircraft guns over the years has proceeded in a number of steps, all attempting to solve the two basic problems: first, to obtain the hit, and second, to obtain the kill.

Take a hypothetical situation with a machine gun, not unlike those used in the early days of air combat, with a rate of fire of 600 rounds per minute (RPM) and a muzzle velocity (mv) of 300 metres per second (m/s). The interval between the individual rounds in a burst is 0.1 secs. If an aircraft was flying directly through the burst at right angles it could conceivably fly through the burst unscathed if its length was, say 7 metres – not untypical of aircraft in the Great War – and its speed was 180 kts. It shows that fly-through shots at high angles, which occurred frequently, would be unlikely to put sufficient shot on target to give any reasonable chance of its destruction (Figure 4.2).

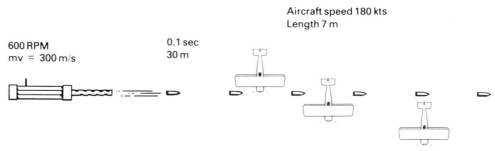

FIG 4.2.   Fly-through machine gun burst

The situation could be made worse when there was a requirement for interrupter gear to allow for firing through the propeller disc. In this instance the point at which the gun should have fired may coincide with the position of the propeller blade before the muzzle and that round would have been suppressed, giving gaps in the firing sequence (Figure 4.3).

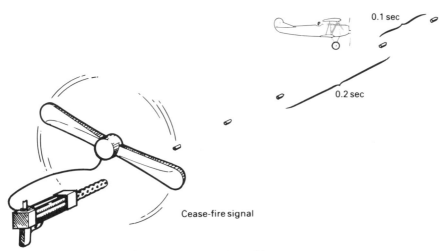

0.1 sec

0.2 sec

Cease-fire signal

FIG 4.3.   Effect of interrupter gear

This would be bad enough if it were the only source of the miss. Unfortunately, the manufacturing tolerances of the gun itself give a dispersion and may be in the order of two or three mils – for the purpose here, a mil is one measure displacement in 1000. Additional to that there is the vibration which is set up by firing long bursts, due to the inadequacies of the mounting in the aircraft. Finally, there is, perhaps, the greatest source of error, that put in by the pilot in his handling of the aircraft. The result is that the overall bullet pattern may overlap the target by some way and the bullet which should have been the one in the 0.1 sec sequence to obtain the hit could be the one which was thrown wide by the dispersion (Figure 4.4).

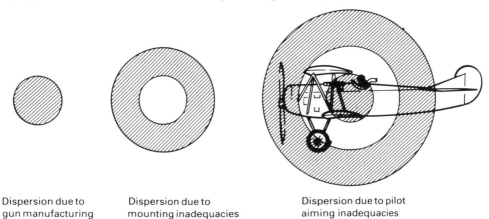

Dispersion due to
gun manufacturing
tolerances

Dispersion due to
mounting inadequacies

Dispersion due to pilot
aiming inadequacies

FIG 4.4.   Factors affecting bullet pattern

The initial answer to this problem was to increase the number of guns (something which has been seen to have caused the early demise of the great Immelmann). This was still the case until quite recently and it will be recalled that the Spitfire had eight Browning 0.303 machine guns in the early models, the P-51D Mustang had six Browning 0.5 inch as did the F-86F Sabre, an aircraft which saw service in combat in the Korean War.

The alternative approach to adding more guns to obtain the necessary concentration of shot was to produce guns which fired more rapidly. From the 600 RPM of the early machine guns, cannon such as the British 30 mm Aden and the French 30 mm DEFA, both developments of a German WW2 design utilising the revolver principle, achieved impressive rates of fire of 1,200–1,400 RPM. It was the use of the Gatling principle of multi-barrels and feed mechanism which allowed the current very high firing rates to be achieved and the modern cannons fitted to aircraft such as the F-15, F-16 and F-18 fire at rates of up to 6,000 RPM and at 100 rounds fired every second makes the chance of flying through a burst unscathed remote.

Obtaining the hit is only part of the problem. The hit must kill. One of the drawbacks to the use of the machine guns of the early days was that the small round had little killing power unless it hit a critical component. Complicating this still further was that the earlier aircraft were not so dense as the modern aircraft and there were large areas where the airframe enclosed unused space. In World War Two there was a case recorded of a Messerschmitt Me-109 which returned to base with no less than 300 holes made by 0.303 bullets yet it not only recovered successfully but, within the month, had been repaired and returned to the front-line.

The explosive cannon shell improved the lethality of the hit greatly. Given good fusing, which would allow the round to penetrate sufficiently to detonate in a confined or enclosed space, the explosive shell could give the kill with the single hit. Specimens on test ranges have shown that tail sections can be blown off airframes by the effect of a 30 mm round correctly detonated and in flight, under combat conditions, it might be expected that the airframe would already be under strain from the flight loads which could assist in emphasising the effect of damage caused by a strike.

Fusing is a difficult thing to get right. If the round detonates too soon, the maximum effect can be obviated. The ideal is to bury the round as far into the structure as possible before activating it. Whereas this is generally easy to see with fuselage structures, it is less clear with wings and tailplanes which, certainly in plan view, comprise the bulk of the target area. If the fusing is designed for deep detonation, a strike on the flying surfaces could pass through and detonate in free air behind the surface losing much, if not all, of its effect on the structure. Many US pilots had poor fusing to thank for their survival in Vietnam when they were able to return after rounds had penetrated their wings and tailplanes and detonated well clear on the dead side.

The step between the solid shot 0.303 in or the 0.5 in round and the 20 mm or more cannon shell is greater than at first appears. Not only has the explosive composition to be allowed for but the fusing can also pose a complex engineering problem. The fuse has to be able to do its primary task of detonating the round at the optimum time after the hit but it must also ensure that the round is safe to handle on the ground and does not arm in the air before it is fired. Space is at a premium, particularly in the smaller calibre shells, and the design has to be able to be built economically to allow production in great numbers. With guns firing at 100 rounds per second, a thought has to be given to cost. A recent contract was announced for M758 fuses for the 25 mm cannon used by the United States Army. 1,741,896 fuses were ordered at a cost of $9,000,000–$5.17 each – which, considering that a modern fuse would impress a watchmaker, says a lot for the techniques of mass production.

It was unlikely that once the ability to put explosive fillings into aircraft cannon shells had been conferred, the designer would not wish to play variations on the theme. A variety of fillings now exist; high explosive, high explosive-incendiary, armour piercing and armour piercing-incendiary, for example. In addition, some rounds will have the option to be fitted with tracer which involves a bright burning composition at the base of the shell. Tracer tends not to be used for every round but for one-in-four or five. Although these options give great choice there can be difficulty in getting the choice right for the occasion and it is customary to belt-up a mix of rounds to cover as many eventualities as possible.

The task for the designer of the rounds is thereby magnified, for these rounds with different fillings and fuses and some with or without tracer, all have to have the same ballistic characteristics if the sighting solution is to be valid in all cases. Modern sighting systems, with high electronic content, give the opportunity to alter the ballistic allowances according to the rounds loaded but the pressure on the designer to produce ballistically constant rounds is still there where mixed belting is practiced.

There is also a conflict for the designer caused by the trend towards *multi-role* capability because the design drivers for the air-to-air weapon are not necessarily those of the air-to-ground weapon. Air-to-air targets, by their nature, are elusive and hard to hit but, once hit, are *soft* targets in weapon terms. Air-to-ground targets, on the other hand, are generally less elusive but are harder and here more emphasis needs to be placed upon weight of charge. This need for weight of charge points to the use of the large calibres. The difference between the amount of explosive which is carried in a 30 mm shell is far greater than the 1.5 factor which could be supposed in comparison with the 20 mm shell. The explosive content tends to increase volumetrically and there is very much greater *volume* available in a 30 mm, as opposed to a 20 mm shell.

The problem arises in obtaining high muzzle velocities. Because of the elusive nature of the air-to-air target, the time-of-flight of the shell must be kept to a minimum to ease the sighting solution and a lower profile shell assists in this aim. As the 20 mm shell can provide sufficient *bang* for the air-to-air case, the requirements are closely compatible. The air-to-ground target, being less elusive, is handled adequately without going for very high muzzle velocities *per se*, not to the extent of compromising the charge weight. Where the weapon system demands high muzzle velocities and a high charge weight, or a high mass, as in the case of the GAU-8 gun on the Fairchild A-10, then a very large weapon results. The gun on the A-10, which fires a heavy 30 mm anti-armour round relying upon kinetic energy for its effect, is the same size as a Volkswagen Beetle and needs to be to get the combination of high muzzle velocity, high calibre and high rate of fire. It would be difficult to see such a weapon being compatible with an aircraft optimised for the air-to-air role.

The multi-role aircraft, as in so many other areas, has to compromise, and the selection of the cannon is no exception to the rule. The specialised air-to-air fighters, such as the F-15, and F-16, have the 20 mm weapon while the equally specialist ground attack A-10 has the 30 mm GAU-8; the Tornado – the *Multi-Role-Combat-Aircraft* – has a 27 mm Mauser cannon based on a revolver, rather than a Gatling, principle.

In the air-to-air case, high muzzle velocity is of great importance because of the difficulty of obtaining the hit. Ideally, of course, a weapon with an extremely long range and a negligible time-of-flight would be the ideal; science fiction material it could have been assumed only a few years ago. Now it is more than a prospect for the future. It can be confidently predicted that the laser weapon will find its way into the air-to-air arena well within the lifetimes of many reading this book. The prospect of *point-and-shoot* weapons will increase lethality enormously and combat as it is known today, with equipment similar to todays, will be unlikely to feature on the scene.

Meanwhile, higher muzzle velocities will be produced as metallurgy provides the means to withstand higher combustion chamber pressures and chemistry matches the trend and produces better propellants. A technique which brings a propellant to a very high temperature by the passage of a sudden electrical charge and in to which, after it forms an ion plasma, an oxidiser is introduced, is already in test and has demonstrated muzzle velocity increases up to 25 per cent. Because the range of a weapon is governed largely by the *mV-squared* factor (mass × velocity squared) this technique could offer the prospect of doubling the range of current systems dependent upon the aerodynamics of the projectile. Perhaps more important is that firing at current ranges would be done with a considerable increase in accuracy.

The effectiveness of aircraft guns is also being increased by the advances made in the computation of the sighting solution. The huge strides made in the capacity of airborne micro-electronics allow more factors to be taken into account in the calculation of a sighting solution and enables those allowances to be made more often and faster. From the days when a sighting system would merely provide an index of where a round might hit under pre-ordained release conditions and at a pre-determined range, modern systems offer a *hot-line* sight which indicates to the pilot the path of the bullet steam through the air at any given moment. Achieving hits with such aids is easier than before and so opens the way to less experienced, or even less gifted, pilots obtaining air-to-air kills. With constraints on training flight time biting so deeply on so many air forces it is to systems such as this that air forces must turn to maintain their operational efficiency.

The target itself has made the task of the air-to-air weapon easier in making itself more vulnerable. Older aircraft used to be filled to a high degree with empty spaces through which a solid shot passed without great trauma. Now aircraft are filled with things which in their own right go *bang*. The Spitfire took-off with a little over 80 gallons of fuel. Even the amazing P-51D Mustang, with a range of over 2,000 nm, took-off with only 265 gallons yet the modern MiG-31 Foxhound has 5,385 US gallons with a further 820 US gallons externally mounted – and it all burns!

Hydraulic systems, hardly needed by aircraft which operated well into the subsonic regime but vital to handle the high dynamic loads of supersonic flight, operate regularly at 3,000 pounds per square inch (psi) pressure and the trend is towards 4,000 psi and higher. Not only services are lost when such systems are hit; a fractured hydraulic accumulator operating at 4,000 psi could be a destructive round in its own right.

Electrical systems are as vulnerable, if not more so, as increasing use is made of electronics for control. Some of that control is of a quite fundamental nature. Modern aircraft of *relaxed* stability do not fly at all without their flight control computers on line and as the trend develops towards networked systems, all interconnected by a data bus, the vulnerability of that connecting system must give pause for thought. Even engine control is being digitised to great effect thermodynamically but if, in the event of an electrical disconnect, the engines run away to self-destruct, as in one design now in service, what price the survivability in a combat environment?

It is aircraft design trends such as this which are making air-to-air weapon designers question whether the air-to-air round, even as large as the 20 mm, may be necessary in the future. Perhaps the increasing vulnerabilities of the targets themselves will allow the trend to be reversed and the air-to-air round made smaller rather than larger. With the high proportion of burnable fuel in modern designs, it may be that a smaller incendiary round would have equivalent effect to a much larger high-explosive round.

Maybe the future air-to-air weapon will not need to be a gun, or even a laser. What would a directed micro-wave pulse do to the heavily micro-computer dependent modern fighter? What would an electromagnetic pulse do to the circuits and memories of a computer laden aircraft?

AIR TO AIR WEAPONS

The large formations of heavily armed aircraft used to prosecute the strategic bombing offensive in daylight during World War Two provided the incentive for the development of air-to-air guided weapons. Certainly the Luftwaffe fighter losses were heavy and increasingly so with the advent of the P-51 Mustang, used in the long-range escort role. Two missiles were well into development when the war stopped in 1945; one, the Henschel HS 298 was radio command guided, and the other, the Ruhstahl/BMW X-4 was wire guided. Fortunately for the Allies they were not used operationally.

During the late 1940s and the 1950s most of the leading aviation nations pursued the development of air-to-air missiles. The US started development of the Sparrow, Falcon and Sidewinder series, France produced the radar-guided MATRA 511 and the radio-command AA20, the Soviet Union fielded the radar guided AA-1 Alkali and the UK produced the Firestreak IR missile.

There is a comprehensive collection of AAMs world-wide and there is little value in cataloguing them here; there are excellent missile directories produced from time to time by the leading aviation magazines. What is more useful is to consider some of the factors common to missiles of a particular group and to see how these strengths and weaknesses affect the use of those missiles in a combat environment.

INFRA-RED (IR) MISSILES

When discussing IR missiles the unit of wavelength used is the micron (μm) which is one-millionth part of a metre. Figure 4.5 shows the pattern of radiation across the

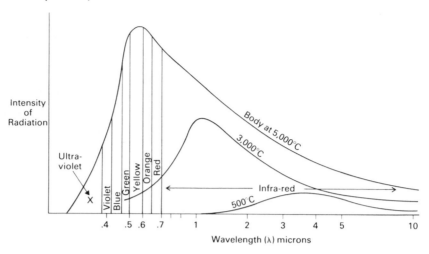

FIG 4.5.   Radiated electromagnetic energy of a body at varying temperatures

infra-red part of the electromagnetic spectrum of a body at a temperature of 5,000°C, 3,000°C and 500°C. It can be seen that at the higher temperature the peak emission is in the visible range and the body would appear *white hot*. As it cools, so it moves further towards the red end of the visible spectrum and becomes visibly *red hot* until it cools beyond the visible spectrum but still emits radiation in the invisible *infra-red* part of the spectrum.

The wavelength of the maximum intensity of radiation increases as the temperature of the body decreases and this can be seen by Wien's law which states that the wavelength of maximum radiation is:

$$\lambda_{max} = \frac{2900}{T}$$

where T = the absolute temperature of the body.

From Wien's law it can be seen that the wavelength of radiation from the hot metal of a jet pipe, typically 500°C, would be:

$$\lambda_{max} = \frac{2900}{500 + 273}$$

$$= 3.75 \, \mu m$$

The hot metal of the inside of jet pipes is commonly viewed from anything up to an angle of 30° off the tail and missiles optimised for this frequency, such as the early IR missiles, were restricted to attack from the rear over this small angle of 30° each side of a dead astern. Further, jet pipes can be concealed by structure, particularly during manoeuvre, and designs such as the F-4 Phantom and the Jaguar show how over-hanging tail planes can provide concealment of the jet pipes under some conditions.

The limitation caused by reliance on jet pipe emissions can be overcome in part by homing on the emissions emanating from the exhaust plume. The carbon dioxide in the exhaust radiates around 3 μm and the water vapour at around 4.2 μm. The exhaust plume radiates in all directions and theoretically gives an all-round detection capability but in practice the exhaust plume is also shielded from ahead and from the sides. Effectively, exhaust plume seekers will have an enhanced rear angular capability but not necessarily a head-on or all-aspect capability.

Another source of radiation from the target can be the skin heating which results from air friction at high, normally supersonic, speeds. An aircraft flying at Mach 1.25 at low level, or one flying at about Mach 1.7 at high level will exhibit a skin temperature rise of about 65°C. The higher skin heating at high level is partly compensated by the lower ambient temperature. Wien's law shows that the wavelength of maximum radiation for this temperature is much higher than the 3 to 4.2 μm of the exhaust plume and is in the 8.6 μm range.

Chemicals capable of reacting to IR radiation are required in the missile head. Such chemicals need to react quickly, to be able to detect small amounts of IR radiation and to have high cut-off points. 'Cut-off' is the point at which the chemical ceases to react to IR radiation and can be increased, normally by about one micron, by cooling the head by about 200°C. Two commonly used chemicals in IR missile heads are Lead Sulphide (PbS) and Indium Antimonide (InSb). Lead Sulphide cuts off at about 3 μm uncooled and 4 μm cooled while Indium Antimonide cuts off around 6 μm; cooling does not improve this but does enhance the detectivity. Indium Antimonide heads can therefore detect the exhaust plume radiations at 3 μm and 4.2 μm, most of the hot metal radiation and a good deal of the leading edge radiation.

Just as hot carbon dioxide and water vapour radiate IR energy, so do the cold gases present in the atmosphere absorb IR energy. This atmospheric absorption affects the transmissivity of IR radiation and the pattern seen at Figure 4.6 shows a series of transmission windows.

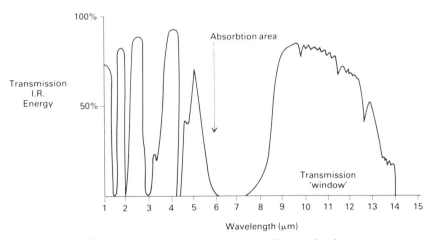

Fig 4.6.   IR transmission – a 1 mm path at sea level

It can be seen that thermal imaging devices working at normal ambient temperatures of about 15°C (10 μm) are little affected by atmospheric absorption. The emission from leading edges between about 5.5 and 8 μm are badly affected and it is likely therefore that missiles optimised in this area would be looking at the 4 to

5 μm band and relying upon high detectivity in this band to produce reliable head-on acquisitions. While the general pattern of the transmissivity remains the same, at higher levels the percentage of energy transmitted increases. It can also be seen that a higher speed target will help in acquisition as the shorter wavelengths from its hotter leading edges will bring the emissions out of the poor band between 5.5 and 8 μm.

IR emissions are also affected by atmospheric scatter caused by particles or droplets in the air. The closer the droplet size is to the wavelength, the greater the losses through scatter. IR generally penetrates haze or smoke, which has small droplets or particles, better than optical wavelengths but both are equally affected by large particles found in rain or cloud.

This gives rise to one of the major disadvantages of IR weapons over radar weapons – they are not all-weather capable. They are, however, highly discriminating and IR missiles will have less difficulty than radar missiles in selecting one of a number of targets on which to home. Radar missiles can, under some circumstances, receive radar returns from two or more targets and home to a mean point, missing all the targets.

Before dealing with radar missiles and from that leading on to some new and interesting aspects of the modern air battle, consider some of the constraints in the use of missiles. It is too easy to look upon the air-to-air missile as the wonder weapon but the limited history of air warfare in which missiles have been used tends, if anything, to prove the reverse. First, the air-to-air missile is a complex weapon and depends on a number of complicated functions to operate reliably and effectively and to give a successful result. Some are outlined in Figure 4.7 and it can be seen that even if individual functions operate at high probabilities, the number of functions involved still gives quite low overall probablities of success.

Event	Probability of Success	Cumulative Probability of Success
Aircraft system produces valid firing command	0.95	0.95
Missile fires	0.95	0.90
Missile guides	0.95	0.86
Missile within valid parameters	0.95	0.81
Fusing operates successfully	0.95	0.77
Warhead activates	0.95	0.73

FIG 4.7.   The effect of a variety of individual high probabilities on overall probability of success

It is seen that in this example overall probability is only seventy-three per cent despite high probabilities being assumed for the individual component events. Many would argue that overall probabilities as high as seventy-three per cent could only be looked for in new generation missiles and then only in fairly benign combat, or test, conditions. Few commanders would bank on better than sixty-five per cent, the prudent ones would at least consider thirty to forty per cent and those conscious of the Vietnam experience would not be surprised at overall figures of ten per cent.

There were many reasons for the Vietnam experience not least of which was the decision taken by the United States to send everyone to Vietnam once before anyone went twice. This was highly equitable but resulted in a massive cross-training programme because the throughput of fighter pilots was greater than any other. Consequently, not only were the experienced fighter pilots 'tour-expended' early on but thereafter the type and role experience of the crews in Vietnam was less than ideal. With the equipment of the time, the very difficult judgement on whether a valid missile firing could be made was almost completely pilot orientated and in this very tricky area, experience was all-important. As a result, many missiles were fired outside their capability, so artificially affecting the results. A further factor was the situation arising from a poor identification capability and the need for positive identification that a target was hostile before firing. By the time the range had closed to the point where that could be done, the opportunity to use the head-on radar Sparrow missile was squandered. This artificial rule of engagement, at a stroke, did much to negate the major technological advantage possessed by the United States. Yet another problem was the confidence factor. For whatever reason, missiles were being fired and obtaining no, or few, hits. Pilots then took to firing more than one at a target – a standard *salvo* was two AIM-7 Sparrow for example – yet if the shot was outside parameters, this merely served to make the overall figures look even worse.

The judgement of missile firing envelopes is a difficult task requiring experience and regular practice. Figure 4.8 shows a typical missile firing envelope for a rear-

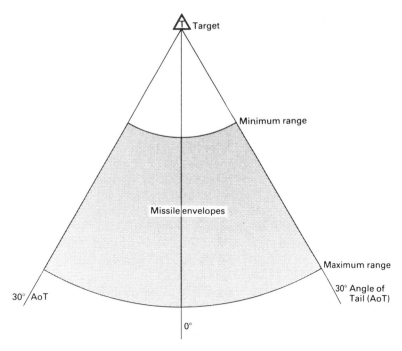

FIG 4.8.   Typical missile firing envelope against a non-manoeuvring target

hemisphere IR missile with a capability over a thirty per cent semi-angle. The minimum range is determined mainly by safety considerations; the missile has to be fired from the aircraft with locked control lest a control hardover should jeopardise the aircraft. In addition, the warhead is inhibited for a period to allow it to clear the aircraft sufficiently so that an inadvertent detonation would not cause self-damage to the aircraft. A time must also be allowed thereafter for the missile to guide satisfactorily to the target. Together, these factors constitute a minimum range. Typically, such a range may be in the order of 300 metres.

The maximum range tends to be a factor of either the ability of the seeker to acquire a sufficiently strong signal from the target to allow guidance or, alternatively, the ability of the missile to actually fly the distance between launch aircraft and target. This latter ability will be determined by the altitude – missiles tend to fly further at height – the speed of the target and the overtake speed of the launch aircraft. A well designed IR missile will try to match a number of these parameters; for example, if the pilot receives an indication of seeker lock then at that range the missile should be able to fly the distance.

Figure 4.9 shows the complication occasioned by a manoeuvring target. In this simplified case it is seen that as the target turns so does its vulnerable tail area move with it until it may cease to coincide with the launch aircraft, thereby denying an acquisition.

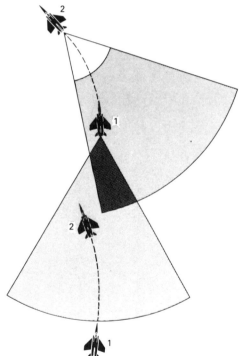

Fig 4.9.   Target manoeuvre negating a missile acquisition

This situation can be further complicated if the missile has some form of proportional navigation law in its guidance system. Modern AAM have the capability to pull high lateral 'G' loads, typically in the order of 35 'G'. Although this sounds more than enough to defeat an aircraft restricted at best to 9 'G', it is important to realise that it is the turning radii which largely determines the ability to execute a successful engagement and a 9 'G' aircraft at 400 knots will have a considerably smaller turning circle than a 35 'G' missile travelling at Mach 2.5. Figure 4.10.

Vehicle	Speed	'G'	Turn Radius (ft)
Aircraft	400kts	9	1,588
Missile	M2.5	35	6,929

FIG 4.10.   Turn radius at low level

Under certain engagement geometry the missile can be placed in circumstances demanding of it a *square corner* which could be outside even the high 'G' capability it possesses. Such a case is illustrated at Figure 4.11 where a high speed missile is fired in the foreward quarter against a target with the missile attempting to keep the target at its dead-ahead position throughout the engagement. This is not utilising proportional navigation and it is said to have a navigational constant (K) of 1. In other words, a sight-line spin of, say, 1°/second is accepted at face value by the guidance system. By introducing various degrees of proportional navigation and by increasing the K-factor, much more efficient profiles can be flown and the *square corner* can be avoided. A K-factor of 2, for example, would involve the guidance system assuming a sight line spin rate of 2°/second for an actual case of 1°/second. In this way a *lead* is built into the flight path.

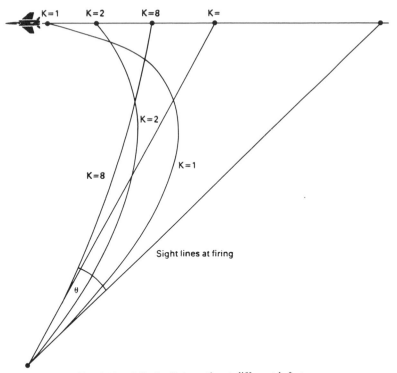

FIG 4.11.   Missile flight paths at different k-factors

A proportional navigation law with a K of infinity would seem to be the ideal and equates to a full lead prediction profiled in which the angle between missile seeker head and the target is kept constant throughout the interception. Unfortunately there are technical reasons for not using such high constants and K-factors of between 4 and 7 are common in practice. Figure 4.11 also shows a further advantage of using proportional navigation in that the missile flight path to the target is shorter, so effectively increasing the range of the missile. Comparatively, the missile impacts earlier which, in modern air combat conditions, can be an important advantage.

The individual characteristics of the missile and the geometry of the attack will have to be taken into account in determining whether the missile seeker head has sufficient gimbal capability to keep the target sighted throughout the flight path. A missile with a K-factor of 1 will effectively be looking dead-ahead and keeping the target in its near-12 o'clock position. As the K-factor increases so does the missile seeker head have to be offset to keep the target in view. It can be seen from Figure 4.11 that in the case of the extreme K-factor of infinity, the seeker head would spend its whole time in flight offset at the angle Θ.

The firing envelope against a manoeuvring target tends to be highly skewed and this can make the accurate determination of valid firing opportunities even more difficult. Envelope diagrams always appear to be very pure but in practice they apply only to the specific conditions outlined. They also assume perfect knowledge of the target's flying conditions, something which is rarely better than an estimate in practice. Figure 4.12 nonetheless shows a typical skew of the firing envelope against a

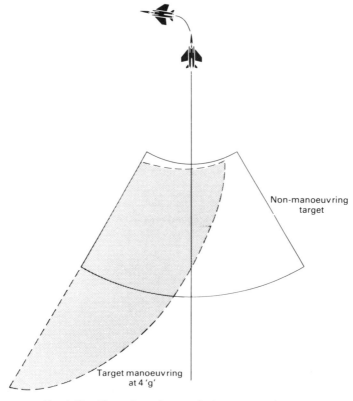

FIG 4.12.   Skewed envelope against a manoeuvring target

manoeuvring target and the shape is influenced for two reasons: the first is that the missile can 'cut-the-corner' and therefore the flight path will be shorter than in the straight and level case. The second is that the target turn effectively increases the missile speed. This can be seen better by reference to Figure 4.12a which shows the relationship between target, fighter and missile speeds in accordance with firing aspect.

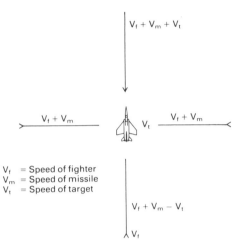

$V_f + V_m + V_t$

$V_f + V_m$ V_t $V_f + V_m$

V_f = Speed of fighter
V_m = Speed of missile
V_t = Speed of target

$V_f + V_m - V_t$

V_f

FIG 4.12(a).   Missile closure speeds

It is this later relationship which gives the different shape for engagement envelopes of missiles capable of head-on attack, be they IR missiles capable of sensing leading edge heating, or radar missiles. Such an envelope is seen at Figure 4.13a. At Figure 4.13b the envelope which results from a high speed target can be

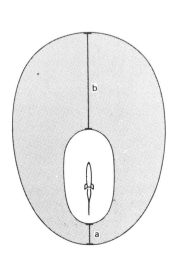

FIG 4.13(a). All-aspect missile
envelope

FIG 4.13(b).   All-aspect envelope
against a very high speed target

seen. This shape is caused by the possibility that high sight line spin rates on beam engagements may exceed the seeker head limitations and also that the 'G' requirement on the missile may exceed the aerodynamic limitations. At Figure 4.13c the envelope resulting from the extreme high speed case shows that the target may actually be getting away from the missile and that the only valid shot may be to engage where target speed is additive to the total engagement. These considerations could apply to aircraft of the SR-71 type which are capable of flight in the Mach 3 region.

FIG 4.13(c). Degraded envelope against a very high speed target

RADAR MISSILES

Although modern IR missiles have a capability at all-aspects against supersonic targets, and for those missiles the envelopes mentioned above are equally valid, the more normal missile to use at all-aspects, particularly against subsonic targets, is the radar missile. The term *radar missile* covers a variety of different types all having their strengths and weaknesses. these will be examined briefly, restricting comment to those suitable for air-to-air use but not forgetting that the surface-to-air missile has many of the same strengths and weaknesses and should be borne in mind when dealing with the general principles.

The IR missile, already discussed, is an example of a passive homing device in that it senses the IR radiation from the targets. Passive homing can also be utilised in torpedoes in the acoustic band and can be used similarly by a radar missile to home onto a radar emission from the target. This can take the form of an Anti-Radiation-Missile (ARM), designed to home on to a ground radar or an airborne intercept radar, or a Home-on-Jam system, designed to home up the beam of a jamming source which could be used to deny accurate range or bearing information to an aircraft or missile system.

As with IR homers, passive radar homers have the advantage of increasing accuracy as they approach their target because the energy of the homing signal increases the closer they get to it. Further, as no assistance is required from the launching aircraft, once the missile is fired, the fighter can withdraw – a 'launch-and-leave' weapon. The lack of any fighter emissions also means that the target is not warned of the approaching threat. On the other hand, passive homing missiles can be countered fairly easily; the target emission can be stopped or simple decoys deployed. Furthermore, passive homers can lack resolution under certain circumstances and tend to attack the centroid of a raid rather than home onto a specific target.

Semi-active missiles home on the energy reflected from a target illuminated by the missile system's own radar. This can be in the form of a ground-based illuminator, in the case of a SAM, or can be a function of the Air Intercept (AI) radar in an airborne system (Figure 4.14). Target returns again increase as range is closed and long ranges can be obtained if the target illuminating radar is of sufficient power. Countermeasures are possible but are generally more complex than in the passive homing case. The semi-active radar missile can be tuned to a particular frequency and this can include a factor for target doppler effect. Jamming is consequently more difficult. Even if a jamming situation exists, it is possible for an engagement to succeed if the illumination is powerful enough. Throughout flight the missile continues to rely upon the reflected energy from the illuminating radar and this means that a semi-active missile is not *launch-and-leave*. This can have serious side-effects in the total beyond-visual-range (BVR) air combat. A problem over the resolution between formations of targets can arise. Furthermore, the energy may be altered when the passive warning receiver of the target is illuminated.

To overcome some of these problems and to strive for a greater engagement range, which is becoming increasingly necessary, AAM are now tending towards active homing. The AIM-54 Phoenix in use with the United States Navy on the F-14 was an early active homing missile and the Advanced Medium Range AAM (AMRAAM) currently under development also uses active homing. In an active missile a self-contained radar within the missile head transmits when close to the target and homes on to the reflected emissions of its own illumination. Active missiles tend to be complex and can be expensive; the size can be further increased because the need for active homing is derived from the long-range capability. In consequence, the motor and guidance (including provision for mid-course guidance, which can be inertially based) can be large and complex in their own right. Phoenix, for example, is over 13 feet long, has a body diameter of 15 inches and weighs nearly 1,000 pounds; it costs close to $1 million.

Missiles of this size can present operational problems particularly when associated with carrier-based aircraft where recovery to the ship will often be weight critical. In air defence operations from a carrier group, where combat air patrols tend to be the norm, aircraft will probably return to the ship with unexpended munitions more often than not. An F-14 with a maximum load of, say, six AIM-54 Phoenix will therefore have to land-on with nearly 6,000 pounds of Phoenix alone, before gun ammunition and IR missiles are considered. Add to this the weight of prudent fuel reserves to cater for battle damage or poor weather and, even from super-carriers, landing weight limits can be, or come close to being, exceeded. The option of jettison is not practicable at the cost or the scarcity of such missiles. Such large and heavy weapons also produce an aircraft performance penalty. Although an aircraft may be tasked to engage at long range, it may become involved in shorter ranged, high-agility combats in which high weights and drags could determine the outcome.

Such considerations affected the design specifications for AMRAAM. While this missile is unlikely to have the extreme range of Phoenix, which has been launched at

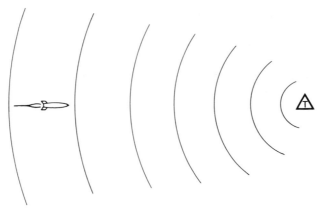

FIG 4.14(a).   Passive homing

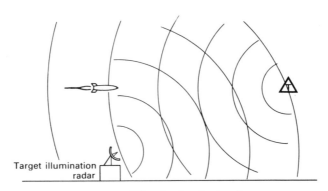

FIG 4.14(b).   Semi-active homing

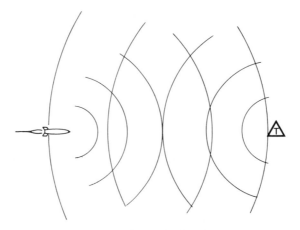

FIG 4.14(c).   Active homing

FIG 4.14.   Homing methods

over 100 nautical miles, it will be much lighter and will have less drag. Body diameter is more than halved at 7 inches and the launch weight will probably be one-third that of Phoenix. The lower frontal area results in less drag and this assists in producing higher speed – another increasingly important aspect in air combat at long range. It has been calculated that an F-16 fitted with the AIM-7 Sparrow missile – in use on F-4, F-15 and other types – instead of the preferred AMRAAM, would suffer a ten to fifteen per cent penalty in acceleration times and in fuel consumption.

Technology is close to the point when it can produce the missile specified by the operator. Phoenix at one end of the spectrum and the new AMRAAM and Advanced Short Range AAM (ASRAAM) at the other, show the wide variety of options available. It may be that the prudent operator should specify a weapon as advanced as possible but, on the other hand, this may not be a cost-effective thing to do. Indeed, it could be most wasteful because in the complex and highly interactive business of air combat, it is rarely one factor which dominates but the combination of many. In the beyond-visual-range (BVR) engagement it is important that systems are matched; aircraft performance can be negated by poor radar performance; an excellent radar, in its turn, can be under-exploited for lack of missile range.

The provision of a *matched set* of aircraft performance, radar performance and missile capability is too often taken for granted yet it is a major task falling upon those involved in the specification of operational requirements and procurement. The old saying that fifty per cent of the cost is involved in achieving the last ten per cent of the performance, while debatable in the absolute, is generally accepted as about right.

Many air forces remain without full control over their own fate. A force updating its missiles may be offered a long-range missile but lack the funds to purchase this and, at the same time, to undertake the radar update necessary to exploit fully the improved missile performance. An aircraft, once fielded, normally has a fixed volume available for the radar and, more particularly, a fixed radome size. It may not be possible to change the dimensions of antennae materially even when the minaturisation of electronics allows for greater data processing to be undertaken in any given area than was previously possible. In this there may be more scope for radome modifications on the slower, older aircraft than on the newer high speed designs where air flow about the nose area, affecting intakes and wing roots, can be most critical. A look at the nose treatment of the Nimrod AEW 3 shows the liberties which can be taken with the slower, more tolerant designs but the possibility of undertaking the same surgery on F-16 or F-18 would be unthinkable to the same degree.

Within the constraints of a minor work, let alone a chapter within it, the detailed examination of the complex interfaces between the individual items in the BVR air combat 'matched-set' cannot be tackled without some simplification. Even allowing for the lack of purity which such simplification brings about, the main relationships can be investigated and, where interest is sparked, more detailed investigations can be initiated. Consider therefore, the archetypal BVR missile combat and examine the major factors which apply.

Clearly aircraft performance is important – but how important? Radar detection range is equally important, for this is effectively the eyes of a BVR engagement and it has been long proved that, to the human, the eyes are by far the primary sensor – so is it with radar in a BVR situation. But the mechanisation of the weapon system is also an important factor when closure speeds can be numbered in the multi-Mach regime. From a first detection, how long does it take to lay an attack and to release the missile? Too long and the opponent gets away the vital first shot which, if the missile has an active homing head, effectively doubles the odds against. Then there is missile range. A long range detection matched to a short range missile merely accentuates anxiety.

Consider the situation in the cockpit of an interceptor which picks up a return ahead. A modern air intercept radar and its associated data processing system should quickly give a fair approximation of the target speed and height. The first, and by far the most important, decision to be made is whether or not the target is hostile. Much has been talked of JTIDS and NIS[1] and IFF MK 10 and the like (all Identification Friend-or-Foe (IFF) devices) yet such black boxes remain less glamorous in the procurement priorities than the more tangible, and understandable, EFAs, ATFs etc[1] yet without an effective IFF, regardless of which exotic fighter is being flown, *time* starts to be squandered following the initial radar contact. In any air combat *time* is the vital ingredient of success; it is the life-saver or life-taker and cannot be sacrificed needlessly. One senior NATO commander has said that his fighter force would be twenty-five per cent more effective with a reliable IFF; his staff only disagreed with him on the extent of the disadvantages – they thought he was being conservative. Over a force of 3,000 aircraft at $25 million each even a large sum is invested wisely if it can improve effectiveness by such an impressive factor as twenty-five per cent.

So is the contact hostile or not? If in any doubt, the fighter must accelerate from the cruise speed on Combat Air Patrol for two reasons: first, fighter speed adds to missile speed and increases missile reach; second, if the BVR missiles miss, and a prudent fighter pilot will always assume this, then the speed is needed to convert to what could be a stern chase or even into a high agility dog-fight. In this very demanding arena, however, there is nothing done without a penalty and the acceleration will use fuel, will commensurately reduce CAP time and could reduce the time available for close combat, where *persistence* is becoming more important.

The next major decision needed is when to convert the radar from a scanning to a tracking mode. Here knowledge of the enemy is important. Will the enemy have a radar warning device which tells him that he is within the scan pattern of an interceptor? Will it be sufficiently advanced to tell that the returns received come from a potentially hostile fighter? When the target is locked-up for missile launch, will this too be displayed? If it is, what counter will the target have available to it? Can it turn 90° to exploit the 'doppler-notch'? Will it turn away, hoping to make the missile manoeuvre or extend beyond its range limit? Will the target's mission allow it to divert from track and still achieve its offensive purpose? Offensive tasking agencies are the same world-wide and customarily task to the full declared range capability of offensive aircraft and combat fuel packages.

When to fire first? It is a bold and confident pilot who does not launch at first opportunity. The single-shot-kill-probability of missiles is not sufficient to trust to only one and a number of missiles may need to be despatched; with some weapon systems this takes time, and if the radar detection has been late, the need to arc-off to position for the line astern re-attack may put pressure on to launch radar-missiles

[1]   Joint Tactical Identification and Display System (JTIDS); NATO Identification System (NIS); European Fighter Aircraft (EFA); Advanced Tactical Fighter (AFT).

early. This will be even more so if the target must remain illuminated by the fighter radar to permit semi-active guidance and when radar gimbal limits could become critical if the launch is left too late.

Then there is the enemy. Is he an offensive aircraft reluctant to become engaged in a missile duel lest the main purpose of the offensive mission be compromised? Or is the target blip an escort fighter with every bit as capable a BVR missile system as the CAP fighter? If so, he probably has an inestimable advantage; while the fighter has doubt about the identification of the target blip – is it an offensive aircraft, or escort, or even returning friendly – the escort fighter, if only from the profile of the CAP pattern, almost certainly knows that his blip is hostile.

Such considerations must weigh on the mind of the fighter crew. Answers to some can be found by equipment, some by procedures, even more by instinct or intuition but, regardless, they take *time*. Such is the source of *reaction time*.

To attempt to identify some of the relationships and to seek a vehicle for discussion, consider a *simplified* and *stylised* BVR missile engagement. *Stylised*, because the direct head-on engagement is considered; *simplified*, to avoid a mathematical treatise where inappropriate but, for example, assuming a figure for missile *average* speed when, in fact, a missile would fly more to the profile in Figure 4.15.

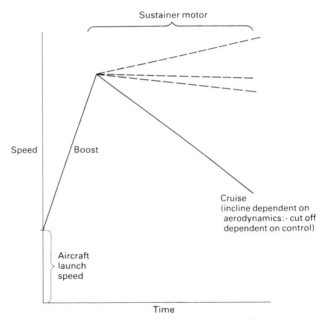

FIG 4.15 Typical AAM missile profile

Consider an engagement in which:

Fighter speed   = Mach 1.0
Target speed   = Mach 0.8
AAM speed   = Mach 2.5 over launch speed
Fighter Radar Range = 50 nautical miles
AAM fly time   = 60 seconds
System reaction time = 30 seconds

Then the following engagement would result:

Figure 4.16a shows that of the 50 nautical mile radar range, 4.77 nautical miles and 30 seconds are taken up by the reaction time. The AAM fired at that time will impact 90.42 seconds after first detection at 38.47 nautical miles down range. At this point the fighter has closed to a point 14.4 nautical miles down range. The AAM range (based on a 60 second flight time), while a marginal short fall, is quite well matched to the total geometry of the attack.

Could the *marginal miss* be corrected by a higher launch speed? Figure 4.16b shows the effect of an increase in attack speed to Mach 1.2, which improves a *marginal shortfall* into a *hit* with some range in hand.

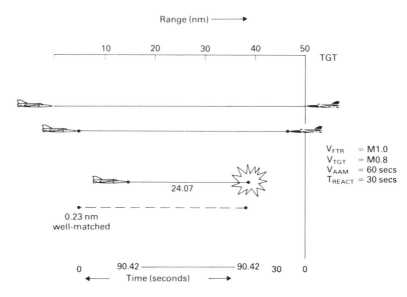

FIG 4.16(a)   BVR missile engagement – missile just falls short

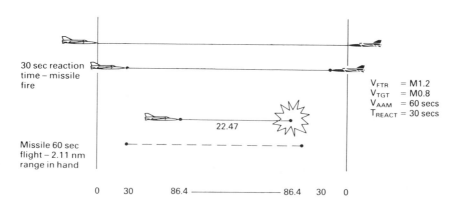

FIG 4.16(b)   BVR missile engagement – missile range sufficient due to increased fighter speed

But what is the effect of aircraft performance? Consider the case when reaction time, AAM performance and radar range is the same but aircraft speed is different. Look at the situation where BLUE is twice as fast as RED at Mach 1.5. As AAM flight time to impact is a function of fighter speed, AAM speed and target speed, it can be seen that, at least to a first approximation, there is little difference between the missile being fired from the fast aircraft or from the slow aircraft. There is a small increase in missile reach when fired from the faster aircraft (Figure 4.17). This tends to suggest that there is something in the suggestion that, in the technological age, weapons and systems are more important than vehicles.

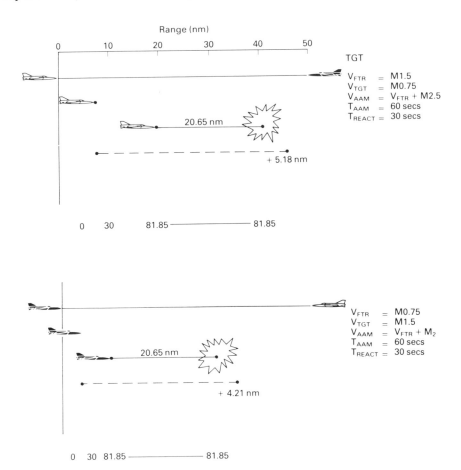

FIG 4.17   BVR engagement showing effect of aircraft performance

What, therefore, if the Blue side place their investment in the aircraft while Red update their old slow aircraft with a longer-ranged, faster missile and some data processing – or an IFF system – to reduce the reaction time. Figure 4.18 shows that the parameters for Blue stay as before but Red, by increasing missile speed by Mach 1.0, thereby increasing reach, and by reducing reaction time by 15 seconds, now impacts Blue at 63.7 seconds, some 18.15 seconds before Blue's missile would impact

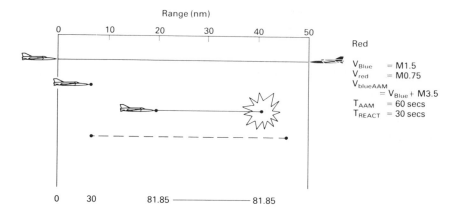

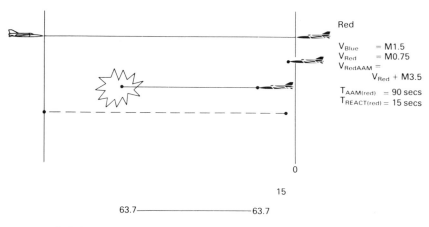

Red's investment in a better missile range and speed
is under-exploited by the limitation on radar
range. The system is not well 'matched'.

Fɪɢ 4.18   BVR engagement showing effect of missile range and speed enhancement

Red. If the Blue missile was relying on the Blue radar emissions for semi-active
guidance, the Blue missile would stop guiding after Red's missile impact. If,
however, the Blue missile was an active homer and had gone active before the 18.15
seconds time difference, Red would still be faced with a threat notwithstanding the
destruction of its opponent's aircraft.

The active missile will introduce a new dimension to the air combat arena. In a trial
of multi-aircraft combat, conducted some time ago, it was found that some tens of
missiles were launched and in flight within a few seconds of the start of the
engagement. Semi-active models would go ballistic if the launch aircraft was
destroyed but active missiles, in quantity, could be difficult to counter, particularly if
other threats were present – SAM and AAA – causing the formation to manoeuvre.

Discussion on missile air combat too often presupposes a single fighter engaging a single target when, in practice, this is the least likely case.

THE DEVELOPING COMBAT SCENE

The factor most feared by combat pilots is the one most difficult to quantify – that of confusion. Studies of past air combats have shown that this is truly the killer. The World War Two poster warning against '*the-Hun-in-the-Sun*' indicates that the basic lessons hold good with time. In the modern BVR battle electronic *eyes* may have to reinforce the human eye but the *principles* remain the same.

Progressing from the BVR combat into the modern high agility visual combat will call for quite different piloting skills and technical equipment. The BVR battle is largely a conflict between systems and sensors and, as such, electronic warfare will have a large part to play. The high agility air combat will be less the game of chess and parallel more the physical strains of the rugby scrum.

Increasingly modern fighters can not only achieve 'G' loadings in the region of nine but can, under a wide range of circumstances, sustain such levels. Even given 'G' suits, reclining seats, physical fitness and, above all, regular practice there are few, if any, pilots who can sustain such high 'G' levels for anything more than a few seconds. Those air forces operating such high performance equipment are finding new problems; one claims that a term of duty on the squadron of high agility fighters results in a collar size one larger than at the start due to the physical strain imposed on holding aloft the body's single most heavy object, the head. Others are becoming increasingly concerned at the so-called '*G*'-*induced unconsciousness* where, unlike the gradual onset of blackout associated with normal 'G' loadings, and its rapid relief when the load is reduced, a sudden onset of very high 'G' may cause an equally sudden loss of consciousness and, more seriously, an extended period of some ten to fifteen seconds before consciousness is regained. Few scenarios in combat or in flight close to the ground would permit such long periods of unconsciousness without serious consequences.

High 'G' in visual combat may therefore have to be used sparingly and sustained 'G' restricted to levels in the order of five or six. The higher 'G' loads may be limited to those occasions when the nose must be drawn on to the target to sight guns or missile heads for the kill, or for the *in extremis* avoidance of attack.

Two new factors are emerging in the close air combat scene. In the past, the ability to disengage was the prerogative of the passably competent fighter pilot. To engineer a head-on pass, or to develop some angular difference in a low energy situation, was enough to depart the combat before the opponent could react. Sufficient distance could be gained to prevent any parting shot. With high agility aircraft, however, even a 180° angular difference can be taken out in a matter of nine seconds or so and a missile can be fired even earlier than that if the aircraft has an off-boresight capability. Once engaged therefore, is there any escape short of a result? Has gladiatorial combat arrived at the point at which the winner survives and the loser invariably does not? In a field with no recognisable means of surrender, or indeed of offering quarter, the situation concentrates the mind. It also places added emphasis on *persistence*, or the ability to stay engaged, usually dependent upon the available fuel. Economical engines, high fuel-fractions and the skill to use thirsty after-burners economically, will weigh heavily on the ultimate outcome.

Modern aircraft design is tending to favour the Infra-Red missile. Compare the long jet pipes of aircraft such as the Hunter, through the shorter but airframe-shrouded jet pipes of aircraft like the F-4 Phantom and the Jaguar, to those of modern designs where unstable control technology allows weight to be placed further aft and engines can have very short jet pipes right at the end of the fuselage. The jet pipes of F-15, F-16 and F-18 show the trend well. The opportunity for IR shielding is consequently less and this is exacerbated by the trend in engine design itself. Modern materials and, even more significantly, turbine blade cooling, have allowed turbine inlet temperatures in the order of some 1,500 degrees centigrade in the more advanced designs. In short jet pipes this heat dissipates only a little and metal parts in a modern jet pipe, such as the after burner galleries, can be operating at temperatures which only a few years ago would be found only on the turbine disc itself. The IR signature is likely to be very large indeed.

IR decoy flares will help, although these can prove to be less useful against high agility missiles approaching from the beam angles. Data processing in the missile heads themselves, made possible by the advances in miniaturisation, can give the modern missile great discrimination by including logic or *behavioural* circuits. Few if any flares, for example, retain the velocity profile of an aircraft and can thereby be discounted by logic circuits as a valid target.

IR jammers which emit pulsed IR transmissions offer the best option in the short term but good intelligence of the missile operating frequency is required. In the longer term, it is not impossible to conceive a missile head with a *home-on-jam* facility similar to the technique used widely on radar missiles.

Against *missiles*, rather than *hitiles*, there may be scope in seeking counter-measures to the fusing circuits. A proximity fused warhead is no threat if it does not initiate. In some respects this can be easier than attacking the guidance heads from a distance because fusing circuits activate close to the aircraft and size and power requirements for a counter may prove more manageable.

Any modern combat is going to be a highly lethal affair, be it BVR using long-ranged radar missiles, or in the close visual combat more usually associated with IR missiles. Missile expenditure will be high if only because the cumulative kill probabilities are low enough for the wise pilot to seek the insurance of numbers; also that, in the multi-aircraft situation, some missiles are bound to be laid on the wrong target or will be confused. With the modern missile in a high agility close combat, some aircraft will be presented with numerous firing opportunities and may fire-out rapidly. The contradiction of needing large missile loads of both radar and IR missiles while not wishing to accept the weight and drag penalties in combat, is a problem to designer and pilot alike.

Smaller, lighter missiles, typified by the trend from AIM-7/Skyflash to AMRAAM, and semi-buried or conformal carriage will have to be the path to the future for the smaller high-agility fighters but the threat of the very long-ranged missile, fired from the large, even ponderously slow platform, cannot be ignored altogether. For this later design the integral rocket/ram-jet is a natural choice for the motor and it will be interesting to see how this technology proceeds – and which nation embraces it. Ultimately they may have the trump card.

PLATE 9. In Vietnam, the *F-4* was up against *MiG-17* and the *MiG-21* shown here in its later *Fishbed* L (*MiG-21 bis*) form. The *MiG-21* was used in Vietnam similarly to the *Me-262* in World War Two – fast slashing attacks in a hit-and-run mode, avoiding close combat where possible. The *MiG-21* was difficult to see. It is not a large aircraft. *(Photo: United States Air Force)*

PLATE 10. The *MiG-21* is similar in size to the *F-5* and for this reason the United States Air Force Aggressor Squadrons adopted the machine. The Aggressor Squadrons study Soviet tactics and doctrine and fly typical Soviet profiles against NATO forces to better train against the likely threat. 'Aggressor' training is highly appreciated by the recipients. This *F-5* is camouflaged in typical Soviet colours to add realism to the training. *(Photo: Author)*

PLATE 11. The importance of size is shown in this picture of an *F-5* flown alongside the much larger and heavier *F-4*. The small size in total is a problem but this can be exacerbated head-on where some aircraft, including the *F-5* and *F-104* have very fine profiles.

(Photo: United States Air Force)

PLATE 11A. The fine head-on profile of the *F-104* can be imagined from this shot which shows why the design was susceptible to roll-coupling (see text). *(Photo: United States Air Force)*

PLATE 12.   While the design parameters were falling out of the Vietnam War which pointed to the need for high agility fighters, the *F-111* ('F' for fighter) was entering service intended to be a multi-role machine. The *F-111* is now perhaps the most capable long-range interdictor in service in NATO and its prowess as an attack aircraft was proved in the Libyan raid but even its most vocal advocates would not claim that it was a fighter. This view shows how the crew are are encapsulated (literally) in the highly faired cockpit . . .
(Photo: United States Air Force)

PLATE 13.   . . . and this view demonstrates the almost negligible view to the rear.
(Photo: Author)

PLATE 14. The *Tornado* multi-role combat aircraft went through almost the same experience as the *F-111* albeit on European rationale. The version in use by Germany, Italy and the UK is proving to be an excellent interdictor. *(Photo: Author)*

PLATE 15. To produce an air interceptor, however, the United Kingdom has had to change the avionics, redesign the cockpit, use a new radar, lengthen the nose and modify the wings and engines. 'Multi-role' in the Sixties and Seventies, on both sides of the Atlantic, seem to be an elusive goal. The longer fuselage of the *F3 Interceptor* is seen to advantage in this picture. The multi-role genealogy is seen in the lack of a raised or bubble canopy. *(Photo: Author)*

PLATE 16. Vietnam air combat experience spawned the specification which led to the *F-14* for the United States Navy and the *F-15* for the United States Air Force. The *F-15* is a big powerful fighter with lots of lift and lots of thrust – what more does a flying machine need? It also has a large and powerful radar and carries eight missiles in addition to a Gatling gun. The twin fins testify to its design for high angle of attack manoeuvring and this keeps the fins clear of turbulence coming from the proud bubble canopy. *F-15* pilots love their aircraft – and that says a lot about any aeroplane. *(Photo: United States Air Force)*

PLATE 17. Developed as part of a high/low mix plan, that is high capability all-weather *F-15s* and lower cost day-only capable aircraft as a complement, the *F-16* is set to become another of the classic fighters. Already 2,000 have flown and the forecast build already exceeds 4,000. The *F-16* is a dynamically unstable, fly-by-wire design, able to pull, and under some circumstances, sustain over 9 'G'. Although conceived as a pure fighter it is being used to good effect in the air-to-ground role where its advanced avionics make it highly effective. Note the excellent view for the pilot but also the restricted volume available for the radar – a penalty for the chin intake which gives advantage in high incidence manoeuvring. *(Photo: United States Air Force)*

PLATE 18.   The *F-18* was yet another attempt to solve the conundrum of compromise needed to produce a multi-role design. Specified as a fighter/attack aircraft by the United States Navy, McDonnell Douglas have come as close as anyone to date in fulfilling the requirement. With excellent manoeuvrability, a good radar in the APG-65 and splendid cockpit ergonomics, the *F-18* is a most capable aircraft. Seen here, a Canadian *CF-18* fires pods of the CRV-7 high velocity rocket against a ground target. On escape from the target area the *CF-18* will then have a Beyond Visual Range head-on missile engagement with its radar and its AIM 7 Sparrow missiles. *(Photo: Canadian Armed Forces)*

PLATE 19.   Skyflash missiles fitted aerodynamically under the fuselage of a Tornado. *(British Aerospace)*

PLATE 20.   Magic 2. Shown here being fired from a Mirage 2000. *(Matra)*

PLATE 21.   Skyflash. Skyflash air-to-air missile being launched from an
F16. *(British Aerospace)*

5.

Radar

IT may be difficult to accept that radar should feature in a volume on air superiority. It has been conceded that *air superiority* is to be equated in the main to *dog-fighting* and another volume in this series will be examining in greater detail the specialist business of air intercept.* Surely it is in this later field that radar comes into its own?

Indeed it does and radar is the fundamental tool of that trade and will remain so until networked and data transferred systems become the norm in the future. But it is becoming equally essential to the art of close combat for a number of reasons. First, and of the greatest importance, is that the division of combat into *air intercept* and *air combat* is becoming less clear-cut. Before a pilot can distinguish himself under the high-'G' conditions of a dog-fight, he must first have survived the opening salvoes of the interaction, which will increasingly be those fired beyond-visual-range (BVR). Radar, with all its strengths and its weaknesses, bears heavily on the BVR battle and an understanding of those advantages and disadvantages is as essential for the combat pilot in the modern battlefield as it is for him to know about the aircraft or weapons of his enemy.

The second reason for the importance of radar in the close-in fight is the trend towards highly integrated weapon systems in which radar features strongly. Modern head-up displays (HUD) are able to display to the pilot, overlaid on the real world outside the cockpit, an indicator showing where the radar has detected a target. No longer need the pilot drop his eyes into the cockpit to interogate a radar screen for blips and then do the metal gymnastics to convert that raw information into a visual search area head-up. Computers do that tedious task and the pilot is allowed to keep his attention where it should be, out of the cockpit. The result has been a marked increase in the visual pick-up ranges due to the assistance of HUD cueing and this has caused the close-in fight to become a longer ranged affair than in the past. (Figure 5.1)

Even when the combat is joined, there is a role for radar to play. Missile seeker heads tend to have rather restricted angles of view to enable limited signal strength to be concentrated on to the seeker mechanism. Consequently, in a high-'G' combat, the situation arises where the missile is within its theoretical capability to engage the target but the missile head is not picking up the target returns because it is looking directly forward rather than towards the offset target. If the position of the target, as detected by the radar, can be converted into a signal which drives the missile heads to search in the direction of the target, then a missile lock can be obtained where otherwise it would not. (Figure 5.2)

Air Defence by Group Captain M. B. Elsam FBIM, RAF.

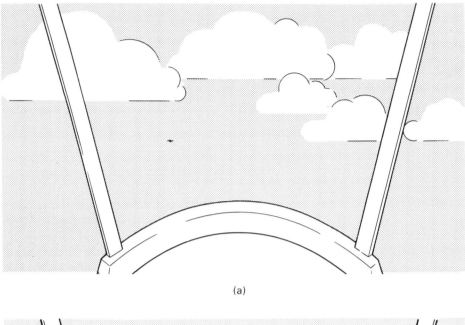

(a)

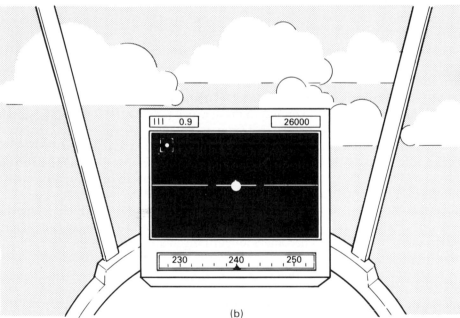

(b)

Fig 5.1.   Modern aids to acquisition: Head-up Display indication of target position

It is not only missiles which can be improved by the application of radar in the close-in battle. The validity of the sighting solution presented to the pilot by the gunsight is greatly dependent upon accurate estimation of the target range. Although modern high velocity guns and cannons have eased the sighting problems from the point of view of assessing gravity drop against range, this improvement has come

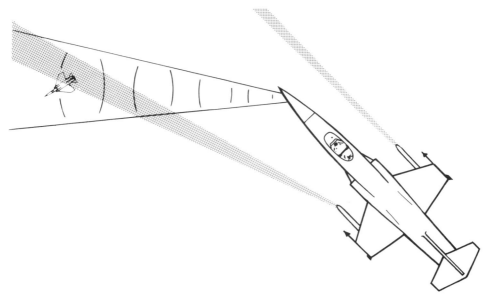

FIG 5.2.   The use of radar to slave missile heads to target

about when aircraft are able to pull higher 'G' loads and the crossing targets are increasingly becoming more difficult shots as greater 'G' loadings are used. Further, modern guns and cannons are presenting the pilot with greater opportunities for the longer ranged shot if the deflection solution, depending on range, can be adequately computed. An accurate range, derived from a radar mechanised for use in high agility combat, can allow many shots to succeed which would in the past have hit only by luck.

An accurate close-in range, allied to the ability to conduct fast and complex computation in the weapon system, allows the presentation to the pilot of a gun *hot-line*. Instead of showing merely one pipper which would indicate the fall of shot at one given range, the hot-line shows the path of the shells through the air and is computed in such a way as to take into account the gyrations of the aircraft and, if the target is being tracked, *de facto*, the gyrations of the target.

The theory is that the pilot merely has to manoeuvre his aircraft to bring the hot-line through the target aircraft and then to fire. As always the practice tends to be some way removed from the theory. No matter how fast the computation, it has to be working on out-of-date information, whereas success of the shot depends more on prediction, or the future behaviour of the target. Of course, the computation can *predict* the future on the basis of the history which it has been working on but that relies on the target maintaining a steady state condition and not being *unpredictable*. As the basic teaching to any fledgling fighter pilot is to be unpredictable when under threat, the hot-line sight is seen to be a great aid but far from the ultimate solution. It will be close to an ultimate solution in the future when matched with a laser weapon where the time of flight of the *shell* is negligible – but then, so is the *hot-line* negligible as well.

THE RADAR FORMULAE

It is not the purpose of this volume to produce a weapons instructor and to introduce the radar formulae is to risk widespread defection of those not of a mathematical mind. However, formulae are only traumatic to those who have to work them out in detail; those unfortunates who earn their daily bread in the fifth place of decimals. There is no point in fighter pilots exhausting their energies in this way. In most cases the absolute numbers are irrelevant; there is little that the pilot can do about them. What he has to do is to work with what he has been given and his energies are best directed to this end than to forever searching for what might have been. It never will be!

The study of the radar formulae should therefore be undertaken to understand the generalities, the interplay between one factor and the other, and to derive from its most general inspection those things which may be possible and those which are impossible. To see also the general relationships between certain factors. Once these are understood, the scientists and technologists can be safely left to argue about the mathematics because the ultimate user can be content that he will understand the thrust of their conclusions.

Forwarned about taking unwarranted fright, consider the basic formula:

$$S/N = \frac{P \cdot A \cdot RCS}{4\pi \cdot k \cdot T \cdot Fn \cdot R^4 \cdot \theta \, (\sin o_1 - \sin o_2) \, d \cdot L}$$

where:

S/N = Signal to Noise ratio
P   = Power to the Antennae
A   = Antennae Gain
RCS = Radar Cross Section of the target
k   = Boltzman's Constant
T   = Temperature
Fn   = Internal *noise* in the equipment
R   = Target Range
θ = Horizontal angle of the swept area
o   = Vertical swept angles up and down
d   = the rate of data update
L   = Line losses in the system

Before discussing the implications of the various interactions in more detail it is necessary to put the formula into a form more useful to the fighter pilot. Although it is not beyond the pilot to talk in terms of *signal-to-noise ratio* it is more normal for discussion to revolve around *range*. Transposing for 'R' then:

$$R = \left(\frac{P \cdot A \cdot RCS}{(4\pi \cdot k \cdot T \cdot Fn \cdot S/N \cdot \theta \, (\sin o - \sin o_1) \, d \cdot L)} \right)^{\frac{1}{4}}$$

Immediately the most important implication of the radar formulae becomes apparent. Range, on the left of the equation, is separated from the other factors on the right of the equation by a *fourth-root* function. Consequently, if the range was desired to be doubled by using increased power, for example, then that power would have to be increased not twice but no less than 16 times:

$$2 = (16)^{\frac{1}{4}}$$

The same argument is applicable to the other factors on the top line of the formulae. An increase either in antenna performance – either size or gain – or in the target radar cross section of the target will both improve the performance of the radar in terms of range but only in proportion to the fourth-root. Very large changes are required in these factors if any meaningful improvement in range is going to result.

Conversely, anything which can be done to decrease the factors below the line will result in a larger number on the right of the equation and therefore a greater range. Many of the factors are fixed as far as the pilot is concerned once the radar is in service. The noise emanating from the internal workings of the radar set (Fn) and the line losses (L) do not lend themselves to great improvement in an in-service equipment, neither does the signal-to-noise ratio. There was a time when operator proficiency made a difference here and some skilled radar operators could break out a target from clutter better than others. More modern systems take the raw signal and analyse it in computers and once the program is written with a particular signal-to-noise ratio the pilot can do little about it. Temperature is a function of the height at which the battle has to be fought rather than any conscious act of the pilot and this factor, too, cannot be looked upon as a reliable variable.

The remaining factor allows some manipulation. It represents the area over which the available radar energy is being spread

$$\theta \, (\sin o_1 - \sin o_2)$$

and the rate at which it is being interrogated (d).

The effect of this can be best illustrated by comparison to the world of optics. Take a torch and attempt to illuminate a distant wall very quickly by a series of wide and rapid sweeps. Although it may well be possible to discern the wall, it will be impossible to make-out any detail. Two ways of improving the situation fall immediately to mind; first, to scan the wall more slowly, allowing the strength of the beam to play on any given point longer, or, second, to play the beam at the same scanning rate but over a smaller section of the wall. The effect in both cases is virtually the same. It is to allow more light to fall on any given point and it is the reflection from this light which is picked up by the eye as an image which is seen.

An alternative would be to scan the whole area of the wall at the original fast rate but to use a more powerful torch (P). Although the torch would play on any given part of the wall for the same amount of time as before, the amount of light being projected is greater, the return is equally greater and the wall is seen better. The amount of light produced by the bulb could be concentrated better by the use of a large spotlight reflector or the amount of reflected light could be amplified by use of light amplification devices like night vision goggles. This is the optical equivalent of increasing the size of the radar antenna or improving its gain.

The wall could, of course, be repainted and the dull matt-black recovered with a shining brilliant white. The effect would be an improvement in the image because the reflectivity would have been improved. In radar terms, the 'RCS' would have been enhanced.

For those who have difficulty working in terms of that part of the electromagnetic spectrum which cannot be seen there is some merit in relating circumstances to the optical case which the average citizen finds easier to comprehend. Homo sapiens is equipped with splendid optical sensors which are, after all, his primary sensor. He is less perfectly equipped to handle the wavelengths in which radar is to be found. Yet, in the fundamentals, optics and electronics have much in common.

RADAR CROSS SECTION

The radar cross section (RCS) of a body can be seen to be an important factor in the radar equation. Its importance has increased of late with the emphasis being placed on *stealth* which, by diverse means, attempts to reduce the RCS.

It can be seen that the RCS factor affects range through the fourth-root factor and it might therefore be supposed that major changes in the RCS would be required if the range factor was to be affected materially. Whereas with antennae performance, or with the power provided to the radar, major changes in magnitude are rarely possible to achieve, the use of the correct techniques can make a substantial difference to RCS, enough to affect the detection range considerably.

Some confusion can be caused by the term RCS and its method of measurement. RCS is referred to as a number of *square metres* and it is easy to assume that the measure is a function of physical size. This is not the case. The standard of measurement is related to the radar reflectivity of a metal sphere which presents an area of one square metre. Radar transmissions striking such a ball would be reflected in a variety of ways, just as a light beam would striking a similarly silvered sphere. That part of the beam striking the point nearest to the transmitter would be reflected as though it were hitting a flat plate, that is, straight back to the receiver. Those beams hitting the periphery of the sphere would reflect very little energy back to the receiver. (Figure 5.3)

It can be seen, therefore, that if the target was a corner reflector in which the arriving beams were reflected more directly back to the receiver, then the received signal would be much greater than that received from the sphere, even though the physical size of the reflector might be much smaller. Shape is therefore more important than physical size.

Other factors affecting the reflectivity of an object include the incidence at which the beam strikes it. The idealistic ball would be unaffected by this consideration but just about every practical flying object is. The smoothness of the surface also affects the reflectivity just as the difference between a silvered surface and velvet would for the case of light reflection. Even the slightest surface unevenness can cause the beam to be reflected in a variety of ways, some directly back to the receiver.

The absorption of the material greatly affects the reflectivity and the manufacture of materials designed to absorb the radar beam internally is now common. It is far from a new technique, being used on the German submarines of World War Two as a counter to detection by airborne radar fitted to maritime patrol aircraft. The technique has developed a long way since and radar absorbent materials (RAM) feature already in the technological battle and will clearly continue to do so in an ever increasing way. Patches of RAM, which can be in a sheet form, can be attached to the more vulnerable, that is, reflective parts of a structure to reduce the RCS. Major

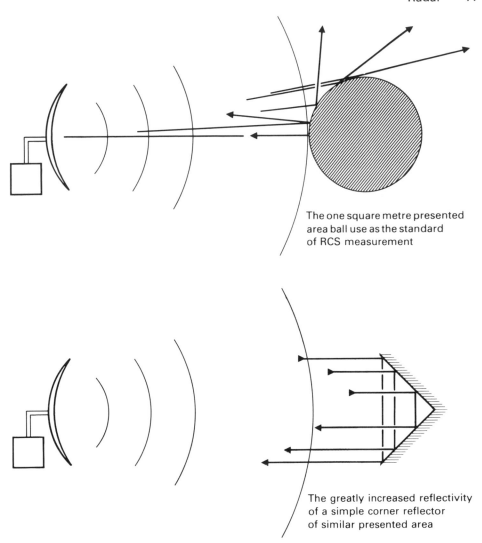

The one square metre presented
area ball use as the standard
of RCS measurement

The greatly increased reflectivity
of a simple corner reflector
of similar presented area

Fig 5.3.   The effect of shape on RCS

reductions in RCS can be achieved in this way. Even greater reductions can be
achieved if a body is designed from its inception with stealth in mind and is shaped to
avoid *corner reflectors* and randomly placed *flate plate surfaces*. When RAM can be
produced which can also take structural load, the prospect of producing shapes with
extremely low RCS will be high indeed. The importance of low RCS in the battle is so
great that the whole subject of RAM and stealth has been shrouded in secrecy but it is
reasonable to assume that RAM capable of being used at least in secondary structure
is now available.

RAM is material which *absorbs* radar energy and should not be confused with
those materials, such as carbon fibre, which are transparent to radar energy.
Consequently, it cannot be assumed, if an aircraft structure contains some of the

modern carbon-fibre components, that it is therefore more stealthy. In fact, the reverse could be the case because the factor which then affects the reflectivity may be the sub-structure beneath the carbon-fibre and that may be metalic, reflective components designed for structural strength rather than for stealth. A carbon-fibre skinned aircraft could, possibly, be of greater reflectivity than a similarly shaped aircraft skinned in metal.

Another factor often ignored in discussion on stealth is the effect of the friendly radar itself. If the radar is transmitting, its emissions can be detected further away than the radar itself can *see*. This is because the emissions only have to travel one-way to the passive warning receiver whereas they have to travel there and back to be received as a signal at the transmitting radar. A radar equipped aircraft using its radar for search is likely to be picked up first by a passively listening target. What price *stealth* in this instance?

The radar dish itself can become a liability if the target is also searching for returns in that, when the dish is pointing at the target, it is the perfect *corner reflector* and will reflect the hostile emissions almost perfectly.

The conclusion falling so clearly from this straightforward analysis is that as stealth becomes a more important factor in the battle, the prudent designer will attempt to move away from powerfully transmitting radars and to try to achieve his detection aims by passive means.

Figure 5.4 shows the effect of stealth on the radar cross section of two aircraft, the B-52 and the B-1. Open sources suggest that the RCS of the B-1A was only one-tenth that of the B-52. The later B-1B was only one-tenth that of the B-1A. The figure shows the B-1B in comparison to the B-52 as a radar would see it. Converted into

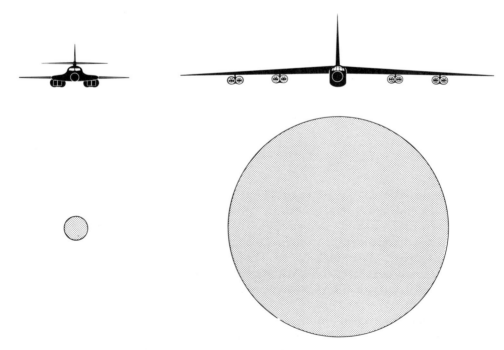

Fɪɢ 5.4.   Radar-eye's view of B-IB and B-52

range terms, a radar which detected the B-52 at 100 nautical miles would detect the B-1A at about 56 nautical miles and the B-1B at only 31 nautical miles. Another way of presenting the argument is given at Figure 5.5.

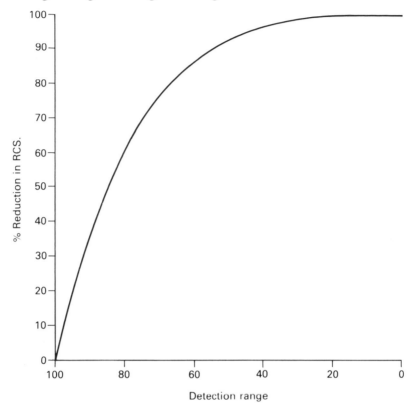

FIG 5.5.   Effect of the reduction in RCS on detection range

It is easy to be seduced, when talking about RCS, into believing that the figures commonly quoted are the only RCS of the target. This is far from the case and the low figures most often heard relate to the head-on case. This is indeed the most important figure in the case of the head-on attack but does not necessarily affect radar detection if the aspect angle of the radar to the target is from the side. Figure 5.6 illustrates the pattern of radar reflectivity which might be experienced over the total presented area of a typical bomber. It can be seen that at quite small angles off the nose, the RCS increases and that it increases dramatically at the beam.

The original passive means of detection in the combat situation was the eyeball and it is still a vitally important sensor. One of the most difficult training tasks is to persuade an embryo fighter pilot that, notwithstanding his impressive radar or other aids, it is the unseen aircraft which remains the greatest threat. Many times in training situations the instructor will find himself alongside the student who, head in cockpit, is still searching for him on the radar.

A more popular detection aid which is currently reinforcing radar but which could in the future replace it in certain circumstances is the Infra-Red Search and Track

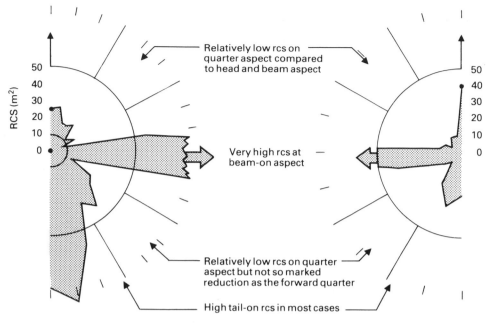

FIG 5.6.   Typical bomber RCS

(IRST) system similar to that fitted on the F-14 and appearing on the new Soviet designs. As more sensitive IR detector material is discovered and more effective ways are found to cool IR heads to make them more sensitive, so the ranges achieved by IR systems are increasing and it becomes a more valuable detection tool. In the past, the disadvantage of an IR system has always been that, although quite good definition could be obtained in azimuth, the equipment could provide no range information. Target position could not therefore be obtained and IRST was considered only as a nice-to-have feature. The combination of better azimuth discrimination coupled with a modern on-board computer has offered means of getting a reasonable range estimation out of the equipment by a form of triangulation. Once the nose of the fighter has been swung through the target azimuth a few times an estimate of range can be made.

It is tempting, but dangerous, to think that an aircraft with radar can see all about it. Radar in all aircraft other than the specialist types such as E-3A AWACS, is highly directional and, as has been seen before, the radar energy has to be concentrated in a beam to obtain the best range performance. Outside that beam, or more correctly, the area scanned by the beam, a target can remain undetected. Incorrect radar handling by the crew can result in a target closing to visual range without any warning. Patrol heights and search patterns become critical in the air superiority environment where the use of the radar in the first instance can betray position and incorrect use can prove to be ineffective.

A classic dilemma is whether to search for the low threat or the high threat. The low threat could be the fighter-bomber attempting the undetected penetration or the high threat could be the high-and-fast Look-Down-Shoot-Down (LDSD) threat which is a difficult target to engage. If too much of a compromise height is chosen for the patrol then small elusive targets at low level will spend too little time in the narrow beam to give a high chance of detection – the stealthier the target the more this factor applies – whereas, if too low a height is selected, to tackle the low target better, then sufficient power is rarely available to gain enough energy to match a high speed, high altitude target. (Figure 5.7)

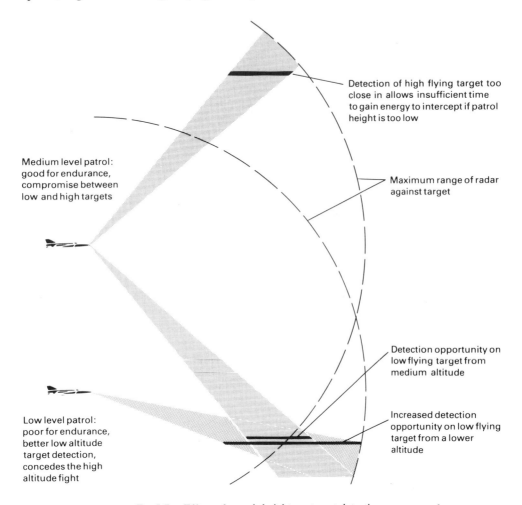

Detection of high flying target too close in allows insufficient time to gain energy to intercept if patrol height is too low

Medium level patrol: good for endurance, compromise between low and high targets

Maximum range of radar against target

Detection opportunity on low flying target from medium altitude

Low level patrol: poor for endurance, better low altitude target detection, concedes the high altitude fight

Increased detection opportunity on low flying target from a lower altitude

Fɪɢ 5.7.   Effect of search height on target detection

The influence of radar on the battle and the design implications of the radar antenna are together major drivers of modern aircraft weight and size. A fascinating philosophical debate must rage before even the first line is drawn on paper in the design office. Is the best answer to opt for the big aircraft which provides large power supplies for a big radar, with its proportionally big antenna, and let stealth look after itself? Or is the best option to go for a small stealthy aircraft with a proportionally smaller radar, with less range, but which can get within firing range of the aircraft with the better radar by utilising its stealth? In the larger Soviet aircraft, a trend towards the first option can be detected and aircraft like the Foxbat, Foxhound, and Flanker are large aircraft (80,000 lbs and 50,000 lbs weight respectively) with large powerful radars. The F-16 is a smaller aircraft (25,000 lbs weight) with a much smaller radar, a design feature falling from its inception as the cheap fighter in the *high-low* fighter mix with the F-15, and the demands for great agility which drove the designers to the chin intake which, in turn, sized the radar antennae.

There is little doubt about the issue should the F-16 engage in close combat with the large Soviet Foxbats and Foxhounds. However, if those two large, fast, but low-'G'-tolerant aircraft were allowed to engage on their terms – long-range stand-off – then the issue might equally be in little doubt. The aircraft designer today cannot practise his art therefore without first engaging in the analysis of the likely operational scenario. If this essential first step is miscalculated then the design, though it may fly perfectly, will prove to be a flawed *fighter* for it will not triumph in battle.

Increasingly, the design decision resolves around this simple balance. A big aircraft with a large powerful radar, which engages from the stand-off with long-range missiles; or the small aircraft which, like the terrier, gets into the fight by stealth and deception and uses superior agility to bring its shorter-range and lighter weapons to bear.

There are powerful advocates for both views. In the high-low mix of fighters procured by the United States Air Force in the mid-seventies both options were kept open. The large F-15, with its impressive radar and its medium-range missiles on the one hand, and the smaller F-16, equipped with the short-range IR missiles on the other. The Soviets, a decade later, are starting to field aircraft which the developing technology allows to have both high agility and impressive radar performance, and the Fulcrum and Flanker both have large radomes housing, presumably large radar antennae. The mid-nineties are likely to see the United States Air Force *Advanced Tactical Fighter* (ATF) in the 50,000 lb class, which aims for excellent radar performance, stealth, high agility and sustained supersonic performance at height. A very demanding specification indeed.

The European nations, conversely, in their *European Fighter Aircraft* (EFA) proposal, are looking towards a much smaller aircraft (20,000 lbs weight) and the French favour the same approach with an even lighter design, the Rafael at about 18,000 lbs. In Sweden the JAS 30 Grippen is also a small multi-purpose design and in Israel the Lavi is in the F-16 class. It cannot go without note, however, that the imperatives driving the designs in the European consortium, France, Sweden, and Israel, owe as much to political, economic and industrial factors as to any purely military desires and it is necessary to study the two primary aircraft manufacturing nations, the United States of America and the Soviet Union, to determine the trends of combat design untrammelled by such confusing, if real life, complications.

It has already been shown that weight or size in itself is not the determinant of stealth characteristics and there is no reason why the smaller designs should not achieve the high stealth ratings needed to live in the powerful and long-range radar environment. There is, unfortunately, a consideration which acts against this worthy end.

First, is that the smaller aircraft, particularly one optimised for the air superiority mission, with engines designed for thrust rather than for economy, will require a high fuel fraction if it is to have the *persistence* which modern combat increasingly demands. There is an understandable, but regrettable, tendency for designers to rely on drop-tanks to carry the required fuel. Although these excellent devices were originally designed to do just what their name suggests – be dropped – they can prove to be so expensive and scarce that pilots will have to jettison them with circumspection if the squadrons are not to be drop-tank-less in the early stages of a war. The modern *drop-tank* is probably one of the most grossly over designed pieces of war equipment in the total inventory.

Second, is that the smaller the aircraft, the more difficult it is to mount missiles conformally. Conformal mounting, or the semi-burying of the missile in the aircraft structure, greatly reduces drag and is highly beneficial. But even in the quite large Tornado (40,000 lbs weight) the Air Defence Version had to have a lengthened fuselage before four Sparrow/Skyflash missiles could be mounted. Although there is a trend, perceived by some, for smaller missiles, the size would have to be reduced significantly if they were to be mounted conformally on an aircraft of the weight of *EFA/Rafael/JAS/Lavi*. The answer, as always, will be to mount on pylons and this, together with the drop tanks, starts to give a shape with a myriad of reflecting centres and stealth in the main aircraft structure becomes irrelevant.

A small aircraft, with a small radar, with small, short-ranged missiles, but with stealth is one thing – without stealth it is quite another. In what is about to become a very lethal battlefield, where such esoteric factors make the difference between success and failure, victory and defeat, life and death, whoever is charged to cast the die had better get it right.

Although a good radar will have as little energy spill into side-lobes as possible, it is almost impossible to suppress them completely. Side-lobes are troublesome things for they too frequently form the path whereby jamming signals enter the radar and they can also form the source for passive warning devices to sense the presence of the radar threat. In the future they may become an even more lethal nuisance because the trend towards miniaturisation, made possible by the advances in micro-electronics, is allowing small anti-radar heads to be produced to home onto the emissions from radars.

The use of these heads on agile missiles in the air combat environment could cause great consternation, not only because the *modus operandi* of such heads means that they become more accurate the closer they home to the target signal, but because it could prove difficult, if not impossible, to determine what sort of head was on the threatening missile. In the average close combat, such missiles will be in the air for only a few seconds, far too little time to go through a variety of counter-measures. Although such threats are not fielded in any great number at present, they will clearly arrive on the scene soon and, when they do, it must place in question the use of the radar in the close combat arena.

Once combat is engaged at visual ranges, other technologies offer themselves to be used to slave missile heads to off-bore sight targets. The *helmet mounted sight* is designed to allow the pilot to place a sighting marker, presented to him on a small screen before his eyes, on the target and the azimuth and elevation of the target is calculated by measuring the position of the pilots helmet. The system is passive with all the advantages that gives in the technological battlefield and, with practice, can result in an input into the fire control system accurate enough for the purpose of laying missile heads.

Clearly, the additional weight involved on the helmet, small though that may be, has to be considered carefully when modern aircraft pulling high 'G' are concerned. To be properly protective, flying helmets have to be substantial things in their own right and any additional weight is undesirable. Under 9 'G', a helmet may already weigh in the order of 18 lbs and if the aiming equipment adds only $\frac{1}{2}$ lb it is enough to increase the burden to an impressive $22\frac{1}{2}$ lbs. Placing a $22\frac{1}{2}$ lb weight on the head and taking a few steps is enough to prove that real physical strength is required to move the head in any way, let alone in the way it needs to be moved in the air combat environment. The helmet mounted sight answers many problems but, unless the design is optimised for low weight, it could result in problems of its own.

A consideration for designers and procurers alike must be cost. It is instructive to consider how cost profiles have changed over a relatively small number of years. At the outbreak of the 1939–45 war the cost of an aircraft was split almost equally between the airframe and the engine. The guns were machine guns of no great cost and the sighting system was little more than a ring and bead. *Avionics* consisted of a four-channel radio set. During the war, the avionic content started to change and the advent of air intercept radar and bombing devices such as the H2S caused the avionic content to compete with airframe and engine for a finite part of the whole. Only recently has the weapon part of the equation made its bid for an equally finite part of the total cost. Although the choice has to be made with care, there are weapon systems about which demonstrate that the cost relationship between airframe/engine/avionics and engine is now equally divided.

From open sources, for example, the cost of the Tornado Air Defence Variant is said to be 'around' £20 million. Its radar, the Foxhunter, has been said to cost £630 million at this stage of its development. The Tornado ADV buy is 165 aircraft and without making complex allowances for spare radars and support, or allowing for those aircraft which are kept in reserve or are in deep servicing, the taxpayer could be excused for thinking that if it costs £630 million to put radar into a 165 aircraft purchase, then the radar costs about £4 million each.

Will this expenditure be necessary in the future? Is radar now an essential part of the design for an aircraft which has to fight and survive in the modern world? Certainly it is increasingly difficult to envisage a fighter without some form of sensors to provide a picture of the air combat battlefield. As that battlefield expands continuously, well beyond visual range, then the pilot's own faculties will not be able to cope. Something will be needed to provide the *situational awareness* of the total scene which will be essential, not only for survival but for the vital first shot and, quite probably, the consequent success.

Passive warning receivers, giving early warning of the approaching radar, will feature strongly in an offensive suite as will, increasingly, other passive sensors such as the IRST systems. But these alone may not be able to present the battle plot sufficiently comprehensively to enable the engagement to be started on the most favourable terms.

What may offer the answer to the individual radar in the aircraft is the netted multi-source sensor system which feeds into a central computer analysis from which the total air picture is derived, the synthesised picture then being fed to the aircraft via data link. The pilot would have his situation plot in the cockpit – but through a data link, rather than through his own radar set.

The solution has its attractions. The pilot retains all his passive aids but is spared the inconvenience of carrying the weight and complexity of the radar set. Weight is important, particularly when aircraft are now being designed by economists rather than by aerodynamicists and are therefore becoming *small* because, to the uninitiated, small equates to *cheap*.

The AWG-70 radar being developed for the later marks of F-15 is said to weigh 550 lbs, a weight which fits better with the 81,000 lb take-off weight of the F-15E than with a ten-tonne EFA. But even this advanced radar is predicted to 'improve' present standards of reliability to a *Mean-Time-Between Failure* of 25 hours which, although indeed an improvement over the norm, still implies a considerable investment in spares, manpower and training – all very expensive items. The prospect of removing weight, cost and manpower from the equation by the fitment of a data-linked air situation picture becomes exceedingly attractive and is probably the path to the future.

RADAR CROSS SECTION

From the radar formula it can be seen that detection range is proportional to the fourth-root of the RCS. Consequently, large reductions in the RCS are needed to show a substantial decrease in detection range, as shown in Figure 5.5. However, large reductions in RCS are possible by the use of Radar Absorbant Material (RAM) and attenuation exceeding 10 decibels (dBs) are possible, even on existing designs. 10 dBs equates to 90 per cent reduction on a percentage scale. It can be seen that a 90 per cent reduction in RCS would reduce the detection range to 56 per cent of the non-suppressed condition. At that point in the graph, relatively small additional reductions would reduce the detection range considerably. A British manufacturer offers on the open market a RAM giving a performance better than -10 dB between 6 to 20 GHz, -15 dB between 8 and 14 GHz and no less than -20 dB between 10 and 12 GHz.

As an example of the reductions in RCS possible when the problem is addressed at the design stage, the RCS of the B-1B bomber now entering service with the United States Air Force is one-hundredth of the RCS of the old generation B-52. Figure 5.4 shows how this would look from the radar-eyes-view. The natural inclination is to put this down to shape – the two aircraft are markedly different in this regard – but this would not explain why the B-1B is only one-tenth the RCS of the B-1A which was virtually the same shape. The SR-71 is another example of a design which had stealth characteristics considered from its inception. Even though this aircraft still looks futuristic, and out-performs most other aircraft in service, the original aircraft first flew as long ago as 1962.

There is a popular misconception that RCS is a function of weight; that a large aircraft is by definition less stealthy than a smaller aircraft. This is not the case. RCS depends primarily upon shape and materials rather than size *per se*. This can be illustrated by the example of a design which reduces the weight by 20 per cent. Weight is closely related to size, more specifically *volume* but at a first iteration it can be assumed that a 20 per cent size reduction would accrue. If this reduced the RCS by

20 per cent the resultant detection range reduction would be only 3 per cent. A much greater pay-off could be obtained by using RAM on a larger design.

As an indication of what the combination of shaping at the design stage and the use of RAM and other structural material makes possible, early reports of the proposed United States Air Force Advanced Tactical Fighter suggest that a frontal RCS as low as 0.1 square-metres is being aimed at. This compares with the current RCS of a fighter-bomber in the order of 10 square metres and of a fighter of about 5 square metres.

PRACTICAL RADAR CROSS SECTION

The radar cross section of a target is usually quoted as the head-on case and in the scenario of the air intercept or in the initial engagement geometry of an air combat, the head-on case is a useful start point. The head-on case may not, however, be the smallest RCS. Not only are there the reflections which can be caused by radar antennae in the nose of the target but large intakes can form good reflective areas. Cockpit transparencies allow reflectivity from the insides of the cockpit, an area rarely designed with stealth in mind.

It is not unusual to obtain the smallest RCS at angles off the head-on/tail-on aspect of about 30 to 60 degrees. Most targets exhibit very large RCS at the beam-on aspect where the *flat-plate* effect comes into play. In some cases the more modern aircraft are worse in this regard than older designs. Larger vertical stabilisers are becoming the design norm, even to the point of using dual fins – F-14, F-15, F-18, Fulcrum, Flanker, Foxbat – and some modern bombers are slab-sided. The radar cross section of two typical bomber aircraft are shown in Figure 5.6.

It is this initial fall-off in RCS as the aspect increases off the nose that can give rise to confusion. In this circumstance the RCS is decreasing at the same time as the visual target is increasing.

At best such RCS plots are illustrative. It is virtually impossible to estimate accurately the RCS of a real aircraft by theoretical calculation and even the use of models is suspect unless they are an absolutely correct representation of the aircraft. Even then the smallest discontinuity in the skin of a specific aircraft could give a quite different overall RCS. One study showed, for example, that the change of aspect on a test aircraft of only one-third of a degree gave a difference of 31.6 square metres in the RCS.

THE ELECTRONIC REVOLUTION

The miniaturisation of high capacity electronic circuits is having a major impact on development over the whole field of weaponry. Already terms such as *smart* for a guided weapon are having to be superceded by *super-smart* and some writers are using the odd *brilliant* to enthuse over the capabilities of the later inventions. The radar in the F-15 series shows a good example of what has happened in the area of electronic development over a short timescale.

Introduced in 1974, the original F-15 entered service with an AWG-63 radar, a hard-wired signal processor, and a 16K data processor. Soon after the 16K capacity was upgraded to 24K. In 1979 a programmable signal processor with 96K of memory was installed. Now the AWG-63 is planned to be replaced by the AWG-70 version of the radar. The AWG-70 will utilise technology which gives a 4-to-1 increase in computer density and the signal processor will provide 5-times more processing with no change in weight, power requirement or volume from the original version. The AWG-63 was introduced with the capability of conducting *7.1 million-complex-operations-per-second* (MCOPS) – the AWG-70 will start with a capability for 33 MCOPS and have a growth capability to 44 MCOPS.

For all but the expert, it is difficult to appreciate what 33 million-complex-operations-per-second really means. There comes a point at which the human perception reaches its limit of understanding. This can be compared better to something more akin to the grasp, even if still in the field of *high-tech*. The Apple IIE is a popular and not inconsiderable personal computer. The 33 MCOPS capacity of the AWG-70 radar will represent the capacity of no less than 200,000 Apple IIE computers. Such a store of computers would occupy more than a warehouse – or two – whereas the processor in the AWG-70 will occupy a volume of one cubic foot and weigh 60 lbs.

It has been estimated that if the motor industry had have made the same advances as the electronic industry over the last two decades, a Rolls-Royce would cost only three pence. Unfortunately, it would be miniaturised to be only one-half inch square!

RADAR ABSORBENT MATERIALS

Radar Absorbent Materials (RAM) are becoming popular as a means of reducing the radar reflectivity of structures and can be used in two ways; the first, as an addition to structure in the form of stick-on panels at those parts of an airframe identified as having particularly bad shaping giving rise to reflective centres, and the second, but as yet less popular, as a structural medium which not only reduces the reflectivity by absorption but is strong enough to take structural load in its own right.

A typical RAM consists of a sandwich of three layers; two are part-radar-reflective and contain a third dialectric material between them. The radar waves pass through the first layer and are then reflected to and fro between the top and bottom layers. The effect is for the incoming waves to be partially cancelled out by the outgoing waves. The purpose of the dialectric material between is to contain the waves sufficiently to allow the cancellation to take place.

Although effective and offering impressive reductions in radar reflectivity, the current RAM using this technology is rather tailor made to a particular frequency. That frequency is determined by the distance between the outer reflective layers and the form of the dialectric used. A change in radar threat frequency could quite alter the degree of protection provided. Some modern search radars which operate over a wide band of frequencies would have a poor, or non-existent, return at one setting but would receive a usable signal at another frequency. What is required, therefore, is a RAM which has resistance to a wide frequency spectrum.

Some work in the United States suggests that a RAM based on the use of salts as a dialectric rather than the more customary ferrite materials, will provide protection against a wide range of frequencies; a reduction of 80 per cent has been claimed. An important futher advantage is that materials based on the salts rather than on the ferrite inner core could prove to be only one-tenth the weight of the earlier material.

An interesting cost balance has to be drawn. The cost of RAM treatment for a tactical aircraft varies with the source consulted but lies between £20,000 and £80,000. When this is set against the costs of additional power needed for a protective ECM equipment to provide a similar level of protection for the un-suppressed aircraft, the economics are seen clearly to favour the RAM fitment.

6.

Basic Fighter Manoeuvres

'. . . easy! It's all just a matter of ribbons and bubbles.'

AIR combat is a subject which stirs emotions personal and corporate. It is perceived as the most glamorous of the warlike arts and, as such, has been subjected to media hype. It makes good copy. It is a field of readily identifiable heroes, for a *kill* in air combat can be counted and revered far more easily than a kill from a bomb dropped from the distant and anonymous bomber. League tables can be drawn up and changing fortunes celebrated or mourned as with Liverpool or Charlton Athletic. All the world loves a winner! Further, bombs dropped by bombers tend to kill civilians and that, somehow, is still not considered *fair* or *gentlemanly* whereas airmen killing each other can be accepted as a natural order of things. After all, the gladiators were equally popular with the fun-loving crowds.

From the perception of the fighter pilot, the glamour of air combat depends on whether he is winning or losing. Being a combat pilot in war is one of the most lethal occupations and technology is making it more so. The stakes are high and its unforgiving nature makes them even higher; for example, in air combat there is no internationally recognised way of surrendering – a white flag cannot be raised at Mach One. Of course, a premature ejection is a possibility, and there is some evidence that this has been resorted to in the Middle East, but it is a dubious solution over the North Sea in the middle of both winter and war.

Another reason for the attraction of air combat is its mystery. Good air combat pilots stand out amongst their fellows on the squadrons and, invariably, seem to emerge from practice combats with killing film regardless of what lesser mortals do to frustrate their purpose. There is an element of gamesmanship in some of these virtuoso performances and the art of cheating has been developed by some into almost an art form. Not necessarily a bad thing for, once in the cockpit of a fighter aircraft, the sly, low-down, evil-minded cheat can endear himself to his squadron commander, particularly if those qualities result in success.

The others who succeed tend to be those who understand the fundamentals of air combat and, can *read* an air situation and apply those fundamentals to it. Reading the air situation becomes difficult as the number of aircraft in a combat increases and good combat squadrons – and not all are by any means – are the ones where this vital factor of *situational awareness* is developed and practised.

Success in air combat does not depend on being the best pilot. Bishop claimed to be the highest scoring *ace* in both the British and the German air forces because, as he openly admitted, he had destroyed more allied aircraft in landing accidents than he killed enemy in the air. Some excellent pilots, who impress with their smooth and accurate flying will make poor combat pilots if their skills are not matched by their knowledge of the combat manoeuvres, and by an ability to read the sky about them. Before World War Two, the Italian Air Force were renowned for their aerobatics but this helped them little in combat, where their smooth and predictable flying made them easy targets. Smooth flying may be very necessary to milk performance out of the edge of the envelope but being predictable with it is a sure recipe for disaster:

'Never do ANYTHING for more than 15 seconds'

. . . and some say that long is pushing the luck.

Already, the discussion is leaning towards *fundamentals* rather than *secrets*. Aircraft performance, as has been seen, is governed by the laws of aerodynamics and physics and the scope for conducting original stunts is limited. As with chess, there are a number of possible moves and the game has to be played within them – bishops cannot move directly up the board because it is not allowed. Yet there are the chess *aces* or masters who, consistently, can so use the permitted moves in combination that they triumph over lesser mortals. Much of their success lies in the ability to think ahead a number of moves, to force their opponent to react to their initiative – in air combat terms, they possess better *situational awareness*.

Rather than in the field of aircraft manoeuvre, the secrets can be found emerging in formation *tactics*. In the air war in South East Asia the north Vietnamese, following their Soviet tutors, used decoys, not an original tactic, for it was used to effect by the Germans in World War One. The decoy could consist of a MiG-17 flying vulnerably low and slow beneath a formation, tempting a singleton or a pair to detach for the easy kill. But high and fast behind would be the MiG-21s waiting for the force to split, to lose cross-over and cohesion, and allowing them to turn the tables and obtain an easy kill with the fast slashing attack and departure.

Be it individual aircraft combats or the larger interactions with number of aircraft, there is merit in avoiding complexity. A number of tactics which look so fine in the coloured chalks of the briefing room end up with chaos in the air because the very complexity requires every unit to perform perfectly. It just does not happen that way. As the electromagnetic spectrum increasingly becomes a battlefield in its own right, the use of radio to control complex tactics is equally likely to fail. The simple plan, executed well, has a lot to commend it. It follows the KISS principle:

'Keep It Simple – Stupid'

The success of a squadron in combat will depend on a number of things, not least of which is the importance placed by the squadron commander on air combat training. There have been squadron commanders who have concentrated training on those aspects of the overall task in which they themselves excel – if that does not happen to include air combat then the squadron suffers. The squadron also needs at least one good instructor who knows both theory and practice and, of vital importance, can *teach it*. This man does not have to be the best pilot on the squadron, or the best air combat pilot, but he has to know how to put the concepts across in a convincing manner.

Too many air forces now rely upon such a man emerging naturally from the herd; for the qualities required to teach this most difficult subject to develop automatically. It is asking a lot – too much – and, apart from the exceptional pilot who will always emerge from the large sample, air combat instructors have to be trained formally if the skills are to be taught and absorbed thoroughly by a large force.

Like many other aspects of the air war, the truths come home to roost when the fighting starts and losses mount. It has already been seen that the Royal Air Force went into the Battle of Britain with outdated tactics compared to a battle-experienced Luftwaffe fresh out of Spain. During the conflict that followed, the Royal Air Force formed the Central Fighter Establishment to pursue tactics, weapons development, and leadership training within the fighter force. Twenty years of relative peace was sufficient to destroy this child of necessity and the unit was disbanded in 1965. It is, therefore, over two decades since the Royal Air Force last produced a fighter combat leader from a course dedicated solely to that purpose – before some of the current fighter pilots were born. The Royal Air Force is not alone in being in this situation.

The United States services, both United States Air Force and United States Navy, needed to be put into the embarrassment of low exchange ratios in the air war in Vietnam before they too grasped the nettle and accepted that formal training of air combat leaders was necessary. The film 'TOP GUN' – if stripped of its romance and Hollywood characterisation – gives some indication of what is involved and has brought to popular attention the United States Navy Top Gun School, the formation of which showed an almost immediate effect on the exchange ratios in Vietnam half-way through that conflict. The United States Air Force have parallel organisations at Nellis Air Force Base which is acknowledged, even by non-US airmen, as truly *the home of the fighter pilot*.

In NATO, an initiative taken at the end of the seventies started the *Tactical Leadership Programme* in which crews of the six Central Region nations, all but one not having schools of their own, join together to conduct post-graduate leadership training. Limited resources and the difficulties of training realistically in the densely populated reaches of North West Europe present problems but it is better than nothing.

Over the years, one of the most difficult problems to tackle has been the start-stop nature of the training. Air combat training in the Royal Air Force has been discontinued as a training exercise three times in the last 30 years. At least with aircraft such as the European Fighter Aircraft being supported by politicians – if not designed by them – as a *combat* machine, there may be cause for hope that air combat training is now here to stay in the minds of the senior management. Another time, because the loss rates in training were too high, ignoring the obvious corollary that if loss rates were concerning in peace using film-*bullets* what would they be like in war using real bullets? If loss rates are high, more training is required, not less. In all, air combat training has travelled a tortuous path through the years of peace and lessons and teaching techniques are best found in those air forces which have been shot at rather than in those which have succeeded in their deterrent purpose. The Fighter Leaders School of the Pakistan Air Force, patterned closely on the now defunct school of the Royal Air Force, is a case in point.

TRAINING

Air combat training starts with gaining a true confidence in the aircraft and is why this phase of training should not be started too soon in a pilot's tour on the squadron. A great deal of harm can be done to a pilot's self-confidence if his air combat tuition starts with a series of crushing defeats due to his inexperience.

Aerobatics and hard manoeuvring are flown to investigate the edges of the performance envelope but primarily to gain a *feel* for the aircraft. Perhaps because aircraft have become more system orientated, and cockpits are full to overflowing with the knobs and dials of modern technology, there is a temptation to be hypnotised with their messages various and to ignore the outside world. Yet it is in the outside world that the threat to well-being lurks and to ignore it is to invite surprise and potential disaster. An AI (airborne intercept) radar will help little with the threat closing fast in the six-o'clock no matter how proficiently the radar is manipulated. Pilots (which will be used also as shorthand to include crews) must get their eyes out of the cockpit. BVR combat is a system affair but close-in-combat (CIC) is predominantly a visual matter.

If a pilot is to get his eyes out of the cockpit then he must have some help in knowing what the aircraft is doing, particularly when it is flown close to the limits. In the past there have been the honest aircraft which could be flown with eyes out of the cockpit because their handling qualities were such that they gave indication of what was happening through the stick. The *nibble* of the *Meteor* ailerons as the critical Mach number was reached; the buffet pattern of the *Hunter* in the low speed regime, are both examples of the *talking* aircraft.

One of the penalties for the increased performance of more modern aircraft has been some handling qualities which are far from benign and which can result in loss of control unless great care is taken to stay within the limits outlined by the flight clearance. It is difficult in some circumstances, for example, to know accurately enough the angle of incidence (alpha) of the Jaguar without reference to the instrumentation, yet if flown aggressively outside the alpha limits the aircraft can easily *depart* into uncontrolled flight which, in that particular design, is what has been described as a *wild ride*.

The Jaguar is a design which is long and narrow. It is over 50 feet long but has a wing span of only 28 feet. It resembles in this respect the F-104 Starfighter which was nearly 55 feet long and had a wing span of only 22 feet. It was with the F-104 that brought the phenomenon of *roll-coupling* came to popular attention. Roll-coupling is explained in Figure 6.1.

Methods of helping the pilot to keep his eyes out of the cockpit can include audio warning devices – horns, bells, whistles or even voices can be used to warn of high alpha, low speed, or ground proximity, being triggered in turn by incidence probe, pitot pressure or radar altimeter. Some aircraft are equipped with stick shakers which give a tactile indication of approach to the stall boundary.

The latest designs, which utilise control inputs through a computer, can be programmed to prevent the pilot entering unsafe areas of the flight envelope and while this can give worry free handling, in a combat environment there is always need for the pilot to be able to over-ride such safety systems. Although an over-stress, or

Aircraft resemble darts and can be shown as a weight with destabilising area in front and stabilising area behind the centre of gravity, the later area generally reinforced by a fin or fins.

Long 'thin' aircraft with short wings can have a weight distribution resembling two dumb-bells at right angles, the larger of the two being that representing the fuselage.

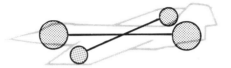

If the aircraft is flown at a high angle of attack and then rolled, the effect is to throw the fuselage 'weights' further away from the line of flight until the 'spin', or roll, is about the line of the wings instead of the line of the fuselage. In practice the aircraft would have broken up some time before this point is reached.

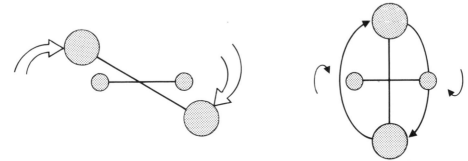

FIG 6.1.   Roll coupling

even a flight departure, is not to be encouraged they are by far the lesser evil to striking the ground or having a mid-air collision.

Another feel that the fledgling combat pilot must acquire is for *relativities* and for *rates*. The great majority of flight training in the early stages is understandably conducted as a single aircraft. Apart from some formation flying, he will rarely have encountered aircraft passing very close to him travelling in the opposite direction. The first experience can be memorable because closure speeds can be very high indeed. Further, such high rates of closure can be deceptive and an approaching aircraft can go from being a dot on the windscreen to filling it in a remarkably short space of time. (Figure 6.2)

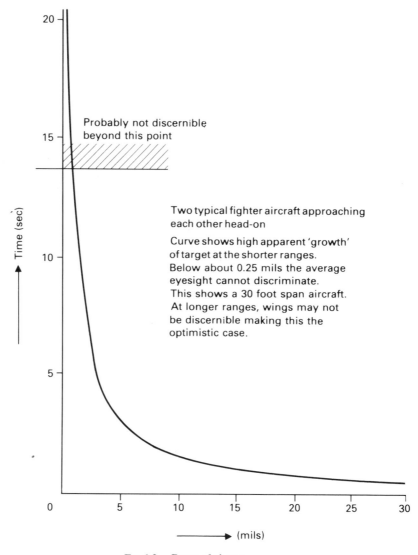

FIG 6.2.   Rates of closure

He must also retain, instinctively, a sense of his relative position to other aircraft in the combat and, most important, to any cloud in the area which can be used for concealment or escape, and, essentially, the earth – for the hard unyielding ground remains the primary killer in aviation. In the excitement and absorption of an air combat, the odd 10,000 feet can be lost un-noticed through a mis-read altimeter, and more than one pilot has penetrated a cloud layer thinking it to have an 11,000 foot base to find to his concern that it had a 1,000 foot base.

RIBBONS

Discounting for the moment CIC weapons with a head-on or front-quarter capability, the general thrust of air combat manoeuvring is the same today as it always has been.

'Fighter pilots have to rove the area allotted to them in any way they like and when they spot the enemy they attack and shoot him down: anything else is rubbish!'

von Richthofen

Much of that attacking still entails gaining a nose-to-tail clearance to the rear of the target aircraft and air combat manoeuvres are designed to bring about that end. So, how is it done and, as important, how is it explained?

Imagine that as an aircraft proceeds through the air it unfolds behind it a carpet or ribbon. The length of the ribbon it unfolds in any given period of time will depend on the speed of the aircraft. If left lying about the imaginary sky the ribbon will trace a record of the flight path of the aircraft. If it is marked with a time base it can be compared with other aircraft ribbons to show relative position during combat manoeuvres. In this way it is useful for illustrating text on the subject.

It can be used further to explain some of the principles if a little imagination is applied. The manoeuvrability of an aircraft can be equated to the pliability of the ribbon. A highly manoeuvrable aircraft could be represented by a ribbon similar to those used to tie hair and which can be turned through sharp angles, indeed, tied into a knot – supreme *manoeuvrability* it might be thought. A large transport or a bomber ribbon might be more akin to thick cardboard or linoleum and would prove impossible to knot or to bend through small radius corners, just as the aircraft themselves have limited manoeuvre in the air.

Figure 6.3 shows the ribbons produced by two aircraft, one at 300 kts and the other at 600 kts. Clearly, if these two aircraft started off with wing-tips level, the faster

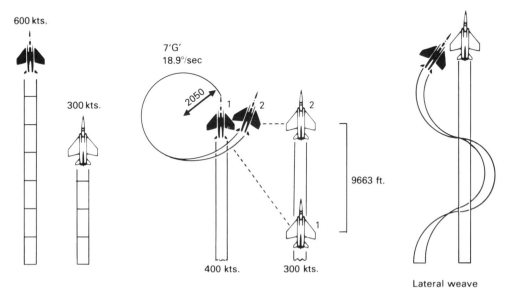

FIG 6.3.   The 'ribbon'

aircraft would soon pull ahead and build up an automatic nose-tail clearance advantage for the slower aircraft. The faster aircraft would have twice the *forward travel* with its ribbon than would the slower aircraft.

How, therefore, to *tie-a-knot-in-it*? The most obvious way to do so is to describe a full circle, either in the form of a loop or, horizontally, in a turn through 360 degrees. Alternatively, a series of turns could be flown which allows the ribbon to be distributed either side of the line of advance. The disadvantage in this case can be the need to reverse the turn.

In a reversal there is a loss of optimised turn at the point of reversal; in some designs this is aggravated by the ineffectiveness of the ailerons or spoilers at high angles of attack. In such aircraft it can prove profitable to temporarily unload the 'G' while the reversal is executed and then pull into the turn in the opposite direction afresh. While the 'G' is relaxed, optimum turn is not achieved, indeed, if the 'G' is relaxed completely, there will be no turn at all. This may be thought to be a marginal disadvantage in view of the short time the reversal takes to accomplish – and in most types it is – but small margins combine to tip the balance if a number of such turns are to be conducted one after the other.

A way of avoiding the turn reversal problem is to keep the turn in the same direction and to distribute the ribbon in the manner of a *tube* rather than as a *snake*: in other words, use roll instead of turn. These options are shown in Figure 6.4. In all

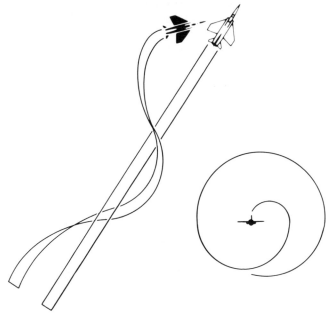

FIG 6.4.   Barrel roll

cases the aim is the same; to make forward travel less than the total length of the ribbon. He who can do that best will gain nose-tail clearance and with it a tactical advantage.

Very rarely will a combat begin from a close formation position. Even in training combats, the participants will each turn out by 45 degrees for an agreed amount of time before reversing to search for the opposition and to start the combat. Until the highly instrumented air combat ranges came to the scene it was in this procedural split that some of the best cheating occurred. A few of the tricks will be mentioned here simply because this volume is aimed, *inter alia*, at the junior officer who may not yet have started his combat training.

The split is designed to start both aircraft off with equal advantage. The point of this is that, at the turn, both should know the geometry of the split and therefore where, in broad terms, to look for the hostile. Whatever can be done therefore, to leave the other fellow looking in the wrong place must be to advantage. Flying a barely detectable number of degrees off the agreed heading on the split can make a good difference, as can flying either slower or faster than the agreed speed. Flying faster, for example, results in a greater split distance than expected and the opposition will get increasingly concerned when the merge does not take place at the right time. This results in him having to split his search over the 360 degrees rather than concentrating on the direction of the cheaters approach. A considerable advantage is gained.

Equally, by dropping height or, alternatively, applying full power and gaining height, the opposition is left searching in the wrong area of sky and, depending on the background – cloud, land or sea – an advantage can again be had for the taking. Against new – and junior – students a split can be arranged which results in the junior man searching for his instructor into sun after the reversal. This used to be a sure way of proving superiority but in these modern days it is less so. Young officers emerge from an education system which teaches them to question, have little respect for their elders, encourages original thought, and seemingly positively urges them to seek *fairness* and *rights*. They have been known, consequently, to actually *complain* at being left looking into sun at the merge. The life of an air combat instructor is not what it was . . .! Figure 6.5 reveals all.

A great psychological advantage can be obtained over the student by *reverse cheating*. It calls for great skill and more than a little manipulation but is well worth the effort expended. It is necessary, a few hours before the flight, to implant into the young-Richthofen's mind that climbing after the split is undetectable and confers great advantage. This information should be communicated in the spirit of brotherly camaraderie. The student is usually touchingly grateful, which can be turned to further advantage when there are chores to be done. The instructional sortie later is flown to the point where the split is conducted a few hundreds of feet below the contrail level – a piece of information omitted by the instructor from the sortie briefing. After the split the student, with his instructor's tips well in mind, applies full power and climbs – immediately entering the con-level and producing behind him beautiful, long, white trails which can be seen by the instructor for 20 miles, while he in turn remains a mere speck in the sky below the contrail level. The student lands in awe of the instructors prowess for he is soundly beaten notwithstanding his cheating – and no wonder!

Is this not shocking and contrary to the norms of officers and gentlemen? Of course it is but modern air combat is a far too lethal pastime for officers and gentlemen – the time to be that is after the victory, sipping a half in the Mess in celebration. There is a need to win first, and to accomplish that all the skill and cunning which can be

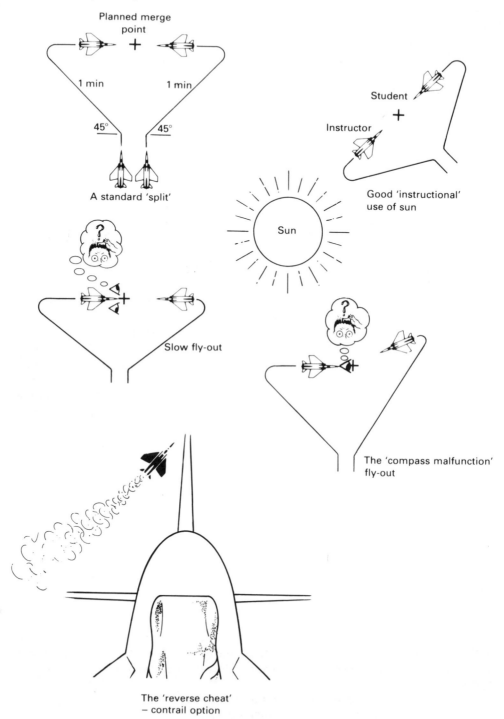

Planned merge point

1 min   1 min

45°   45°

A standard 'split'

Student

Instructor

Good 'instructional' use of sun

Sun

Slow fly-out

The 'compass malfunction' fly-out

The 'reverse cheat' – contrail option

FIG 6.5.   Cheating at the split

mastered needs to be applied; a little practice in cheating is not too out of place in training for the event.

As can be seen therefore, air combat can begin with a variety of different situations and few of them in practice are ever as had been imagined in theory. Very rarely indeed will aircraft merge with equal advantage – even if the speed and height were equal, the geometry of the start would be likely to confer advantage to one or the other. If, exceptionally, the physical conditions were the same, there would remain the different characteristics of the two aircraft types.

TURNS

Playing the turn is like matadors and bullfighting. The aim in defence is to expend as little effort as possible to ensure that the attacker cannot – just cannot – gain the advantage. To use energy to achieve any more than that is wasteful and energy conservation in an air combat is vital, if for no other reason than that of fuel. In the offence it is a cunning bull which is called for. One which may, at times, need to walk into the attack rather than charging into it. One which must know when it will pay to squander energy for the kill and when it must be conserved for the re-attack. When, in other words, the full instantaneous turn-rate must be used or the discipline of the sustained turn applied to a further plan.

There are three types of pursuit turn: *pure pursuit, lag, and lead.*

Figure 6.6a illustrates the *pure pursuit* turn. In essence the nose of the attacker is kept pointing at the target and this eventually leads to an intercept, that is, the two aircraft would meet IF the required performance needed to fulfil the geometry was available. As can be seen from the diagram, this may not necessarily be so, for the pursuit curve can lead to a tightening of the turn in a number of circumstances. This can result in the attacker not being able to match the turn performance required or can result in a speed loss caused by the tightening of the turn, which can allow the target to extend away from the attacker.

An advantage of a pure pursuit turn which is often understated is that, with the nose pointing to the target, the attacker is presenting the smallest frontal area. This makes him difficult to see. Small aircraft, or those with fine profiles – F-5, *Jaguar* – can be extremely difficult to see in such attitudes. Conversely, if seen in this state, the target knows that, at least, he is safe from a guns attack because the attacker would have to increase his aspect to pull lead if the burst was to have a chance of hitting. The requirement does not apply to missiles.

A *lag pursuit* turn is flown when the attacker places his nose behind the target. This tactic is adopted if it is necessary to slow or to stop the rate of closure, if it is required to maintain a particular separation from the target, or if it is desired to maintain or to decrease the angle-off-the-tail (AOT) of the target.

An advantage of the lag pursuit turn is the ability it confers to maintain energy advantage over the target while still remaining in its rear hemisphere. Figure 6.6b. Throughout the manoeuvre, as always, the fighter pilot is looking for the opportunity for the kill and he must decide whether there is any point at which he can convert his excess energy into instantaneous turn-rate to *square the corner* and bring his weapons to bear. If he decides not to, then it is important to retain energy and the lag pursuit turn permits him to do so.

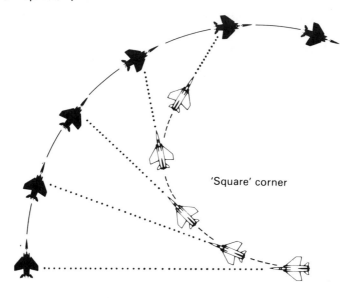

'Square' corner

High overtake – 'squares corner'
Low overtake – danger of target extension

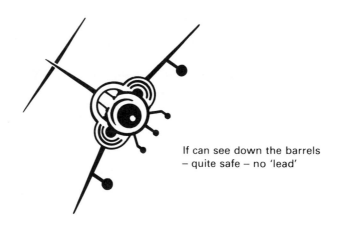

If can see down the barrels
– quite safe – no 'lead'

Attacker aspect in pure pursuit

FIG 6.6(a).   Pure pursuit

Care must be taken in the degree of AOT accepted once on the outside of the turn. If the separation distance is too high, or the AOT is very great – that is approaching 90 degrees – then the target, by reversing his turn, could present the attacker with a difficult problem. If the target is armed with short-ranged IR missiles – as a fighter-bomber might be – then the tables could have been effectively turned.

Attacker aspect – lag pursuit

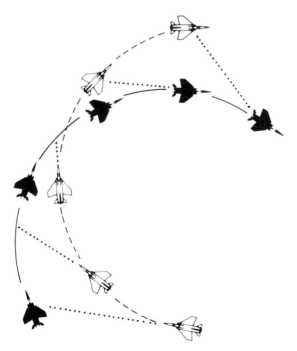

FIG 6.6(b).   Lag pursuit

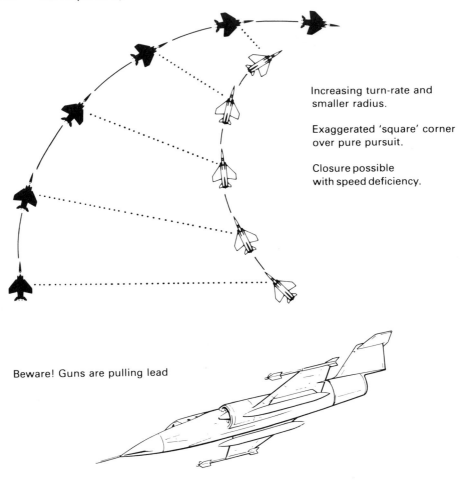

Increasing turn-rate and
smaller radius.

Exaggerated 'square' corner
over pure pursuit.

Closure possible
with speed deficiency.

Beware! Guns are pulling lead

Attacker aspect in lead pursuit

FIG 6.6(c).   Lead pursuit

In a lag pursuit turn the visual clues are more pronounced than in the pure pursuit turn and the effect as far as gun solutions are concerned are the same. The target should be looking down upon the top surfaces of the attacker and in this state a gun solution is unlikely to be possible. Not impossible, because some aircraft designed for air combat or air interception have their gun-lines elevated above the fuselage datum line to assist in bringing the guns to bear in a turning, deflection shooting situation. An aircraft that doubles in the ground attack role is less likely to have such gun geometry because raised gun lines would have the effect of artificially lowering the dive angle and making the aircraft go shallow – a very dangerous effect and a design feature not appreciated by the ground-attack pilot. (Figure 6.7)

Lead pursuit is flown when the nose of the attacker is positioned ahead of the target. It is used primarily to close on a target which may have a speed advantage or when it is desired to close on a target swiftly (Figure 6.6c). A convenient way to judge

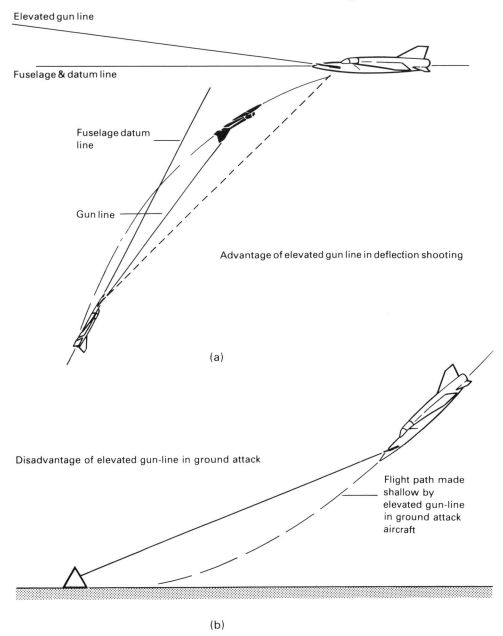

Elevated gun line

Fuselage & datum line

Fuselage datum line

Gun line

Advantage of elevated gun line in deflection shooting

(a)

Disadvantage of elevated gun-line in ground attack

Flight path made shallow by elevated gun-line in ground attack aircraft

(b)

FIG 6.7.   Gun lines

the correct lead for the optimum closure is to pull lead on the target until it seems to be stationary against a distant object or horizon. It can be seen that this is a visual method of achieving the proportional-navigation for which missile heads are programmed and which was explained previously when discussing air-to-air missiles.

The degree of lead flown may be governed by the available look angle over the nose of the attacker's aircraft. In some interceptions quite large lead angles may be required and may be greater than can be flown while keeping the target in sight. Great care has to be exercised if it is decided to risk continuing the interception while going blind to the target. The first danger is mid-air collision – an expensive way of obtaining a kill and not appreciated during training – but an equal danger can be the risk of a change of flight path by the target, using the concealment of the nose to gain a time advantage.

Two options are immediately available to him: the first, to take advantage of his possible speed advantage and to turn away from the attacker, unloading and extending the range; the second, to turn into the attacker forcing a high AOT fly through or even to gain nose-tail clearance himself. As a general rule it is extremely unwise to lose sight of an enemy in an air combat; too much can happen, too fast.

In a lead pursuit the tendency is for the attacker to have to increase his rate of turn and to tighten his radius as he closes with the target. There is also the effect of moving forward on the target in terms of relative geometry – AOT tends to increase – thereby placing the attacker in a vulnerable position for a counter. In all, lead pursuit needs to be flown with care. From the target's viewpoint the lead angle needs to be watched carefully when the range closes because the attacker has the lead angles necessary for a successful guns sighting solution and inside 1,000 metres this may have to influence strongly the action taken to counter the closure.

CONES, TUBES AND DISCS

So far the discussion has referred to manoeuvre in the horizontal plane. Air combat is far from a two-dimensional affair, however, and the third dimension has to be visualised. Further, there are many occasions when the fight needs to be visualised, not in relation to the earth or the horizon, but to the plane of the target aircraft – its extended wing line. There is some merit, therefore, in getting into the habit of reading the air combat situation in terms of *cones, tubes, and discs*.

The disc is the easiest and has already been covered; it is the horizontal plane. Cones and tubes refer more to the geometry based on the target aircraft. The tube is the vertical plane through the target flight path and can be visualised as the path described in the air if the target aircraft turned and climbed at the same time; eventually it would have *swept* a cylinder in the sky. The cone is the imaginary plane swept by a target in a turn with an infinite wing span. Figure 6.8.

Taking a target in a steady level turn it can be seen from Figure 6.8 that if an attacker wished to maintain a given position in reference to it then, visualising the tube, he would have to be inside the tube if he was slow, and would have to be outside the tube if he was fast; how much inside or outside being proportional to how slow or how fast he was. To match the turn performance of the target *at the same speed* the attacker would have to fly a flight path coincident with the tube, not necessarily on the same disc as the target but, high or low, on the same tube.

If the attacker wished to fly predominantly using the target as his reference there is advantage in judging the geometry in relation to the wing-line of the target. In this case the CONE is being used and to retain a constant relative position to the target the attacker will need to move up and down the cone depending whether he is fast or slow in relation to the target. The CONE constitutes a series of different speed discs which allow the attacker to maintain a constant position on the target.

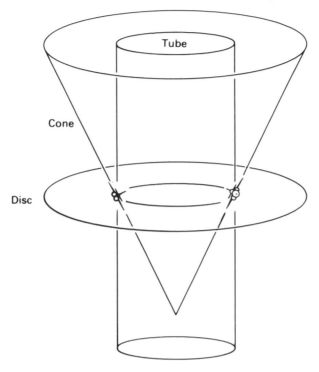

FIG 6.8.   Cones, tubes and discs

This visualisation is useful to apply some simple mathematics to gain some idea of the sort of settings which *balance out* in the combat environment. The most common error in the initial stages of combat training is to over-correct and most of that is caused less by any lack in piloting ability or skill as in not realising the major effect quite small differences in geometry can have over the ranges involved in an air combat. A pilot who has worked for five minutes gaining a telling advantage can squander it all by pulling 1,500 feet too high or going 1,500 feet too wide during his manoeuvring.

Knowing what to do and not being able to do it is one thing – we are all human – but being able to do it and not knowing what to do is stupidity, and potentially lethal.

Take an example. Figure 6.9a shows the geometry applying to a target flying at 400 knots TAS and pulling 2 'G' in the first instance and 6 'G' in the second. Included is the position of an attacker who has gone high and wide to the extent suggested above, that is, 1,500 feet. It can be seen from the table at Figure 6.9b that although there is a considerable difference in the target condition between the 2 'G' and 6 'G' case the difference in speed necessary to hold a constant position on the target when in the plane of the wings *up-the-cone* is only one knot – some 40 or so knots additional to target speed in both cases. The relative insensitivity of this parameter makes it commendably easy to judge accurately enough in the melee of a combat given a little prudent homework on the ground.

The task of the attacker who prefers to play the disc is far more acute. If he swings wide in both target conditions by 1,500 feet this becomes a direct addition to the

V = 400 kts. TAS
G = 2

G = 6

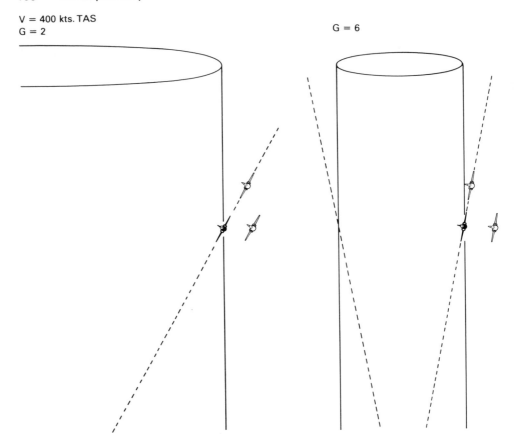

FIG 6.9(a).   Change of geometry with 'G'

| Case 1 | Target | Attacker | | Case 2 | Target | Attacker | |
		1500' high	1500' wide			1500' high	1500' wide
Speed kts tas.	400	441	472		400	442	649
'G'	2	2.15	2.27		6	6.61	9.65
Radius (ft)	8200	9066	9700		2400	2654	3900
Turn rate °/sec	4.72	4.72	4.72		16.13	16.13	16.13
Bank (°)	60	62.4	64		80.4	81.3	84.05

FIG 6.9(b).   Sensitivities in disc and cones

radius of turn and he is faced with the need for considerable performance if he is to retain a position on the target aircraft. Against the 2 'G' aircraft the attacker will need an additional 72 knots to hold relative position but against the 6 'G' target he will need a speed superiority over the target of 249 knots and will need an aircraft stressed to accept 9.65 'G' – or more than the F-16. Put another way, error in judgement in the disc is more sensitive than error of judgement in the plane of the wings, or the cone.

As has been seen in the discussion of pure, lag and lead pursuit turns, it is not difficult for the target to force the attacker into an overshoot. Both pure and lead pursuit turns result in a tightening of the turn and this can be easily misjudged, causing the attacker to be thrown wide. If he stays in the plane of the disc he is straight into the area of great sensitivity of error. If this occurs therefore he is much better advised to reduce his bank angle and to pull high into the cone.

Although this is clearly self-evident by reference to a diagram while sitting comfortably in a chair before the fire, it should be remembered that in both the conditions discussed above the fighter is the same 1,500 feet separated from the target albeit in different planes. Between cloud layers, in conditions of poor visibility and light at low level, or in the deadly *goldfish bowl* conditions over the sea, where there is no effective horizon and the sea surface is not readily apparent, the target may have to be the practical *horizon*. In these conditions the use of the plane of the wings is much easier to accomplish than to judge angles off the wings to use the disc. Particularly at low level, the use of the inside of the turn while in the plane of the target wings has to be done with great caution; too many pilots have fallen foul of the trap of closing on the inside of the turn, low in the target's wing plane, looking upwards at their target, and running into land or sea with disastrous results. The target *might* kill you; the ground almost invariably *will* kill you if you run into it. The old fighter pilots – the survivors – *always* know where the ground is.

THE YO-YO

Leading on from the discussion of the different types of turn and their applicability to varying closing speed conditions the argument can now be extended by the use of the vertical and what has just been seen about discs and cones.

There is something to be said for always presenting an attacking, or threatening, posture to the target aircraft. The very experienced opponent may be able to judge the situation with such finesse that he may be unaffected by the presented menace – the Matador's approach to the Bull – but he will be the exception to the rule – more people watch bullfighting than wield the cape – and the target will normally take some sort of precautionary action to reduce the threat presented. This is very much what is desired for, while the target is taking action to counter the threat, he is being *reactive* and while he is being reactive it is difficult for him to take the *initiative*. Much of the secret in air combat is to retain the initiative and to compel the target to remain reactive.

In presenting a threat from the horizontal turning condition, however, it has been seen that there is the possibility of the fly-through situation as the turn tightens to beyond the capability to match. As soon as this point is reached, the wings can be levelled and the excess energy remaining can be used to climb up above the target in the plane of the cone so retaining nose-tail-clearance and retaining useful energy advantage. By pulling over the top, in the case of a considerable excess energy, the vertical-egg effect can be used to tighten the turn radius and to present a further threat to the target from the high rear. The excess height can be traded for speed to increase closure, this time with moderate AOT and the target finds itself poorly placed.

This manoeuvre is known as the *high-speed yo-yo – high-speed* for obvious reasons and the *yo-yo* merely shorthand for the use of the vertical to absorb, or more correctly, *save* the excess energy. If, at the end of the re-attack the situation is found to have developed into a high angle and high speed closure, the high-speed-yo-yo can be executed again. Provided the required performance margin is available, the manoeuvre is an excellent way of keeping the initiative and making the opponent stay reactive. It is particularly likely to occur when two aircraft combat, one with a high-power, high-speed characteristic and the other with less performance but with better turning characteristics.

The *low-speed yo-yo* uses exactly the same theory and use of the geometry of the situation but in the reverse sense. In this case the problem is not the surfeit of energy but its lack. It may occur when an aircraft is in the rear of a target but cannot close to a killing position. It was a common occurrence in combat between gun-armed fighters but has become less common now that the missile can close distance and take out much of the excess AOT.

The low energy attacker turns into and down the plane of the cone, picking up two immediate advantages as he does so. First, the act of descending allows him to use the component of his weight as thrust and does something to offset his initial energy deficiency – he goes faster because he is going down. Second, because he is descending on the plane of the cone, his turning radius is decreasing and this has the effect of increasing his AOT on the target and gives, *de facto*, closure albeit on a lower disc than the target. The further the attacker has to descend to obtain the closure, the greater will have to be the AOT build-up before the energy is used to pull-up the nose to the target to obtain the killing burst. As with the high speed case, if the first attempt is unsuccessful the procedure can be repeated, and in practice this tends to be the case, with each manoeuvre biting off small parts of the total deficiency.

A note of caution is necessary. If an attacker becomes involved in a number of high speed or low speed yo-yos he becomes very *predictable*. In a one-on-one situation, with the initiative retained over the target, this is no major disadvantage, but if there is any possibility of the target having friends about the sky, it is taking unreasonable risks to attempt any more than a couple of high speed or a single low speed yo-yos. Air combat is not the place for heroes; one-for-none is a far better kill ratio than three-for-one – especially if you are the *one*.

THE COUNTERS

So far the target of the brave attacker has been remarkably compliant and has been assumed to pursue his steady and predictable progress despite the threats presented. In reality this is unlikely to be the case and as much attention has to be paid in combat training to the defence as to the offence. While no combat pilot worth his salt will wish to remain on the defensive longer than is absolutely necessary, circumstances beyond his immediate control may give the enemy the chance of the first pass and this must be countered successfully before the battle for the initiative can begin.

To attempt to teach the *ab initio* combat pilot the counters to all the possible combinations of attack he could face can be counter-productive. First, there are just too many combinations and the young man, while searching his brain for the right chapter of the accepted wisdom which matched his situation, could find that the rapidly changing picture had outdated his mental processes or, worse, he was already being engaged. Second, *book* solutions to situations make them *predictable* and as has already been suggested, being predictable is as lethal in air combat as is being ignorant of its essentials.

It is far better therefore, if the situation is *read* correctly and countered by applying the basics – the fundamentals – many of which have already been touched upon. But what factors need to be read?

At first sight of the enemy aircraft the defender must know, even in the broadest terms, how that aircraft rates against his own in the important areas applicable to the combat scene: power-to-weight ratio, wing loading, sustained turn rate, instantaneous turn rate, handling characteristics, weapons – numbers and performance. From this assessment – falling from the work done on the ground – will emerge certain possibilities and, more important, those things which under no circumstances should be attempted.

For example, if the attacker has greater power-to-weight ratio by a large margin, any use of the vertical will tend to give him the advantage. The unrestricted use of the vertical could be denied him by flying close under an overcast or alternatively just above an undercast – use cloud to take away at least one-half of the vertical option. If at low-level, then get lower and use the ground in the same way – to remove half of the vertical. Of the two options the low-level is best simply because, if the attacker makes an error, the ground could get the kill and as most fighter pilots do not train extensively at low-level they are less content in close proximity to the ground as are, say, the fighter-bomber fraternity whose natural operating area it tends to be.

It is most important to make a quick and realistic assessment of the enemy's weapon performance. Nothing but disadvantage lies in flying profiles designed to break the lock of a missile, and so squandering energy, when a better knowledge of the enemy missile capability would have shown that, under the particular conditions, no missile threat was posed. In Vietnam, this failing was actually used to good effect offensively by some United States pilots who, frustrated at the low kill rate of the AIM-4 missile, which tended to fly through the jet efflux rather than to hit the airframe of the target, fired those missiles at long ranges to make the opposing MiGs break to avoid the missile which so enabled the attacker to close for the follow-up guns attack. Accountants would no doubt blanch at the thought of an expensive missile being used in this way but a *kill's a kill* even if it is obtained by the gun.

Low-level is a good place to be if the enemy is likely to use missiles in preference to guns. Radar missiles can be working in a very *noisy* environment and the proximity to the ground may dissuade the opponent from manipulating his radar with quite the same expertise he might have done at the higher levels. Infra-red missiles could also find themselves operating in a confused situation at the very low levels and, in this regard, the peacetime habit of avoiding towns and populated areas should be discounted. The IR emissions which are likely to come from the average industrial area could be camouflaging for the evading aircraft. *Wiens Law* says nothing about applying only to air combat aircraft and if the mouth of a furnace happens to be emitting at 3 to 5 microns it is a foolish fighter pilot who looks a gift horse in the mouth.

In both cases there can be difficulty with fusing if the flight path to the target takes the missile too close to the ground. The launch itself can give problems; many missiles fall some way low of the parent aircraft before motor ignition and this could cause ground impact if the geometry of the attack can be kept very low by prudent evasion. The difficulty of the gun attack at very low levels is apparent when it is considered that if the attacker can be made to turn at low level the natural tendency will be for him to fall low on the target during a guns attack – not by much, but by enough, given a little luck.

Mother earth can therefore, prove to be friend as well as foe – if used intelligently.

Because an enemy aircraft *can* do certain things it does not follow that it *will* do them. Reading what the enemy is actually doing is important, particularly assessing its energy state. At a distance it can be difficult to estimate speed, more so if head-on or tail-on and by the time the head-on aspect starts to change, it is usually a little late for the assessment to matter greatly. The position of lift and braking devices tell much; an attacker with dive brakes extended is killing rather than conserving energy. Is he going for a slow speed fight? Few aircraft can extend flaps and other high-lift devices at high speed and these can provide a clue but beware of those few aircraft starting to appear which can – those with *mission adaptive wings* and some of the more advanced fighter types may be able to use flaps and slats at quite high speeds.

Generally, the variable geometry, or moving wing, aircraft can prove helpful when a pilot is reading a fight. Most of such types have very strict conditions attached to the movement and positioning of the wings. One such type is so constrained that, at the lower end of the speed spectrum, the wing position is almost a massive air speed indicator, showing to the world in what speed bracket the aircraft is flying. If the wings are outstretched the aircraft is slow – as they start to fold back the pilot is accelerating and vice versa. A great boon to the intelligent opponent. Swing-wings have been popular with Soviet aircraft designers in the past – Fitter, Flogger, Fencer – but it is noticeable that the new generation of combat aircraft – Fulcrum, Flanker – have not embraced that technology.

It can be seen that, for the defender, the AOT is an important measure because it can be exploited if an opponent allows it to get too large in certain circumstances. Consider the straightforward lead turn or the movement forward on the target of the attacker in a low speed yo-yo. If the target remains on his predicted course, the attacker may be safe but the rapid deceleration of the target, which at the same time turns into the attacker, can alter the geometry quite substantially. If the attacker has been too bold and has allowed the AOT to increase too far, then the tables can soon be turned.

SCISSORS

The turn into the attack to force the overshoot is one of the basic combat manoeuvres and is the starting gambit to one of the better-known tactics – the *scissors*. Figure 6.10

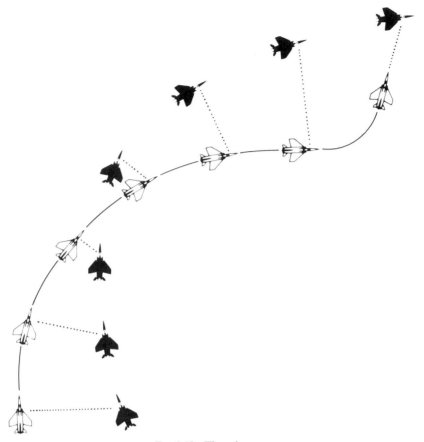

FIG 6.10. The scissors

shows how the scissors is entered and it can be seen that from the point of initiation it becomes a matter of which aircraft can produce less *ribbon* and can make it deflect furthest away from the line of advance. Initially, it is important in the scissors to kill energy as quickly as possible to force the attacker, who in any event probably has the higher initial energy state, to fly through and ahead of the defender. The reversal should then gain the advantage and a repeat of the procedure should result, in an ideal world, with a steadily decreasing AOT and a final positioning for the guns solution.

The scissors was at one time a popular combat manoeuvre; less so now as the realisation that *speed is life* argues against the slower speed tactics, but also because it was primarily the tactic of the gun-armed fighter. The scissors is flown, even with modern combat aircraft, at very close ranges, frequently far too close to allow the use of the missile armament which has to be looked upon in many modern types as the primary weapon system. To be involved in a scissors in, say, an F-4 Phantom and rendering useless the combined capability of a large and effective pulse-doppler radar, four Sparrow/SkyFlash and four AIM-9 missiles, must, on face value, be of questionable benefit. Notwithstanding, United States pilots in Vietnam obtained kills with guns in slow speed tactics against MiGs.

But the reason for the unpopularity of the scissors has been seen before; the sky is full of aircraft – or at least must be assumed to be – and once the energy is dissipated to engage in the scissors the aircraft participating are highly vulnerable to the fast slashing attack from a disengaged fighter. It is no longer the aircraft which is being engaged which is necessarily the greatest threat.

With the scissors in mind, the methods of *tying the knot* can be recalled. There are different planes in which this manoeuvre can be flown. The rolling scissors and variations of the vertical scissors each have their advantages and disadvantages. Aircraft handling characteristics are most important in the scissors and if the descending vertical scissors is contemplated, for example, the drag comparison between the two aircraft must be considered.

It must be warned, however, that the vertical scissors is not to be entered into lightly. Even with all the drag devices fully deployed, modern aircraft are still descending fast towards the *great earthy killer* and at a time when so much attention is having to be given to the other aircraft. The temptation to allow pride to overcome common sense and to continue the descent until the other aircraft *chickens out* has proved irresistible to some deceased before now.

The most dangerous time is, strangely, in training when the fight may be taking place between similar aircraft. Here aircraft characteristics are similar and the battle can turn into a gladiatorial one between two pilots. With dissimilar aircraft, differing drag characteristics and handling qualities normally soon decide the issue in the vertical scissors.

In Korea, the scissors was used extensively between the MiG-15 and the F-86 Sabre, with the Sabre emerging the better aircraft, not through performance *per se* – indeed the MiG had better power-to-weight and lower wing loading – but because the Sabre had hydraulically operated controls which made it handle so much better in the low speed gyrations.

. . . AND BUBBLES

As has been suggested, there is every disadvantage in executing a manoeuvre or tactic which may cost energy if it is unnecessary to do so. Most of the occasions when that occurs are connected with the avoidance of suspected missile shots from the opponent. The great problem in conducting realistic combat training is the simulation of weapon shots while the combat is still taking place. Shots are called – but few will believe such calls in the heat of the combat. The Air Combat Manoeuvring Ranges can simulate the kills reasonably realistically but these facilities do not exist in such numbers as to provide daily training. It can be difficult therefore to build up a picture of the weapon envelopes of the likely opposition.

There are two ways of doing this; the first requires the pilot to visualise the weapon envelope of the opponent about his nose and to try to visualise his relationship to that envelope. This is very difficult, not least because the performance of the enemy weapons and therefore the shape of the envelopes, are materially affected by the performance and manoeuvres of the target.

The other way therefore, is to imagine that, as with the ribbons, the aircraft is trailing behind itself an *area of vulnerability*. A moment's thought, and reference to the weapons chapter, will show that this area of vulnerability will closely equate to a large *bubble* and its behaviour will approximate to that of a bubble produced by a ring dipped in soapy water and moved gently about the sky in a resemblance of the gyrations of the target aircraft.

At first sight, this may appear a childish way of representing something on which life or death may ultimately hang, but the problem is that the variations in the area of vulnerability are so numerous and affected by so many factors that to attempt to calculate them in anything other than the broadest terms in the heat of a combat would be impossible for all but the super-human. A few moments spent with the childs toy – preferably where no one can view the proceedings – investigating how the bubble lags the movement of the ring will soon give a very good understanding of some of the complex relationships involved.

In the air it is easier to imagine what is happening to IR plumes and missile envelopes as the turning fight progresses. Eventually, computer programmes will probably display such envelopes in the new multi-colour glass display cockpits – and very useful they will be for those pilots who are good enough, or stupid enough, to spend their time with their eyes in the cockpit long enough to study them.

WHEN ALL ELSE FAILS . . .

When all else fails and either youth and inexperience take their toll, or, there in the mirror is the *Red Fokker* and the be-goggled reincarnated von Richthofen, what to do? What is the air combat equivalent of the *survival kit*.

Prayer is recommended, but if the skies do not immediately open, and sunbeams do not appear forthwith, a few of the following techniques might be considered.

Whenever possible *point at him*. The fronts of aircraft are like the fronts of nasty dogs – all the sharp bits are there which can hurt. No fighter pilot contemplates the muzzles of his opponents guns or the seeker heads of his missiles happily. There is always the opponent who will be lucky and looking at the front of your opponent can make you feel uneasy. Adrenalin is not the best thing in the world for quiet calm contemplation of the tactical options.

Whenever possible *fly at him*. Everyone knows that if a bee stings, the bee will most likely die. The bee probably knows this too. But still people get hysterical when there is a bee around because they fear being stung. They have little sympathy or thought for the bee who may at the same time be committing *hari kari*. Indeed the most frightening thing is someone who does not fear death, for what becomes his natural constraint? By flying at the opponent, the aim is to unnerve him. Further, by having to avoid your aircraft he will have to come away from his optimised handling which is causing the problem in the first place. Do bear in mind that these are tactics when all else has failed – they are *not* recommended for day-to-day training.

Whenever possible, *fire something*. No matter how combat hardened – and in the next war there will probably be insufficient time for anyone to reach that state – it is verging on the positively unpleasant to have someone fire a weapon at you. It is very *adrenalin-pumping* stuff. Aircraft cannon leave a distinctive trail of smoke behind them and the muzzle flash can be impressive, more particularly in low light conditions. Equally, missiles start their flight with much flash and smoke and, if impressive from the side, it will be far more so from the front. As missile flight paths are so difficult to predict, an opponent would be ill advised to ignore the round until, at least, it had become clear that it was not guiding. But by then, who knows, he may have conducted a missile break or throttled back. Every little helps when all else has failed . . .

Whenever possible *gain energy*. Even if the opponent is manoeuvring for advantage, if there is the chance to unload and accelerate at all it must be taken. Even if the increments are small they add up over time and increase your chance to take the initiative. *Never* stop fighting – there is no way to surrender – and he may run out of fuel and have to disengage.

In desperation, *do opposites*. If his nose goes up – put yours down. If he dumps energy – you try to gain it by unloading. Try to estimate what he wants you to do and try not to do it, indeed, try to counter it by doing the opposite thing. It will be unlikely to turn a poor situation into great victory for it necessarily has to be reactive and therefore the initiative can rarely be regained, but it might prevent the rout.

But this is all defeatist talk! The aim is to put the other fellow in that predicament and it can be done with a modicum of skill and a lot of hard groundwork:

Know your aircraft.
Fly it well.
Know your weapons.
Know your enemy as well as you know yourself.
Read the sky.
Know your geometry.

. . . put it all together and . . . you are an *ace! Easy!*

7.

Formation Manoeuvres

Too many hounds are the death of the hare.
Erich Hartmann
(352 kills. World's highest scoring ace)

ONE-ON-ONE combat is a necessary teaching medium. It is a fighter pilot's version of the boxing ring or the tennis singles; a lone struggle against a solitary opponent with all the machismo, skill, finesse and ultimate sense of achievement which that implies. Rather than the stylised and controlled contest of the boxing ring, practical combat is more akin to the crowd riot where the danger comes from the blow to the back of the head. It calls for different disciplines and, occasionally, for modified techniques.

Erich Hartmann's comparison with hares and hounds equates closely to the sentiments expressed by a range of experienced veterans. Adolf Galland spoke with feeling about the situation facing the Luftwaffe at the end of the 1939–45 war, when they were so overwhelmingly outnumbered. Lenin put it quite simply, but effectively, when he said:

Quantity has a quality of its own.

The skill involved in air combat is to turn an opponent's advantage into a disadvantage; to convert vice into virtue. The art, and occasionally the science, is to turn the tables.

To take an example from another field: in Central Europe the Warsaw Pact have the virtue of massive conventional superiority on the ground, but the vice of that virtue is that to apply it, as the offensive alliance, they have to *move*. By applying interdiction to that movement the NATO Alliance can extract a price and thereby present a deterrent. The virtue is turned into a vice. Such relationships, and the opportunities they provide, should be looked for in *all* military fields.

TWO VERSUS ONE

Consider first the simplest of the multi-aircraft interactions, the pair versus the singleton. Where the singleton is attacking the pair, the basic principles of mutual support can be demonstrated.

It is often imagined that the fighter pilot, particularly those who fly single-seat aircraft, are the archetypal individualists and *loners*. It is true that many of the older *aces* certainly were but that was probably at a time when the combat scene was relatively straight-forward and when aircraft performance and weapon reach allowed the individual to maintain a reasonable *situational awareness*. Performance of both modern aircraft and weapons has reached far beyond that point, and to survive in battle today *teamwork* is required.

Developing teamwork is made difficult by the widely separated nature of the fighter formation, but engendered by high standards of flying proficiency, hard and continuous training, and firm self-discipline. It can call for the same type of self-discipline shown by the footballer, considering himself to have a fair shot at goal, passing the ball to his colleague who has a better angle.

Figure 7.1a shows an attack developing against a pair separated for mutual support and cross-over. The distance required for the separation is determined by the look angles available in the aircraft design and the weapon capability of the expected opposition. If the enemy is armed with short range guns, the separation distance can be kept small, so easing formation manoeuvre; if, however, the enemy is missile equipped his firing range is extended and the distance out has to be greater to provide more extensive cross cover. As it can never be guaranteed to detect the threat at the first theoretical opportunity, the distance out is often increased when facing a high speed threat which could close to a weapon solution in a short timescale.

Having detected the threat, Figure 7.1b shows the defenders separating further to force the attacker to commit early to one aircraft or the other. As soon as this occurs the aircraft so threatened turns away from the formation to lead the attacker into a flight path which allows the unthreatened aircraft to obtain a *sandwich*.

Although a straightforward tactic, the sandwich has to be nicely judged to be successful. Closure rates have to be assessed carefully and due allowance made for the corner-cutting effect acting to the advantage of the attacker when the turn is initiated. It is imperative that the trailing formation aircraft engages the enemy before the enemy closes to shooting distance of the lead aircraft. It can be seen that of the many qualities demanded of the fighter pilot, a good feeling for closure rates and angular relationships is well to the fore.

If the manoeuvre is executed too soon, or if the separation has been too wide, it is possible for the attacker to spoof the formation into believing that a commitment has been made, then to transfer attention to the trailing aircraft of the formation. Figure 7.1c illustrates.

The sandwich as shown was more popular in the age of guns and cannon rather than that of missiles which, in extending the range of engagement, has made the separation distances large and the performance needed to exploit such tactics correspondingly greater. This has particular significance at the lower levels where most aircraft are limited to a fairly narrow band of speed at the high speed part of the flight envelope.

A further factor in the missile age is that in turning away to initiate the sandwich, the lead aircraft turns his jet pipes directly at the missile heads of the attacker, thereby easing his infra-red acquisition. Against a IR-missile equipped attacker there is, therefore, much to be said for the inward turn-about which keeps jet-pipes turned away and, in many cases, shrouded by aircraft structure. This is shown in Figure 7.2. A further advantage accrues here if the defenders are armed with IR missiles capable of a head-on or front quarter engagement. The attacker is faced at the completion of the turn with double the firepower that would have been the case in the traditional sandwich.

The two-on-one situation, this time applied to the attackers, gives all the options put so clearly by Erich Hartmann. A numerical superiority in addition to the positional advantage to the rear should give the *hare* little chance for, whichever way

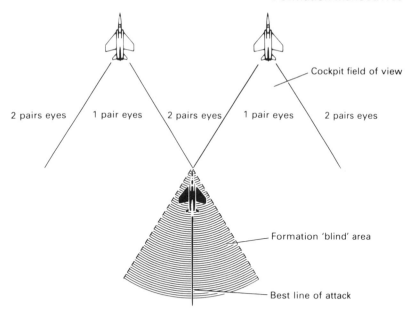

2 pairs eyes   1 pair eyes   2 pairs eyes   1 pair eyes   2 pairs eyes

Cockpit field of view

Formation 'blind' area

Best line of attack

FIG 7.1(a).   Single aircraft attack against a pair

FIG 7.1(b).   The 'sandwich'

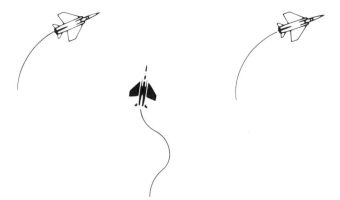

FIG 7.1(c).   Counter to the sandwich

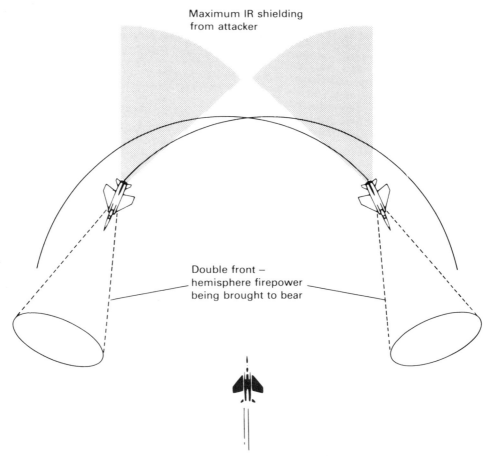

FIG 7.2.   Counter in the Missile Age

the turn is made, it should be to the advantage to one or other of the attackers. Figure 7.3 illustrates.

The ill-placed defender in this instance – unless he possesses a machine of superior performance by a wide margin – will need to minimise his disadvantage and to attempt to spoof the opposition into throwing away some of their advantages. Played in the horizontal plane, the defender must concede the advantage to one or other of the attackers. It is therefore in his interest to play the manoeuvre in the vertical if at all possible. At high level the option will be to go up, and to execute an Immelmann turn of one variation or the other, or to go down in a pull-through manoeuvre, taking full advantage of the characteristics of the *vertical egg*. This later course could be particularly useful if a missile shot is expected as the pull-through, or *split-S*, allows a tight radius turn and possibly the shielding of jet pipes. Furthermore, power can be reduced to cut even further the IR emissions. Against some IR missiles, the fact that the heads are pointing earthwards can further confuse, and lock-on may be broken by spurious ground returns.

At low-level these options are reduced to one – the pull-up – but here there is a high chance of cloud cover being available for escape from visual attack; cloud also

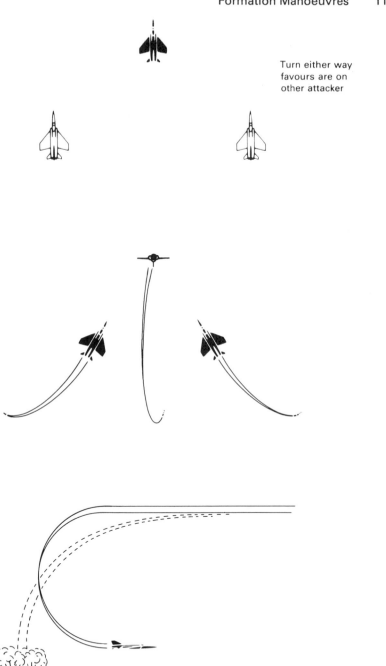

Turn either way
favours are on
other attacker

FIG 7.3.   Hares and Hounds

affects the guidance of IR missiles. Cloud becomes an excellent asset in such circumstances and, at low level, pilots should always be aware of the escape route into cloud – just as they were in the 1914–18 war.

If pull-ups or split-S manoeuvres are contemplated and if a slow enemy closure speed allows some finesse, the defender will wish to control his speed to that which allows the best possible turn radius – or best rate, depending on the circumstances – while at the same time encouraging the attackers to fly at speeds outside their best turning performance. A short burst of afterburner, or a short jettison of fuel which leaves a vapour trail, can both cause the attackers to accelerate in the belief that the defender is trying to escape with speed alone. The purpose here is to leave the attackers faster than their best turn speed.

The defender may at the same time wish to descend gently to a height which allows him to conduct a split-S – just – but which would not allow the attackers at their higher speed to complete the manoeuvre without striking the ground. If cloud is penetrated at any time during such manoeuvres, the defender should have planned in advance a change to his flight pattern while in the cloud cover. *Predictability* is lethal in combat. Whenever the chance occurs to be unpredictable, it should be taken.

TWO VERSUS TWO

Much of the theory which goes with the two-versus-one case holds good for the two-versus-two case except that the argument is taken one stage further. Figure 7.4a shows how the simple sandwich can become the *double-sandwich*. The advantage none the less always remains with the formation which has the aircraft at the end of the sequence; this is partly because of the obvious advantage that this aircraft, not having an aircraft in the rear, is unthreatened but also because the only aircraft in the total combat which cannot bring weapons to bear is the one in the front.

In the illustration, white has twice the firepower *potential* of black. Further, the front white aircraft can break out to the left leaving the trailing black aircraft with a difficult choice. Either he continues the turn with the possibility that the white leader could reverse and leave the situation with two whites behind two blacks – Figure 7.4b – or he could follow the departing white.

This later course has two major disadvantages. First, that to reverse a turn allows the pursuing aircraft to cut the corner and possibly to achieve a killing shot. Generally, if a reversal is contemplated, it should never be flown in the same plane but made to be as complex a manoeuvre as possible. In the instance under discussion, the black trailer is governed too much by the flight path of the white leader – and the discipline of the white trailer off his tail – and the opportunity to fly a complex manoeuvre could not be guaranteed. The second disadvantage is that, even if such a plan was feasible, it would still leave the lead black aircraft out of the fight for an appreciable period, thereby leaving black trailer with a two-on-one situation.

Forcing the black lead aircraft out of the fight for a period gives the white section a meaningful advantage but one which they must none the less exploit without delay. In this case the black lead aircraft could be expected to re-position as soon as was possible and the tables could be turned with two whites on one black and with a black fighter loose in the melee with all the possibilities there are then for the opportunity shot. Figure 7.4c.

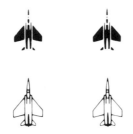

FIG 7.4(a).   The Double Sandwich

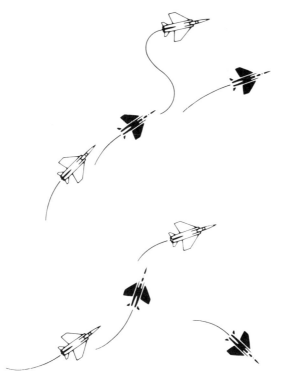

FIG 7.4(b).   The Breakout

Fig 7.4(c).   The 'Loose' fighter

It can be seen how critical *time* can be to the options being opened and to their exploitation. The flight leader must be always conscious of this factor. A clock in the cockpit is invariably provided but the most important *clock* in a combat, where adrenalin runs freely and time gets amazingly compressed, is that which runs in the head of the good flight leader. Part of *situational awareness*, together with the feeling for the conventional three dimensions, is the feeling for the *fourth* dimension – time.

In a combat with modern aircraft, using fuel at prodigious rates, the clock is replaced by the fuel gauge. The amount of fuel allowed in a mission for high powered combat can govern the time that the aircraft can remain engaged and can prove to be a far more compelling discipline than tactics or weapons. It determines *persistence* – a word of increasing importance to the modern combat pilot.

VARIATIONS ON A THEME

Two variations on the theme will be examined to illustrate how large formations can provide a defence against attack: the first, purely defensively, perhaps against an enemy with superior performance; the second, to enable an aggressive purpose to be achieved while fighting off attack.

Raoul Lufberry, already mentioned, saw early in the history of air combat that an aircraft, or a collection of aircraft, flying a tight circle, could be difficult to penetrate without providing an opportunity shot for one of the circle. It was a variation of the circle of wagons drawn up to fight off marauding Indians in the Wild West or the defensive posture of the porcupine. Figure 7.5. Great care had to be exercised in breaking into the circle without falling prey to the guns of the aircraft following the intended target.

While this was a perfectly legitimate tactic to use when out-performed, or even when out-numbered, it had its drawbacks. Like the Wild West wagon train, or indeed the hapless porcupine, while going around in small circles, or when *curled* into a defensive ball, progress in a straight line is limited. The Lufberry circle can be

FIG 7.5.   The Lufberry Circle

looked upon therefore as, at best, a temporary expedient to some outrageous fortune.

In the modern world it is even more flawed. Lufberry developed his tactic in the age of guns but in the age of missiles the attackers might not need to penetrate the defensive circle. Obtaining IR missile acquisitions against the outward pointing jet-pipes, all reflecting the high power needed to maintain a tight circle, might obviate the need for the attacker to enter the immediate threat area. If the IR missile has not made the Lufberry circle obsolete, the radar missile fired from some distance away certainly has.

A method of achieving many of the advantages of the Lufberry circle, while maintaining the freedom of action to proceed about more aggressive business, was seen by the West for the first time in Korea. The North Koreans, capitalising on the better high altitude peformance of the MiG-15 over the F-86 Sabre, and initially operating to Soviet inspired doctrine of the large formation, were seen in a formation to become known as the *Train*.

The Train consisted of pairs of aircraft flying line astern separated by about 2,000 to 3,000 metres while flying stepped-up in sections by about 2,000 feet. The theory was similar to that applied by Lufberry but in this case the defence was provided in line rather than in the circle.

With the gun armament of the day, and the similar top speed of the two aircraft involved, the tactic was effective. When trying to break in at any point in the Train the attacker could expect to find a section, or a number of sections, in his rear with a height advantage which could be traded for an overtake speed (Figure 7.6).

FIG 7.6.   The Korean 'Train'

There is a tendency for operators in the West to underestimate the tactical doctrine of opponents, particularly those from the non-Western world. The tactician who developed the Train deserves some respect, however. He matched a series of pros and cons and derived a tactic which could have been more successful than it was. The MiG-15 had a better power-to-weight ratio than the F-86, a better time-to-height and a lower wing loading gave it a better ceiling. The F-86 was fuel limited when operating from bases in South Korea and had only 20 minutes endurance about the Yalu river. If it was required to climb to great heights, that endurance would be further reduced. If the F-86s stayed lower, to escort the fighter-bombers better, one of their major tasks, then the Train could be flown lower while still retaining the height advantage and still placing the F-86s at a severe disadvantage.

The tactical doctrine was therefore well conceived. Why did it not succeed?

Training! The control of large formations requires skilful leadership which is developed only by hard and conscientious training. That training must develop qualities of initiative and determination if a complex aerial situation is to be controlled and directed against an aggressive and individualistic foe. To date, such qualities have not sat easily within a communist system. Air forces trained within the Soviet system and which follow the Soviet doctrine rely on set-piece tactics, well rehearsed, and flown exactly. However, when the inevitable unforeseen happens, such training can fall down and the opportunist, trained to exploit the situation as he sees it, will win the day.

So it was in Korea and the phase of the Train soon passed to be replaced by the North Koreans imitating the American tactics of flying with smaller, but more controllable, sections of four and eight aircraft. A lesson is there for the learning. To succeed in the air combat arena, an amalgam of qualities is required. Notwithstanding how excellent the equipment, or how well conceived the tactical doctrine, if the man has not been adequately trained, then both are as nought. With American training and experience at the time, it is for thought provoking conjecture as to what could have come about if the tables had been turned and the US pilots had been flying the MiGs. The Train might have gone down in history as one of the great tactics – but history is a hard taskmaster and few now remember it.

'STICK – SEARCH – AND REPORT'

Few fighter pilots have not been brought up through their formative years without *stick – search – and report* being drummed into them as the Holy Grail. It is well established in the short history of fighter combat and started before the end of the 1914–18 War when the danger from the unseen enemy at the deep six-o'clock was first recognised and mutual cross-over introduced as an answer to the threat.

As then perceived, it epitomised the duties of the perfect wingman. *Stick!* First, he must stay with the leader for, if he did not, then the leader had to divert attention to finding his errant wingman and thereby, had to lose concentration on the main purpose. There was annoyance in this; the same annoyance suffered by the owner of the dog which will not stay to heel – and there have been element leaders which have considered the problem in just such terms!

Search! The much maligned wingman, with his front screen adequately filled with his leader, was expected to divert the majority of his attention to the rear, often in cockpits which were ill-designed to make rearward vision easy, and – *Report!* – to transmit, promptly and clearly, any developing threat from that hemisphere.

No mean task! Indeed many experienced fighter pilots would concede that, even with the benefit of hindsight, such early days placed heavy demands upon them. As increasing proficiency drew its rewards, and they became leaders themselves, the accolade came as a welcome relief from the arduous wingman duties.

The theory should have been questioned long ago but airmen are no different to others, and accepted norms are put to the test as infrequently as they are in any other established profession. None the less, expecting the inexperienced wingman not only to match the maximum performance manoeuvres of his more experienced leader but also to do so with the majority of his attention directed over one or other shoulder, should have been enough to question the wisdom of the doctrine. Many young tyros failed to attain this demanding standard and, for the crime of losing the leader regularly, penance was exacted, varying by squadron. In some it was banishment to the dark worlds of bomber or transport operations, even worse, to training duties; to others it was more practical – *Arbeit macht frei* – and crewroom coffee bars and floors sparkled with the sweat of young fighter pilots who were still to learn how to *stick – search – and report*.

THE RADAR-MISSILE AGE

It was the advent of the radar-missile age which put serious question to conventional wingman tactics. Aircraft such as the F-4 Phantom, flying in trail in close formation, seemed to make little sense when both aircraft were weapon systems of great potency in their own right. Conventional doctrine effectively halved their firepower by expecting the wingman merely to trail the leader, giving little opportunity for the second aircraft to optimise its own weapon system.

At the same time – and this development was happening during the Vietnam era – closure speed advantage to the attacker was greater than at any time since the 1939–45 war and, arguably, closing speeds faster than they had ever been. This needs some explanation because, on paper, the top speed of the MiG-21 and the F-4 were comparable, at least to the first order. In a clinical trial setting there would have been little to tell between the speeds. But real combat has many other disciplines and the F-4s could not go about their business over North Vietnam at high supersonic speeds. Their fuel capacity would not allow that. Where they were operating without the benefit of ground radar stations, and before the days of advanced airborne radar systems such as the AWACS, the MiGs could be *set-up* for a high speed attack. In such circumstances formations cruising at around Mach 0.85 could find themselves under attack by aircraft flying at Mach 1.4 or higher.

Assuming an initial detection at a creditable two nautical miles, remembering that the MiG-21 was a small aircraft, particularly so in the head-on aspect, and that action to break the attack had to be taken before a missile launch at, say, one nautical mile, then there were only 11 seconds available in which to manoeuvre to meet the threat. It was such mathematics which forced so many formations into maximum perform-ance *break* manoeuvres to avoid engagement. Often break manoeuvres result in a loss of cohesion of the formation; where mutual cross-cover is lost, vulnerability increases.

In some cases the necessity to fly at maximum performance to avoid the missile shot caused the offensive aircraft to jettison their offensive loads. In such cases the defensive MiGs had achieved their aim completely, regardless of whether the kill was obtained or not – for their primary purpose was to defend the intended target of the offensive aircraft (Figure 7.7).

Once the formation had been broken up by the first slashing attack, other MiGs would attack in trail but this time attacking a disrupted formation. The possibility of obtaining opportunity kills was enhanced. The more the formation manoeuvred energetically to escape attention, the more energy was lost and the relative advan-tage of the high speed attacker increased. These tactics were identical to those developed by the Luftwaffe's JG44 under Galland in World War II to exploit the advantages of the Me-262 and in many respects similar to the tactics of von Richtfhofen many decades before.

It was a simple attack to execute and could be flown by pilots less well trained than would have been needed to engage in the turning fight to the air combat kill. As the object was to defend the target rather than obtain kills *per se*, the doctrine fitted the North Vietnamese requirements. It is a doctrine which might well be practised by the Warsaw Pact in Europe, for largely the same reasons. The difference will be that low level operations will reduce the overtake speed available and that the loss of half the vertical dimension will restrict the options available to attacker and defender alike.

Weapon system aircraft like the F-4 could be rendered ineffective therefore, either by being tied to traditional wingman duties or involved in large, relatively slow formations which conceded the initiative to the enemy. Once combat was engaged, it was important to optimise radar and missile performance and it was this imperative,

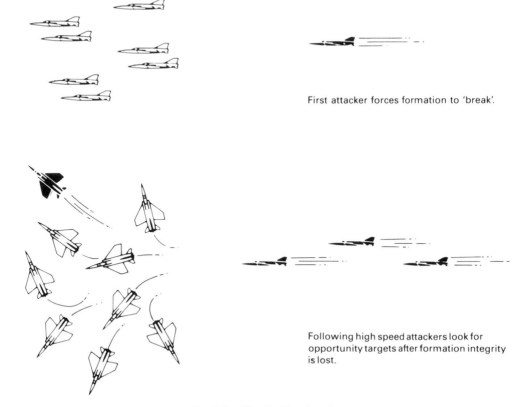

First attacker forces formation to 'break'.

Following high speed attackers look for opportunity targets after formation integrity is lost.

FIG 7.7.   The Slashing Attack

together with the acceptance that aircraft armament fires forward and that the tail area is uncovered, which led to the development of *loose duce* tactics.

Loose duce aims to split a pair of radar equipped fighters in such a way that each is covering the tail of the other with the head-on attack capability inherent with the radar missile. It also attempts to enable one aircraft to disengage to gain energy while the other is prosecuting the fight. The tactic requires considerable teamwork and regular training if it is to be successful but where that price is paid it can present a less well-prepared enemy with formidable problems. Figure 7.8 shows the general principle.

SPOOFERS AND DECOYS

In the days of visual combats the opportunity for spoofs and decoys was limited. Once contact was made visually, that magnificent *computer*, the brain, could quickly assess the initial moves of the opposition even if, once combat was joined, the picture became rapidly confused.

It was the advent of air intercept radar (AI) which caused the fight to start beyond visual range (BVR) and this placed emphasis on the skill of the operator interpreting

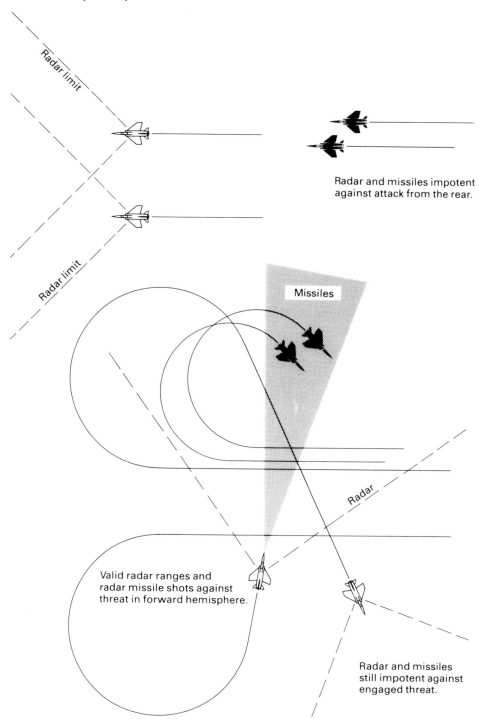

Radar and missiles impotent
against attack from the rear.

Missiles

Valid radar ranges and
radar missile shots against
threat in forward hemisphere.

Radar

Radar and missiles
still impotent against
engaged threat.

Fig 7.8.   'Loose Duce'

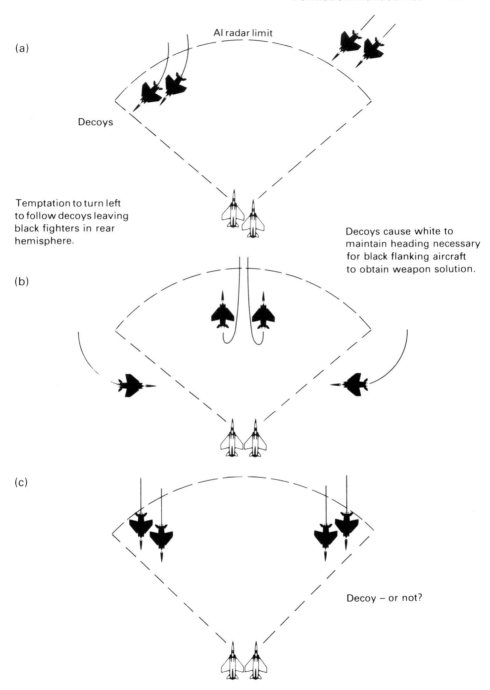

FIG 7.9.   Spoofers and decoys

the radar picture if the initial distribution of aircraft was to be accurately determined. Early radars produced a raw picture compared with the processed display common in the more advanced fighters of today. Discrimination was not particularly good and an attacker could close on what was thought to be a single target, only to find that, at visual ranges, two aircraft flying tight together constituted the target.

Equally, the early radars required a target, detected in a wide sweep search mode, to be *locked-up* onto a selected return. At this point the search mode was largely rendered ineffective and targets appearing after lock-up would not show on the screen. There was the danger of prosecuting a radar contact in one direction and missing a threat developing in another. In single-seat aircraft, where the pilot alone had to fly the aircraft and operate and interpret the radar at the same time, the amount of attention left over for visual search for the unseen attacker was limited. With these early radars the case for the two-place aircraft – particularly in the *all-weather* fighter role – was well made.

Modern radars do much to overcome this problem. The introduction of *track-while-scan* radars allows a target to be locked-up and a weapon engagement conducted while the radar is still searching for and displaying other targets at the same time. Developments such as this coincide with the introduction of more powerful radars and ones with greater discrimination. Some of the better of the present generation radars have little difficulty in breaking out individual members of a threat formation at quite long ranges. A further development which greatly assists the interpretation of the radar picture, particularly for the single-seat operator, is the *processed* picture. Rather than having to interpret the raw radar return, this is now done by the computer, and a synthetic computer generated picture is presented to the pilot.

The result can be a presentation, in a digestible form, of what amounts to a horizontal situation display with the forward battle area clearly laid out for the pilot's interpretation. The computer can also calculate the height of targets, their direction of flight and the rate of opening or closure. Such data, when processed through the weapon computers enables them quickly to calculate, and display, whether the target is, or is not, within weapon parameters. A '*fire*' or '*hold*' command can be shown in the pilot's Head-Up-Display.

While this all makes spoofing and decoying more difficult to achieve, it certainly does not rule it out. A deliberate engagement of a penetrating formation by lower performance aircraft in order to draw away escort fighters and so giving higher performance fighters an opportunity to make a clear attack against the penetrators, is a tactic that was used in Vietnam and, according to some reports, earlier in Korea. The doctrine is not dissimilar to the slashing attack described previously and used by the MiG-21s in Vietnam. The tactic remains essentially the same – in boxing terms it might be described as the feint with the left to clear the way for the right uppercut.

While self-evident to the fireside reader, or the theoretician, who together may be frustrated at the naivety of the pilot so seduced, the timescales involved in the modern combat, for a situation to be assessed and a course of action determined, may be numbered in seconds at the most, and often split-seconds. The decision to engage a crossing target travelling fast cannot take more than a couple of seconds at most if the very question itself is to remain relevant.

A problem of the same nature but one which without the discipline of war and the live expenditure of armament is often ignored, is that once a fighter has expended its ordnance it is no longer a *fighter* but is merely an *aeroplane*. In the escort role therefore, a strict control over the expenditure of weapons may be necessary. If missiles are expended against aircraft not actually threatening the main force, ultimately this may prove to be misguided.

It is sometimes difficult to convince the more headstrong that the task of the escort fighter is not to get kills for their own sake, but rather to prevent the enemy getting kills from the force being protected. As this limits the freedom of action of the escort fighters, it is a role which calls for the highest skills. The sheepdog mentality is required rather than that of the bull terrier.

The total rapport needed between the force leader and the escort leader was one of the reasons cited for having the P-47 Thunderbolt and P-51 Mustang fighters under command of the United States Army Air Force Bomber Force during the 1939–45 war. General Spaatz argued convincingly against placing them under the control of Royal Air Force Fighter Command, not for any narrow nationalistic reason, but to enable them better to concentrate solely on their specialist escort mission.

With modern AI radars therefore, the achievement of decoy is made more difficult and places upon the side using the decoy technique the requirement to use *time* critically. Where real weapons are in use, rather than the simulation of peacetime training, there will be a tendency – strong and understandable – to engage the first available targets. As enemy weapon capability extends in range this may be forced upon a formation leader, who may not be able to afford to accept the first salvo of missiles from one target group while trying to assess its importance relative to another. Figure 7.9 illustrates some of the possible situations.

The figure gives some indication of the difficulties of setting up decoys and spoofers as the AI radar capability increases. An early detection of the threatened formation is essential and any routing variation will make the prediction of the intercept area very difficult. To marshal the attackers accurately enough to succeed in the more complex evolutions requires effective ground control, radar and highly proficient controllers.

Airborne early warning aircraft go a long way to solving the problem of plotting accurately the approach path of the targets, although even this cannot predict ahead a formation which, prudently, is not following a steady course – being *unpredictable*. Ground controlled interception (GCI) tends to be hampered if the engagement is occurring at low level. Thus, in any future conflict amongst nations with an electronic warfare capability, the use of radio to guide aircraft closely could not be relied upon. In this case, only those nations with the capability to exchange data between aircraft by jam-resistant systems would be able to contemplate the complex tactics needed for effective spoofing and decoying.

THE EXPANDED THREAT

Figure 7.10 shows what has happened over the years to the *minute*. At the operational speeds of the day if two aircraft were to fly towards each other from opposite sides of the circle, they would meet in the centre after one minute. It is instructive to see how these distances compare with the distance the average human can see in the air. In the example given, the distance relates to the range a 10 foot

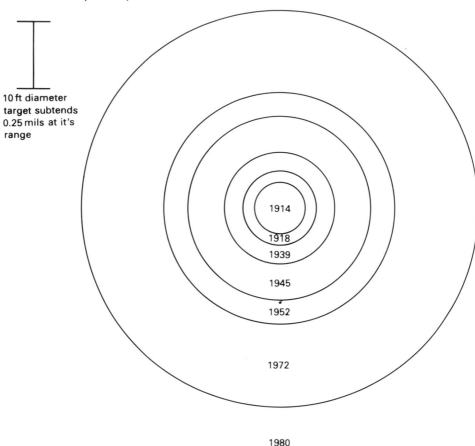

10 ft diameter
target subtends
0.25 mils at it's
range

1914
1918
1939
1945
1952
1972
1980

FIG 7.10.   The expanded threat – the minute

diameter target could be seen by a subject with a discrimination of 0.25 mil – a reasonable average. The representation has little practical value but does bring out the fact that the *area* of vulnerability is increasing at a great rate. On the same parameters, if the area of threat was shown for a modern fighter, such as the F-14 armed with Phoenix missiles, it would be greater than the area of the page itself – by a wide margin.

This is due largely to the speed of modern aircraft and to the *reach* of the weapon systems. Looked at in the context of the long-range radar-missile the thesis is straightforward but it applies equally to the close-in fight, the air combat as popularly conceived, or, as sometimes descriptively called, the *furball*.

In a multi-aircraft *mêlée* of the past, the fighter pilot could conveniently let his attention drift from certain opponents because, if they were on the other side of the fight, perhaps travelling in the opposite direction, it would take some time before they could bring their forward firing guns to bear, even if the enemy was a most skilful adversary. Now, however, the aircraft in similar circumstances may be armed with off-boresight missiles, their heads slaved by radar, and capable of high manoeuvrability once clear of the launcher. Missiles do not extend the area of the fight solely by

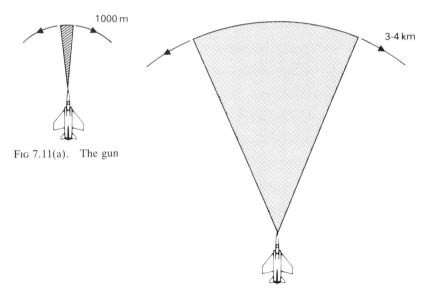

1000 m

3-4 km

FIG 7.11(a).   The gun

FIG 7.11(b).   The early missile

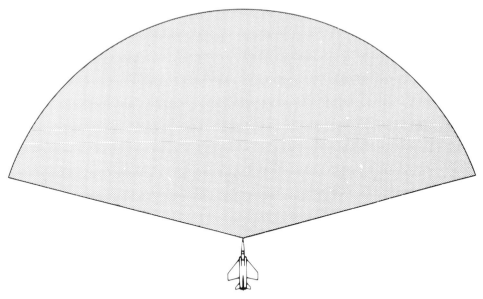

FIG 7.11(c).   Future 'agile' air combat missiles

FIG 7.11.   The expanded threat – the missile effect

virtue of their range capability, their *manoeuvrability* achieves the same effect.
Figure 7.11.

The result of the development of the new generation of agile air combat missiles is
that even the fast slashing attack may have to be executed with circumspection.

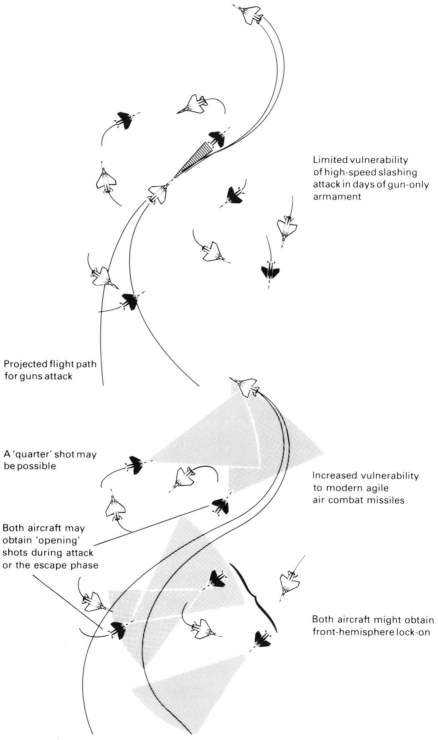

Limited vulnerability
of high-speed slashing
attack in days of gun-only
armament

Projected flight path
for guns attack

A 'quarter' shot may
be possible

Increased vulnerability
to modern agile
air combat missiles

Both aircraft may
obtain 'opening'
shots during attack
or the escape phase

Both aircraft might obtain
front-hemisphere lock-on

FIG 7.12.   The new lethal dimension

Against a solitary target, the attack geometry may be able to be so controlled as to ensure a safe escape after weapons are fired, but when attacking a multi-aircraft *furball* the extended capability of the new missiles may offer many of the target aircraft an opportunity shot. Even high closure speeds may not provide the same defence as of old; that is, before missile heads offered the chance of front-hemisphere engagements and when missile speeds were lower than is common today. Figure 7.12 shows the perception of the old and the new fighter pilot in engaging an existing furball, in the first instance when guns were the only weapon and in the second when the areas of vulnerability have been expanded by modern agile missiles.

The conclusions falling from these new facts of the air combat scene have already largely been identified. Many are old truths; modern technology merely sharpens their relevance. Notwithstanding advances in radar and in other forms of surveil-lance – Airborne Early Warning Aircraft (AWACS), for example – when the fight starts the six-o'clock position is still the most dangerous place, simply because the human being is constructed to look forward primarily and he designs his aircraft with that much to the fore. Von Richthofen's strictures remain substantially true today as they did in the Great War.

Predictability is still to be avoided at all costs. As the area of vulnerability increases, and as weapon systems enable more opportunity shots to be taken, so it is progressively more important to be less and less predictable.

Using energy to turn to gain a positional advantage must become increasingly questionable as the modern agile missiles make the furball a hostile and lethal place to fly. Using energy to turn may need to be limited to those occasions when a kill can be obtained quickly and an escape made expeditiously.

The line between bravery and foolhardiness will become a fine one. Erich Hartmann's advice may be equally applicable to the future conflict in the air as it, from his record, seemed to be in World War II:

'Get your kill, go home for a cup of coffee, think about it, and then fly again the next day'

Unfortunately, such a gentlemanly rate of flying is unlikely to be the norm in future conflicts and fighter pilots can expect to have to fly four or five sorties a day in the initial stages of a modern European war. With the battlefield as lethal as it is now, the strain on those who are ill-trained will be immense and the premium on sound preparation is high indeed in the new air combat arena.

Nations which spend their money on exotic equipment and then economise on training might just as well leave their money safely in the pockets of their taxpayers.

PLATE 22.   This outstanding picture gives the impression of the view afforded to the modern combat pilot by high visibility bubble canopies. The take-off runway is clearly visible partly blocked by the port fin. An F-18 pilot can see directly between the two fins. Note the wing tip AIM 9 Sidewinder rails and the intake arrangements which allows the maximum nose volume to be made available for the APG-65 radar.

PLATE 23. The *Mirage 2000* is the French approach to the modern trend towards high manoeuvring performance. The design features of the Dassault line are seen clearly and Rafale will be the first major break from a well-established evolutionary design path. The designers has given less weight to rearward visibility as is the norm in the latest United States and Soviet designs and that is shown in this view. A marked wing/fuselage blending can be seen as can the exhaust for the powerful engine made necessary by the high sustained 'G' requirement allied to a delta wing. *(Photo: Author)*

PLATE 24.   So what is the opposition? In numbers the *MiG-23 Flogger* rates highly. A powerful aircraft with excellent acceleration characteristics and good high speed performance. The cockpit view is poor by modern standards and the swing-wing, while offering some aerodynamic benefit, shows readily to the opponent

PLATE 25. The *MiG-25 Foxbat* is designed for very high altitude, high speed flight with engagements being made where possible from the 'Sanctuary' which such performance gives. Stressed for the high altitude case it is unlikely that the MiG-25 is capable of sustaining high manoeuvring 'G' but, if used correctly, it should never need to engage on those terms. *(Photo: United States Air Force)*

PLATE 26. The SU-27 *Flanker* is one of the new generation Soviet machines and initial assessments of its performances are impressive. For ready comparison the *Flanker* can be looked upon as the F-15-Ski. It is a large aircraft with a powerful radar and can carry up to 10 radar and/or infra-red missiles. The AA-10 missile is a large long-range weapon and it is likely that the SU-27 will exploit these advantages and attempt to engage wherever possible from 'Sanctuary,' while retaining a high manoeuvrability performance to commit to close-in combat if advantageous to do so. The *Flanker* is thought to have a Look-Down-Shoot-Down capability.

(Photo: Soviet Military Force)

PLATE 27. The *MiG-29 Fulcrum* is the second of the new Soviet fighters. Smaller than the *Flanker*, it can be compared most readily to the *F-16* or the *F-18*. The *Fulcrum* has already been exported by the Soviets and reports in open source speak highly of its performance and handling. Its intake arrangements leave nose volume for a large radar and this aircraft too can carry an impressive weapon load. Note that like the *Flanker* it has a high visibility cockpit and twin fins. *(Photo: Soviet Military Force)*

PLATE 28.   The *MiG.31 Foxhound* is an incremental development of the *MiG-25 Foxbat*. The *MiG. 31* is a two-seat design and this large fighter is probably designed primarily for use in the vast reaches of the northern Soviet Union and over the Arctic, to attempt to intercept bombers approaching over the Pole before they can launch their air-launched cruise missiles. It is unlikely that the *MiG-31* would be stressed for close-in combat and the acceptance of a cockpit arrangement which embeds the crew firmly in the structure testifies to its intended use as an interceptor-bomber-destroyer rather than as an air superiority dog-fighter. *(Photo: Soviet Military Force)*

PLATE 29.   Them! A group of Soviet fighter pilots posing for the camera in their 'dayglo' flying suits. In peace it is very sensible to fly in brightly coloured flying equipment. Following a bail-out over barren terrain, possibly with broken limbs, is no time to be camouflaged. The German Air Force fly with similar suits but, for some reason, they do not seem to have been demanded by aircrews elsewhere.

8.

Operations

'The force will be small and it will not be beyond the capabilities of a few carefully chosen officials to run'
    Trenchard (1920)
    (On the staffing of the
    new Royal Air Force)

TRENCHARD was, of course, correct although at the time he said those words he might be forgiven perhaps for underestimating how history would treat his definition of *small*. The massive retrenchment of the Royal Air Force during the twenties and the early-thirties was followed by the panic rearmament in the late-thirties when the folly of the *ten-year rule* was realised in the face of Nazis expansionism; a rule which assumed that there would be not less than ten years warning of a war in Europe. As a modern society, used to living under the *balance-of-terror*, and facing a Warsaw Pact poised well forward with *surprise* as one of its first principles of war, there could be some excuse for looking back and wondering at the complacency of those days.

Between 1939 and 1945, the Royal Air Force expanded to a force of over one million men and women. Raids numbering 1,000 bombers were mounted and the complement of fighter and fighter-bomber squadrons was extensive. Disarmament after the war was to be expected and proceeded apace, only to be stopped as the intent of the Soviet Union in Europe became apparent. Later, Korea showed that places further away were not to be immune from communist expansion. Arguably, no greater damage was done to the Royal Air Force since its inception than by the infamous 1957 *Sandys* White Paper which, mesmerised by the promise of missilry (even if, at that time largely unfulfilled), reduced the front-line Royal Air Force overnight by a percentage beyond the dreams of Reichsmarshal Goering at the height of the Battle of Britain.

Now only the two Super Powers have large forces of modern aircraft. The smaller the force, the more command and control becomes vital if the capability is to be concentrated where it is required and effort is not to be squandered. Command-and-Control – the *management* of air power – is the field of operations and in this chapter a few of the aspects of the exercise of air power will be examined.

There are enough books about which deal with the *macro* scene – the big-hands-on-little-map approach – and there is no intention to emulate that here. Instead a look will be taken at the inconvenient – those nasty facts-of-life which, on the day, become the imperatives which determine whether the battle is won or lost. They are the factors with which the flight commander, squadron commander and wing commander have to struggle for it is at their level that the discipline bites. It is an area too often ignored by staff colleges – which tend more towards the intellectual stimulus of the macro – with the result that those air forces which have been without the recent education of war can find themselves with a command and control chain which too little accepts the practical disciplines. This can only be to the detriment of achieving the grand purpose.

What follows gives only a flavour of those disciplines. It is the part which involves figures. Indeed, a mathematician may be uneasy at that term being used to denote what is, in the main, common sense and able to be grasped without the aid even of a pocket calculator – but still the determinant of effective operations none the less. Another part is man; that annoyingly unpredictable creature which, in war, regularly turns mathematicians on their head and who is dealt with later.

AIRCREW-TO-AIRCRAFT RATIO

In fielding a force the much-maligned planner must come to some decision on the ratio of aircrew-to-aircraft on a squadron or wing. They rarely start with a clean sheet of paper. The personnel structure of a large force is complex and in those which have embraced a volunteer or careerist approach – the Royal Air Force for example – is even more so. Structure can be difficult or time-consuming to change and what may seem outwardly to be an insignificant adjustment can be traumatic to the career expectations of many servicemen. A predominantly single-seat force on being replaced by a two-seat force can cause, over a short period, a manning demand for a large number of *navigators* – an out-dated term for those who serve as weapon-system operators in the modern warplane. A reverse process can cause a glut of careerist talent but with inappropriate skills.

Apart from the cost, which is in no way negligible, there is a natural pressure on the planner to be economical in the matter of manning the squadrons. Air forces have different standards which they apply and they, in their turn, may vary with the role of the aircraft. Clearly, aircraft tasked with 24-hour operations will require higher ratios than those with only a clear-weather or day capability. Although there are the odd exceptions, Western air forces are generally found to lie somewhere about the ratio of 1.5-to-1 for all-weather/night capable squadrons and 1.2-to-1 for day-only squadrons. That is, in the first case, there will be 15 pilots (or crews) for each 10 aircraft on the strength of the squadron.

There are, however, a number of factors which impinge upon this decision and some of those are becoming difficult to reconcile in the modern world. Some may even be thought to be mutually contradictory.

For example, the *pace* of war has become much greater than ever before, as many of the conflicts in the Middle East have shown. Periods of intense, and possibly prolonged operations will be demanded of a squadron. The week-end rest and recuperation with a pretty girl in London, a favourite of Hollywood producers of World War II classics, is unlikely to be a feature of a Third World War in Europe.

Modern technology has done its best to remove *night* from the battlefield and 24-hour operations, while still not universal, are becoming more popular. 24-hour operations are particularly draining if the manning ratio is not right. Even those units which are manned on the basis of a day-only capability must be assessed carefully. *Day* in the Central Region of NATO in the summer lasts 16-hours, and squadrons deploying to northern Norway could find no *night* at all during the summer months.

Equally, they could find no *day* at all in the winter months. A moment's thought will show that the staff officer who solves this conundrum with a happy average should feature in the New Years Honours List – with a Star of Lenin.

Modern air operations are likely to be fatiguing. Not only will there be the stress and fear to be expected of live operations, and in the very lethal modern battlefield that may be more debilitating than some credit, but operations in the environment of the new *hardened* bases and under NBC (nuclear, chemical and biological) conditions, where the wearing of tiring protective suits is mandatory, fatigue could set-in quickly. Unless proper rest and recuperation can be taken, a force could be worn-out within a relatively few days. To allow the required rest, a force must be manned with sufficient spare capacity.

Unfortunately, this spare capacity then has to be trained in peace and modern training for an air force is expensive and cuts into budgets which are already strained. On amortisation alone a modern aircraft can cost up to £7,000 an hour to run and that is before spares, fuel and operating costs are added. 10 technicians can cost £1 million over ten years and hundreds are required for a full wing. In afterburner, a modern aircraft can burn fuel at a rate which can be measured best in tonnes-per-minute. The imperatives to keep aircrew ratios modest are severe.

The importance of getting the ratios right in peace has also increased because of the difference between the modern situation and that of old. In the 1939–45 war industry was geared to produce aircraft at a great rate; at the end of the war every one of the warring nations was producing fighters at over 1,000 a month, as many as the NATO nations have on line in the Central Region in total in peace. Aircrew training schemes were producing aircrew to match – at home, in the United States, in Africa and wherever the circumstances would allow.

It is difficult to imagine nations producing aircraft such as the F-15 or the Flanker at that rate or to be able to train the replacement crews to match them. Modern flight training can take a year or more; some even takes three years, and the sum of these unpalatable facts is that the next war is likely to be a *come-as-you-are* affair. It will be fought, largely, with what is in the front-line at the time, supported only by a modest reinforcement from the force as a whole and from the in-being supply system.

What therefore is the effect of losses in such a situation? Looking at the aircrew-to-aircraft ratio, it will be seen that in an unreinforced situation, if a squadron starts with a ratio better than 1-to-1 then its ratio will get *better* as losses are sustained. Conversely, the squadron starting less than 1-to-1 will get progressively worse. Figure 8.1. This conclusion is based on a surmise which in the circumstances is not unreasonable. That is, that in combat with modern weapons, the survivable *kill* is less likely than before and a lost aircraft will have to be assumed to be a lost aircrew. Even in those cases where an ejection is possible, the record from a series of peacetime accidents does not point to a high possibility of the survivor being in a fit condition to return to his combat duties within the timescale of a short intense war.

It might be thought that the simple mathematics involved in Figure 8.1 should not be necessary even in a volume aimed at the junior officer and interested civilian and that the conclusions are self-evident. It is included because this simple relationship was not understood recently by a very senior officer serving in an operations post. This was not because he was ignorant or unintelligent, quite the contrary, but because he had never before thought of the relationship in this way. It is too easy in

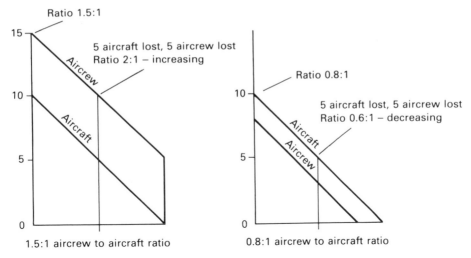

FIG 8.1.   Aircrew to aircraft ratio

peace to ignore the situation which will arise when, in war, losses of aircrew occur. It is not a problem which has to be faced on a day-to-day basis in peace.

SORTIE RATES

Although it is normal to see air forces compared on the basis of numbers of aircraft this simplistic accounting may not tell the full story. It may not be comparing like with like and may ignore the fact that numbers of aircraft matter less than what can be done with them – in other words, *sortie rate*.

Compare two mythical air forces which start a conflict with a numerical relationship not unlike that between the Warsaw Pact and NATO, that is, about two-to-one. Take the comparison a stage further by assuming that the air force with the larger number of aircraft has produced them by reducing quality to obtain quantity.

Conversely, the other side, with its stress on quality, has gone for the more sophisticated and complex design and, while reaping the operational advantages of that, may have more problems in terms of availability and maintainability. See how the macro relationships can change rapidly.

Initially take a simplistic approach,

TABLE 8.1
Effect of Better Availability and Sortie Rate on Total Sorties Available

	Blue	Red	Ratio
Total aircraft	1,000	2,000	1:2
70% available	700		1:2.3
80% available		1,600	
3 sorties per day	2,100		1:3
4 sorties per day		6,400	

By acquiring an aircraft which by its simplicity is more *available* and can be flown at a higher sortie rate because there is less to go wrong, the initial advantage of the cheaper aircraft, which in this example has given a starting advantage of 2-to-1, can be magnified as far as the operational measure is concerned to be 3-to-1. Lenin would seem to have been justified in his strictures.

It would be surprising if life were so simple! If it were the debate about *many/cheap* versus *few/costly* would not have raged so heatedly for so long. The factor which upsets the simplistic mathematics is *attrition*.

Cost and complexity today is most usually to be found in the area of performance – fly-by-wire, for example – and in weapon systems – radars, missiles, electronic warfare suites and the like. It would be strange – and disappointing to many – if this investment in sophistication did not have at least some return in lower attrition, or looked upon from the other viewpoint, higher kill rates. Applying some attrition disciplines to the simple mathematics above what emerges?

Assume that the heavy premium paid for sophistication, which results in Blue having only half as many aircraft as Red, has the effect of, say, halving the attrition rate of the better equipped aircraft compared to the more simple design. For the sake of example assume that Blue and Red have attrition rates of 5 per cent and 10 per cent respectively. Applying the attrition formulae, what transpires by the end of the first day?

TABLE 8.2
Effect of Attrition on Starting Ratios After First Day

	Blue	Red	Ratio
5% attrition/3 sorties per day 700 aircraft at start, Sorties	1,996		
10% attrition/4 sorties per day 1,600 aircraft at start, Sorties		5,502	1:2.8
Aircraft remaining	600	1,050	1:1.75

Already it can be seen that quantity at the expense of survivability, notwithstanding the cost of the sophistication required, quickly starts an adverse trend in the ratios. Consider what happens if the operation is continued for seven days.

TABLE 8.3
Effect of Attrition After 7 days

	Blue	Red	Ratio
5% attrition/3 sorties per day 700 aircraft at start, Sorties	9,232		
10% attrition/4 sorties per day 1,600 aircraft at start, Sorties		15,162	1:1.6
Aircraft remaining	238	84	2.8:1

The sortie advantage, while still there, is some way removed from the starting aircraft ratio of 2-to-1 and the potential sortie advantage of 3-to-1. But of greater concern to the Red commander would be that his force is virtually destroyed by an attrition rate which sounds to the uninitiated as a *modest* 10 per cent.

As an aside, the term *decimation* is associated with the Roman punishment applied to a unit which had rebelled. One man in ten – hence *deci-mation* – selected at random, was put to death by his fellows. It was considered enough to dissuade all but the fool-hardy from mutiny. The risk was pitched at a level considered by most as unacceptably high. In air operations it might be thought that the same applied today.

An attrition of 10 per cent is far from modest, indeed, even at the height of the 1939–45 war, when aircraft and crews were being produced as replacements at a pace, attrition far less than double figures caused commanders to pause for thought. When the United States Army Air Force suffered an attrition of 22 per cent on the raid against the Schweinfurt ball-bearing plants, it was enough for them to suspend deep penetration raids completely and to change their doctrine substantially until an escort fighter, in the guise of the P-51 Mustang, became available.

Modern commanders, with far fewer resources to muster, have to worry them-selves with attrition rates in the low single figures and, with so few reserves, even quite small differences in attrition may cause the best laid plans to be recast – and in a hurry.

It is not the purpose here to make commentary on the future procurement policies – of either side – but the balance between quantity and quality is a fine one. The influence that modern technology is having on that balance can be cruel. Whereas, in the past, such decisions have had to be placed on a scale which ran progressively, but regularly, from the black to the white, there is a tendency for the modern weapon systems to put some step functions into the process. A solution to a procurement requirement could either result in total operational success or total failure without the reassurance of much, if any, graduation between. A heavy responsibility rests on the planners and operational requirement staffs.

'NO WEAPON – NO ROLE'

Weapons grasp the headlines in war; in peace they lack the glamour of aircraft. They rarely pull the crowds at air shows – they cannot execute formation aerobatics with or without smoke! An air force without aircraft is readily seen to be so and can be ridiculed by politician and press alike but who takes the same interest in some insignificant storehouse on the edge of an airfield containing the tools with which the war will be won or lost? Weapons, like good news, seem not to sell newspapers.

Things may change. It is getting more difficult to eulogise a modern crew in the manner of the Immelmanns and Baders when today they engage their enemy out-of-sight and the missile does most of the clever flying tens of miles away. This could seriously cut the available copy and cause the correspondent to search for more abstruse subjects. They are around and *stock levels* and *costs* are good subjects for peacetime debate.

Consider the problem facing the planner in a time of straightened defence funding when contemplating weapon stock levels. In the case of the air superiority force, he will see that there are several trends which vie for his attention. There is a powerful argument for fighters to carry larger numbers of weapons and one reason for that – the probability of kill – will be mentioned soon. Another reason is that the more talk turns towards mounting combat air patrols (CAP) at extended ranges, the more it is important to have a large weapon load on the aircraft. Without this, weapon loads could soon be exhausted and the aircraft would have to return to base to re-arm. Much is claimed for the value of tankers for in-flight refueling of aircraft on extended CAP but, once fired out, the fuel situation is irrelevant – the fighter will have to return to base to rearm.

What is the norm in terms of weapon loads? It is difficult to be precise with seemingly two different design philosophies emerging between the Europeans – EFA, Lavi, Grippen, and Rafael all tending to be small aircraft with commensurately small weapon loads – and the United State and Soviet Union – the Foxhound, F-14, F-15, Advanced Tactical Fighter (ATF), MiG-2000(?) – all much larger. The Grippen, for example, is an eight-tonne aircraft; the Foxhound takes to the air at something over 80,000 lbs or about 40 tonnes. The weight of the ATF is currently aimed at 50,000 lbs and there is talk of a multi-missile capability. The F-14, designed for carrier air defence, a task not dissimilar to the air defence of the United Kingdom, can carry three types of air-to-air missile and can lift a weapon load equivalent to the empty weight of a Harrier. The Flanker is emerging in pictures showing the capability to carry up to 10 missiles in addition to its internal gun armament.

Take as an example an aircraft such as the F-4 Phantom carrying a total of 8 missiles. For the sake of discussion the radar missiles can be costed at around £150,000 and the IR missiles something less than half that cost.

If this aircraft survives, say, 30 sorties in a short but intense war, and on each sortie it expends, on average, half of its missile load, then it will require 60×AIM-7 and 60×AIM-9 at a cost approaching £12 million. It can be seen how the provision of missile stocks for forces of hundreds of aircraft soon give accountants and planners – to use an expressive Americanism – *gas pains*!

Unfortunately, technological development is such that, while able to offer much greater capability, it does so at a price and it is likely that follow-on missiles, such as the *Advanced Medium Range Air-to-Air Missile* (AMRAAM), could cost twice that of the preceding AIM-7 – some sources confidently predict somewhat more than twice. The European developed short-ranged collaborative missile (ASRAAM) can hardly be seen to be priced in the same range as the well-established AIM-9 Sidewinder. The £12 million stock figure could easily double in the modern age.

The problem is confounded even more when an aircraft is fielded as a *Multi-Role Aircraft*. Here again, *no-weapon-no-role* and the 30 sorties would have to have another equally expensive sort of weaponry stocked for the second role if the aircraft was to be, in practice, multi-role. But Maverick, as an example of a ground-attack missile, costs about $300,000 each. 30 sorties worth of Maverick and 30 sorties of air-to-air missiles? Already the missile stocks are costing more than the aircraft in some cases.

The agony of the planner in this instance is, however, that if the 30 sorties are indeed double provisioned to capitalise on the multi-role capability, and the aircraft can hardly do two roles at the same time, then half of the expensive weaponry will lie unused. That is a strange system for optimising budgets to fight a numerically stronger foe.

If an apportionment is made, say 10 sorties worth of air-to-air weapons and 20 sorties of air-to-ground weapons, is the aircraft truly multi-role? If the initial call is for air-defence, as it might be, by Sortie 11 the aircraft is single-role by reason of the reality of only having air-to-ground weapons remaining.

Much abuse is heaped upon those who forward these realities by those who would see in the multi-role aircraft the answer to budgetary and force-structure problems. Yet few would argue sensibly that the designer cannot make a fair multi-role aircraft in the future – even if they have not succeeded particularly well up to the present – the argument is whether air forces can afford to *stock* them, or *train* their crews, or whether peacetime career structures are sufficiently adaptable to develop long-term *expertise* in the force which the requirement for multi-role situational awareness on the modern battlefield demands.

It is in these second-order problems that the question must be put to multi-role capability. There are answers; the first is a copious supply of money, an option not open to many; the second is a corps of professional, full-time aircrew – an *operations branch* in which many, certainly the majority, forsake the chance of high rank for a career in the cockpit.

PROBABILITY OF KILL

If these large inventories of weapons were to be fired at the enemy, surely he would be vanquished early in the battle? The West has thousands of missiles and the enemy only has lesser-thousands of aircraft. Is there a problem?

Ignoring the first requirement of getting the missiles to the vicinity of the target, something which the enemy offensive planner will try to frustrate, there remains the matter of *kill probability*. The modern missile requires a complete weapons *system* to function correctly before a successful kill is achieved. Each of these individual elements within the system has its own probability of success and the overall weapon kill probability depends on all of these.

To avoid infringing security, consider a mythical weapon system and the sorts of factors which would affect the issue.

TABLE 8.4
Cumulative Probability of Successful Missile Engagement – Mythical Missile and Probabilities

Item	Probability of Successful Operation (%)	Cumulative Probability (%)
Aircraft Radar System	95	95.0
Aircraft-to-Missile Interfaces	95	90.3
Firing Circuits	98	88.5
Missile Leaves Rail	95	84.0
Missile Guides	95	79.8
Missile Arms	95	75.8
Missile Fuses	85	64.5
Warhead Detonates	95	61.2
Kills Target	66	40.4

The example in Table 8.4 is for illustration only and the reader can play with his own factors and probabilities – merely multiply all the individual probabilities together to obtain the overall cumulative figure. While those above are not indicative of any particular missile, the cumulative probability is not outside the bounds of reason. A radar missile is being considered here and IR missiles have been proved in practice to be about twice as successful in terms of kill probability than their radar counterparts.

Given the probability of kill of a single missile, the chance of a salvo succeeding is given by:

Pk = 1 − (1 − Pkss)^n

where: Pkss = Single-shot kill probability

n = Number of missiles fired.

From this it can be seen that a two-missile salvo with a Pkss of 0.4 gives 64 per cent chance of kill, a three-missile 78 per cent, and a four-missile salvo a Pk of 87 per cent. It can also be seen why more missiles are needed than targets and why the prudent fighter pilot may not be overly keen to economise on salvo size. This would be particularly so if he was facing an enemy with a missile system better than his own by, say, 20 per cent – that is, the enemy missile system had a probability of kill of 0.6. See how that affects the issue.

A two-missile salvo gives a Pk of 84 per cent, a three-missile 94 per cent, and a four-missile salvo a Pk of 97 per cent. These figures constitute an appreciable increase in lethality and would present a situation demanding a pause for thought. The result could be to conclude that now aircraft can out-perform their pilots and that the operational pay-off for better weapon effectiveness is so high, future investment should be weighted towards the weapon rather than the *vehicle*.

IF THE CAP FITS . . .

Before the discipline of probability mathematics come to the fore, the fighter pilot has a problem not dissimilar to that of Mrs Beaton who, in her famous cookbook, at the start of the recipe for *Jugged Hare*, instructed her readers to:

'First, catch your hare . . .'

There are a number of different ways to bring the enemy to battle to contest *air superiority*. One is to go to him – a variation of the challenge of old of throwing down the gauntlet. The fighter sweeps conducted in the latter months of the 1939–45 war were examples of this in practice. Care would have to be exercised in the conditions of today, however. No longer is the threat only fighters supported by the occasional inject of *flak*. A variety of SAM systems, some impressively effective, now also contest the issue over the other side of the border and fighter sweeps may find themselves taking on odds far greater than the numerical balance of aircraft suggested. This is not to say that fighter sweeps should be discounted. There may be a time to use the tactic and that would be the wrong time and place to have to perfect the techniques for the first time. It has to remain part of the inventory of options.

Another tactic used in the 1939–45 war was the fighter *interdictor*. A fighter joined the returning stream of bombers and, over brightly illuminated airfields, and against aircraft in the slow lumbering configuration for landing, found that there were rich pickings to be had. The tactic had its detractors who pointed out the relatively low kill rates for the effort expended and for the losses incurred. But did they take into account the cost to the other side of *adrenalin*? Or was there some way of calculating the landing accidents caused by pilots, exhausted after the raid, returning to night landings worrying as much about what was behind them as what was in front of them? Such operations lend themselves poorly to be judged by accountants; the psychologist could proffer better opinion.

Clearly it is better, where possible, to fight the air superiority battle closer to friendly airspace. Fuel reserves can be less with diversion airfields more readily available – and this factor acts in the opposite sense for the intruder. Lower fuel requirements equate to lower weight and to better performance. An ascending spiral situation. Against this, in interdictor operations, the higher reaches of the performance envelope may not be needed for use.

Time-on-station is an important issue. Too much time cannot be wasted on non-productive flying if a numerically superior enemy is to be defeated within the constraints of the resources available. The most economical way of using fighters is from *ground alert*. Here fighters stand ready at immediate notice to scramble but do not consume valuable serviceability or fatigue aircrews as is the case with airborne alert. Whether this advantageous mode can be used depends on the degree of warning available.

Consider some first order figures. An intruder is detected by radar at 150 nautical miles travelling at Mach 0.7 – at sea level, 463 knots. Assume that the attacker has 75 nautical miles to travel to reach his target in the forward area. If the radar station takes one minute to assess the threat and to decide on the correct action, and the fighters are airborne five minutes after being scrambled – which from dispersed and hardened bases is not unreasonable – even if they fly at Mach 0.9 (595 knots at sea level) and the attackers spend two minutes over the target, then the attackers are over 60 nautical miles from the target *on their return to base* before the defending fighters intercept them. Figure 8.2 illustrates. The effect that the extended coverage given by the *Airborne Warning and Control System* aircraft (AWACS) has on the effective utilisation of fighter assets, can be seen immediately.

A method used to overcome the reaction time problem is *Combat Air Patrol (CAP)*. By keeping fighters in the air, up-threat, much of the reaction time problem can be solved. Success with this technique demands some careful balancing of factors, some of which are too often ignored in peacetime exercises where many of the imperatives are lacking, for example, the requirement to rearm or where aircraft fire-out before the planned finish of their CAP patrol. CAP can be looked upon by the lazy battlestaff as the panacea answer to all ills where, in practice, it is not.

There are two main disciplines involved in mounting CAPs which the operational commander has to bear in mind. The first is the *circumference effect*, the second is the *cycle time* issue.

A fighter will be able to dominate a certain area of sky by the use of its sensors and its weapon system. Clearly an aircraft like the F-14 with a powerful radar and long-range missiles can patrol a greater area than could a gun-armed aircraft relying upon visual search for detection. For the sake of simplicity of illustration, imagine that this area of domination is represented by a circle about the aircraft's patrol position. In Figure 8.3 it can be seen that as the distance from base increases the number of aircraft required to maintain a comprehensive cover becomes larger due to the *circumference effect* and that this, in turn, is affected by the capability of the aircraft.

Where the direction of attack can be reasonably well predicted, the *arc* covered can be reduced and the number of aircraft required reduced accordingly. Where it

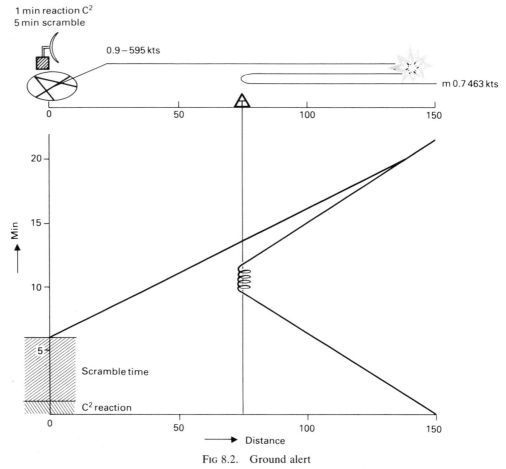

FIG 8.2.   Ground alert

cannot, and as more offensive systems become longer ranged, it progressively more cannot be predicted, then the arcs involved expand to equate more closely to the full circle. All round cover at extended range can soon become prohibitively expensive.

The number of aircraft required to maintain one on CAP is easily calculated. Table 8.5 shows the elements involved and they are all straightforward; turn-round time,

TABLE 8.5
Calculation of Aircraft Required to Maintain One Aircraft on CAP

Take as an example the following conditions:

Turn-Round Time	2 hours
Transit Time	
(to 300 nautical miles at 400 knots	
– there and back)	1.5 hours
On-Station Time	1.5 hours
Total Cycle Time	5 hours

$$\text{Aircraft Required} = \frac{5}{1.5}$$

$$= 3.33 \text{ aircraft}$$

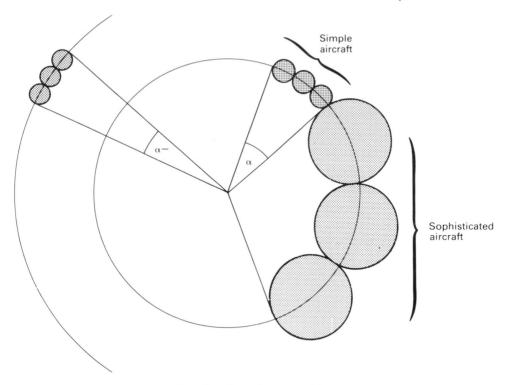

Simple
aircraft

Sophisticated
aircraft

FIG 8.3.   Circumference and Arcs

transit time – there and back – and on-station time. Together they add up to *cycle time* and the number of aircraft required to keep one aircraft on CAP continuously is given by:

$$\frac{\text{Cycle Time}}{\text{On-Station Time}} = \text{No of Aircraft}$$

At first sight, an expensive premium but under some circumstances worth paying for, of course, there may be no other option. Unfortunately, there is more to the story. It would be unusual to place only one aircraft on CAP. There would be no mutual support and total weapon loads may not be sufficient to engage the expected threat. If a pair of aircraft are used the requirement rises to 6.66 aircraft. Serviceability factors must then be taken into account and if an aircraft type produced a serviceability factor of 70% then to obtain the 6.66 serviceable aircraft required for the CAP more than that have to be *possessed*. In this case:

$$\text{Aircraft Required} = \frac{3.33 \times 2}{0.7}$$

$$= 9.5$$

Thus, a squadron requires to possess 9.5 aircraft on strength to maintain a continuous two-aircraft CAP at a distance of 300 nautical miles.

This requirement for large complements of aircraft to mount extended CAP at long range is one of the reasons that the United States Navy favour large super-carriers. It is not because *big-is-beautiful* for its own sake but because defence against the 360 degree threat is so exhausting of smaller forces. Consequently, their Fleet Carriers are of around 95,000 tons displacement and carry between 85 and 100 aircraft, depending upon the mission.

Readers wishing to play with the maritime scenario may wish to note that, as a *general rule*, carriers mount about one aircraft for every 1,000 tons of displacement. This is seen to be true of the American super-carriers and holds good throughout the range of displacements. The new Italian carrier of about 16,000 tons is expected to carry between 16 and 18 aircraft, the Royal Navy's Illustrious class of about 22,000 tons carries about 22 aircraft and the new Soviet carriers, still in build, are thought to be about 65,000 tons and can be confidently expected to carry between 60 and 70 aircraft.

It may be thought that in the example in Table 8.5 some unnecessarily pessimistic factors had been used. Operational turn-rounds can be conducted in timescales much better than two hours – one *Jaguar* base once prided itself on a complete operational turn-round, including crew change, inside six minutes and the Israeli Air Force would probably not be impressed by even that – and surely aircraft capable of Mach 2 can transmit faster than the 400 knots assumed? Both are fair points but if *continuous* operations are contemplated, the turn-round will include minor rectification and servicing to a depth greater than that on an operational turn-round where little or no rectification is attempted. Without this work being carried out the 70 per cent serviceability factor would soon start to be affected.

Ground crews have to be considered also; wearing out ground crews will stop the operation just as surely as the loss of aircraft and they have to be carefully paced. Equally, although the fighter could transit faster, the price would be higher fuel consumption and shorter time loitering on CAP. With a shorter loiter time, more fighters would be required to mount the continuous patrol.

A difficult problem for the planner is that poised if the aircraft engage, and fire-out, shortly after arriving on CAP. A fighter without weapons is not a fighter and will have to be replaced but this will be impossible in the short term and the CAP may have to remain unmanned until the normal rotation time arrives. This could leave dangerous gaps in the cover. The problem which this gives to the defensive planner is certainly not lost on his offensive opposite number who will do all he can to force holes in the cover through which to feed attacking formations. Offensive *saturation* is a tactic which must be expected by the defence. It is a difficult one to counter within the constraints of force availability.

For the airman, the field of operations is nowhere near as enjoyable as flying. But, if it is bungled, through lack of application or through ignorance, or worse, through inadequate battlestaff training, then the skill of the fliers and the excellence of their equipment will be squandered and the war will most assuredly be lost. 'Operations' has therefore, in its own way, a fascination and there are many highly satisfying appointments to be had within its boundaries.

9.

Man, Training and Leadership

A FIGHTER pilot has to be selected and recruited from the population at large. His training has to develop motor skills to a high degree of effectiveness and, despite being a two-dimensional being by nature, he has to be taught to think and to act in three dimensions. He has to develop an individuality which goes hand in glove with single, or at the most, two-seat operation, while at the same time retaining the ability to play his part in the team, indeed, it is teamwork which could determine his fate on the battlefield or, in the converse, allow him to determine that of others. A *team of individualists* is almost a contradiction in terms and is the conundrum presented to those who would lead such a group.

Before attempting to train or lead fighter pilots it does well to ponder on the raw material itself – man. This is necessarily a personal task for it is of little value taking the perceived wisdom of others as the basis for what must be a very individual approach to the matter of leadership. This is not to suggest that role models do not have their place for clearly they do, or to suggest that the other man's point of view should not be duly considered, but only to the point of capturing ideas and techniques; those who try to capture the personalities of their heroes and mentors rarely succeed in doing so.

What follows, therefore, is not forwarded as any school solution. It is merely one man's viewpoint, and other assessments, with all their differing weights and balances, are not only to be encouraged but also welcomed. Similar thought gives rise too often to similar solutions and, in the matter of the selection, training and leadership of fighter pilots there is room for more than one approach. In terms of the leadership issue, it would be a pale and dull world if there was but one stereo-type. Certainly there has not been one in the past.

MAN

From a military viewpoint the balance between man's strengths and weaknesses is finely tuned. As a *machine* he is a poor thing. He tires exasperatingly quickly, his temperature range is restricted to an extent unlikely to be tolerated in a mechanical device; although evolved over milleniums, he still cannot see effectively in the dark, despite half of his existence being spent in that condition; and his need for regular sustenance to stave off debilitating effects is far greater than that of the majority of the higher order animals. His moods are unpredictable and, in any large grouping, a mix of the ecstatic and the clinically depressed is quite likely to be found.

149

He is an aggressive animal, one of the very few of God's creatures to kill for sport rather than for food, for enjoyment rather than for necessity. His intelligence causes him to understand the concept of death, something which is argued as being beyond the understanding of animals who, while understanding pain, cannot envision *death* thereby allowing them the advantage of having no fear of it.

Despite an understanding of death, however imperfect, history records innumerable incidents when man has overcome his fear to perform deeds of great heroism. He is or, at least, he can be, *courageous*, overcoming his natural instincts and doing things which his reason tells him he should not. He can be compassionate and caring and, on the battlefield, place his own safety in jeopardy for both close colleague and stranger alike. He can face overwhelming odds one minute, in the true spirit of Horatius, and can flee like a cur the next with, seemingly, the difference between the two situations leading to his behaviour difficult to discern.

Individually, and in mass, he is capable of great destruction, using his own puny strength but with the economy born of intelligence, or by putting that intelligence to work in more awesome ways, or, again, by collecting as a *pack* and pooling to form a collective evil. This is far from the figment of a purely military mind; the lynch mob of old, the vandal and the football hooligan in the modern era, probably obtain their inspiration from the same base motives.

Yet with all these conflicting qualities he dominates the world as no other creature even approaches. He has produced great art, and prose, and monuments in stone and steel. He has conquered diseases and extended his life span, he has harnessed nature to provide him with power; from the wind, water, the earth's own energy from the hot subterranean rocks, from the hydro-carbons and now from the atom. He has even escaped from what for so long was considered his natural jailor – gravity – and has extended his frontier already to the moon and will, eventually, take even greater steps.

In all, man is a fascinating and impressive creature and forms the backbone of any military endeavour despite the march of technology.

RAISING THE FORCE

In raising a military force, more particularly in a democracy, the perceptions of the populace play a large part. Comment here will be principally directed at the situation in the United Kingdom but similar pressures and conditions can be found, in whole or in part, in a number of the world's major democracies.

Perhaps of first consideration is whether to raise a *citizen* force or whether to field an *elite*. The accepted system in the United Kingdom leans heavily towards the citizen force. The British services are drawn from a wide church. There are rich and poor, northerners and southerners, socialists and conservatives, black and white, and all serve together in a *pot pourri* without thought to race, religion, colour, or creed. The citizen armed force reflects the citizen population.

Because of this (and an advantage therefore of the citizen force) it would be difficult to conduct the plotting necessary for a successful *coup d'etat*; something which has been the scourge of so many other communities. In these cases, as often as not, the military are drawn from specific tribes, or classes, or groups with strong sectional interests. They form a self-interested sub-group within the greater grouping of the national whole. Plotting and scheming in reasonable security becomes far more possible under these circumstances than in the widely-based citizen force.

In the past, the citizen force has served the United Kingdom passably well. Indeed in the two Great Wars, 1914–18 and 1939–45, the full-time standing armies had to be reinforced by conscripted citizen soldiery on both occasions before the issue could be decided. Some scholars have sung the praises of the quality of the average Briton, conscripted or not, who is, seemingly, a fair soldier as soon as the Queen's shilling has been pressed into his palm.

There has been some merit in this thesis. The standards existing in the British society in the past – the not too distant past – were closer to those basic qualities needed to make war *en masse*. Patriotism was something encouraged, pride in a great Empire was engendered, self-discipline and self-denial were considered virtuous, teamwork was prized, consideration for others was more than just good manners, it was based on the Christian ethic from which much of the nation's laws themselves were derived. The firm anchor of the family, the school, the village *et al* gave the feeling of belonging to something wider than mere *self* and the step from identifying with those groups to the similar but different identification with *the Regiment* was not the great gulf that it can be today.

Much has changed, and has changed at a fast pace. The family, as a unit, has less cohesion now than before. One-third of all marriages end in divorce and even those which do not, see offspring fleeing the nest to follow careers and occupations in the four corners of the earth; travel and adventure are the modern norms but can act against family cohesion.

Perhaps the greatest change, is that the world has become a more materialistic place where the reward is too often measured by those things which can be touched, collected, banked. What price care or charity? To offer charity can be considered insulting, to accept it demeaning, regardless of the needs of the recipient. Life in the modern society certainly offers less of a military grounding than it used to. The soldier pocketing his shilling today is far less the natural soldier than he was in the past in terms of the basic qualities and motivations needed in what can be a dangerous profession.

Of course, it may be the military which need to change its perceptions to stay in step with the evolving citizenry. There is merit in that, indeed, the British armed forces are already paid a *military salary* rather than the old fashioned *pay and emoluments*. The military salary is based on job evaluation and pay comparability with *similar* occupations in the civilian markets.

Yet where in the civilian sector do we find what has been termed the *unlimited liability* clause which governs the military man when *push-comes-to-shove*? The upwardly-mobile young executive will scuttle out of the ailing firm for richer pickings at his own volition; can he be compared with the military man who is denied that freedom of choice the day before the war starts, or as the first artillery shells whistle overhead? This poses the question of whether the military in the modern society *can* be compared with fellow civilian citizens, but the greater question which needs to be addressed is whether he *should* be so compared. Has the gulf between the product of the modern society and the qualities necessary to form an efficient military force become so wide that the move towards the elitist force is occurring by default? If so, should not the rewards for those who embrace *Sparta* and reject *Sodom and*

Gomorrah reflect the sacrifice made? Will they not *have* to if the volunteer force is to survive the pressures?

Another problem experienced in raising a military force is a surfeit of peace – most would say, 'Thank God'. The United Kingdom was last invaded in the year 1066 and it can be difficult to convince the modern youth that the world remains a dangerous place with a role for him to play in making it safer. Assuming the age of five to be the start of reasonable recall, very few citizens born after about 1938 will remember much about their homeland being bombed – in 1990 that will make them all over the age of 52 who can, even imperfectly, recall the last threat to their island. Conversely, whenever there is action – Korea, Suez, the Falkland Islands – there is a marked upsurge in recruiting and it can be seen why some who are involved in the raising of forces say that war itself is the best recruiting sergeant.

The difficulties are further compounded by the demographic trends entrenched in the populations of a number of nations, particularly in North West Europe. The military are about to find themselves fishing for high quality personnel in a diminishing pool and, as market forces take their course, balances between quality and quantity will have to be drawn. Already, the Germans are having seriously to consider the recruitment of women into their armed forces if they are to be able to maintain the current strength into the nineties, deeply though it goes against their instincts to do so.

In the Soviet Union, similar trends are to be discerned. They too may have great difficulty in maintaining their present substantial forces on line. Their difficulties are compounded by a major imbalance in the birthrates of the many and various races which make up that diverse nation. The Moslems of the south are showing considerably higher birth rates than the Russians themselves, who are still, in that land of equality, by far the more equal than others. The long term implications for the balance of power in the Soviet state must be concerning to them.

The reasons for this demographic dip are widely debated. The emancipation of women features strongly in the discussions. The life-style advantages of the smaller family are seen more clearly in the new materialistic world. The *Pill* has hardly encouraged procreation, neither have the high divorce rates. It is even suggested that the new acceptance of homosexuality is having its effect and some commentators suggest that in the European republics of the Soviet Union young women can now look forward to four or five abortions. Whatever the reason may be, there are not going to be as many young men about during the next decade as there were in the last, and the maintenance of the military force is going to be more problematical.

Other factors have to be taken into account. No longer is the art of war conducted with pikes and swords; all three military mediums now field highly sophisticated and complex equipment much of which is close to the leading edge of technology. Training costs can soon become prohibitive if the entry standard is too far removed from the high standards required to operate and maintain such equipment. *Dwell Time*, the length of service which is achieved on average, can still make mock of training budgets if even the high calibre entrant stays too short a time properly to amortise the costly training given to him.

Here lies the dilemma. How to find the high calibre entrant with qualities which are increasingly difficult to identify in society as a whole, and to persuade him to stay after training him to the point where he is an attractive asset in a seller's market, while paying him only a *comparative* salary? There are ways, not necessarily based on the ever increasing pay check but rather on *status, quality of life*, dare one say it, *fun*, and an exciting and rewarding career in which these advantages are laid against the disadvantages of the military life; *discipline* beyond the common norm, *professionalism* in the old connotation, *self-sacrifice* for a cause not easy to rationalise to the man in the street.

It can be done – it has been done – but the result looks very much like an *elitist* force; a group that lives within itself, to its own standards which, dangerously, are much higher than their citizen counterparts. In all, elitist forces do not sit easily with democracies; they are more the children of the totalitarian state but, with the pressures about to rear their heads in the maintenance of the military force, the use of the elitist ideal should not be discarded out of hand. It could prove to be the lesser of two evils. It could certainly prove to be a cheaper way of financing a standing force in peace in the technological age.

THE FIGHTER PILOT

With this background in mind, how is the fighter pilot selected from the mass entry drawn from the modern society? With some difficulty! The figures from the Royal Air Force experience are probably fairly indicative of the trend elsewhere. Out of some 1,500 applicants for pilot selection, about 270 are placed into flying training. Of these, 190 or so graduate from flight training and of these, in turn, about 75 will be *fast-jet* quality – that is, fighter and fighter-bomber material. If the young man cutting out the advertisement in the daily paper has his heart set on flying fighters, then he is facing a process with high attrition. Some observers have suggested that the knowledge of this highly competitive situation throughout flight training is a reason why some potentially suitable candidates do not apply in the first instance and *fear of failure* and 'non-competitive' education come into the equation, perhaps.

Flight training to modern operational standards is far from cheap. It has been announced that the cost of training a fast-jet pilot in the Royal Air Force amounts to nearly £3 million. Although many are rejected at the earlier stages in training where the investment is far from this exaggerated sum, it is none-the-less true that the training commitment uses resources and funds which could be spent elsewhere and the search for selection processes which can identify the low-risk student at the start of training is long standing.

As the review of some of the more renowned pilots in Chapter 2 showed so clearly, there is no straightforward standard against which to judge. Even if the emerging knowledge of the chemistry of life in the DNA molecule allowed the *cloning* of fighter pilots, it is doubtful whether the parent *genes*, from which the clone would be produced, could be specified with any certainty. Such a scientific process could hardly be expected either to start, or end up with, the collection of misfits, cripples, weaklings and characters who so prominently featured in the roll-call of *aces* in the Great War, or who pushed the frontiers of aviation so far and so fast in those early days.

Every squadron commander will have his own idea of the ideal fighter pilot – yet another reason for the difficulty of defining a standard – but perhaps there are some, if only a few, common threads. Most would agree that the fast-jet pilot needs to be a good pilot. His trade is to fly a high performance machine in such a way as to exploit the full flight envelope – and at the edges of those envelopes there are aircraft about which bite. The difference between an optimum turn and a flight departure into potentially lethal gyrations is not a wide one in many front-line types. He has certainly to like exploring the full envelope – aerobatics – and he needs to have high standards which he is proud to maintain for their own sake. Occasionally a good, but irresponsible, pilot escapes the checks and balances and becomes a menace on a fast-jet squadron where, often, the machines are single seat and the discipline of the crew is absent.

A primary quality in a fighter pilot is *aggression*. This does not mean that what is required is a suave version of a football hooligan. On the contrary, what is necessary is a *highly controlled and disciplined aggression*. But to recruit to a force which, within NATO, faces odds exceeding two-to-one, it is necessary to avoid those who do not fancy a challenge. There are those who will show apprehension at such a balance and they, hopefully, will be employed elsewhere; the fighter pilot will look at such odds with excitement, arguing that he will fight in a *target-rich* environment and that it will take him only half the time to find his kill than it will take his opposite number. These sterling emotions must be kept in check – rightfully, the task of the wise squadron commander – who will, at the appropriate time, remind his younger charges that General Custer met his sticky end in a *target-rich environment*.

Another factor which is becoming more accepted as the preserve of the competent fighter pilot is the possession of *situational awareness*, not only the awareness of things about him in a daily situation but extended further to encompass what is happening in an air combat. The figures for those killed in combat by aircraft which they had not seen places emphasis on this point. With this in mind, the selection system introduced by the Swedish Air Force may have some relevance. Known as *Defence Mechanism Testing (DMT)* it involves a series of psychological tests designed to detect a subjects awareness of dangerous situations. Whether or not it produces a better fighter pilot could be open to question but, on the training results obtained over a period of time by the Swedish Air Force, it certainly seems to be able to produce him with a far smaller loss rate through training.

In the United Kingdom investigations over a number of years, have come out with conclusions which indicate that some combinations of circumstance produce better chances of success through training than others. These are combined to give a *P-score* which purports to give a guide to potential success. Within that system credit is gained if the subject enters training young, or has had previous flying experience. As these two qualities equate in the common-sense mind to *you can't teach an old dog new tricks*, and, *if he wants to fly badly enough, he will*, there are some who would question why it has taken so long to realise such elemental truths.

The modern trend, however, has been the opposite. In the 1960's, and in the light of the popular upsurge in the desire for tertiary education, the RAF leant heavily towards the *graduate entry*. Whatever the pros and cons of that scheme, one clear disadvantage was that three years at university in the late teens was the last thing needed to assist in getting a pilot onto his first squadron by the age of 21. Consequently, pilots now join their front-line squadrons at an average of 25 years of age which many squadron commanders deplore and which, if modern studies are right, takes them well clear of the youthful category which enjoys greatest training success.

But is great academic knowledge essential to those aspiring to be an *ace*? The past argues that it seems not to be the case. This slim volume should have been shown that to understand the fundamentals only the barest grasp of *mathematics* is required and even then the understanding of the *bottom* line, or even the acceptance of the bottom line, is what really matters, rather than its derivation. In a force of 6,000 aircrew there will be amongst them, almost by random chance, quite enough with a skill in figures to tackle the complexities of air combat mathematics without insisting that they can all do so.

One of the great myths, but held to be a truth by many, is that the fighter pilot needs to be an extrovert. Ignoring the clear message from the past, in which so many of the *aces* have been quiet unassuming men, the Hollywood image can cloud good judgement. The term *fighter pilot* conjures up visions of fast cars, glamorous women and copious quantities of beer but less so for those who know fighter pilots than those who see films about them. There are, naturally, both extroverts and introverts on most squadrons but the rank order of excellence in the air cannot be related to their character on the ground with any certainty. This is not to say that a fighter pilot party cannot be an awesome affair if, to coin a nuclear term, it goes *critical*! There has been many a Station Commander fear for his base, and probably for his career, when his young aircrew have decided to enjoy themselves with single-minded dedication.

TRAINING

Fighter training – and in this term can be included fighter-bomber training – is an expensive pastime. Modern combat aircraft are valuable assets in themselves and are costly to run. A £20 million aircraft may be designed to give a life of 3,000 hours; on amortisation alone an hours flying time costs close to £7,000. This is before fuel and servicing costs are taken into account; a modern fighter at low level, using the afterburner, can be using fuel at the rate of three-quarters of a tonne a minute. The more complex the machines the greater the demand for manpower to service them at a time at which, with the volunteer force, 10 men cost £1 million over ten years and hundreds are required for a latter day squadron. It is a heavy investment.

The currently accepted wisdom is that, to remain reasonably competent, the fighter pilot should fly about 240 hours a year, or 20 hours a month. Many nations do not achieve that goal and suffer from the fact that operating budgets are the easiest for idle accountants to plunder; the shop window remains full of inventories which engender reassurance while only a small, and politically insignificant group, realise their true worth without the essential training to match the capabilities. Within NATO, where the norm is 240 hours per year, there are nations flying much less but few fly as little as the Soviet Air Force which fly regularly at half the NATO rates. It will be fascinating to see in time if the introduction of the modern generation of aircraft into the Soviet Air Force, such as the Flanker, Fulcrum and Foxhound, do not force them to modify their personnel structure and training doctrine in order to exploit more fully the capabilities offered by these advanced designs.

A Soviet pilot tends to stay much longer on the front-line squadron than his NATO counterpart, up to 15 years, and although flying only about 10 hours a month has, until recently, flown those hours on aircraft which are predominantly single role and in an operational environment which is more benign than in the West. Comparisons between the two philosophies are difficult to make with any confidence but it must be assessed how a two-year tour on a multi-role aircraft flying 20 hours a month equates to a 15 year tour on a single-role aircraft flying 10 hours a month. The difference may be finer than those who compare only the hours flown make out.

Quality of training matters enormously. The profession of *fighter pilot* in war must surely be one of the most lethal if matched against a comparable enemy. Even now, when such great strides have been taken to automate and to remove the load from the pilot, whether the fight is won or lost is still a function of his skills. Unless these are honed to a fine pitch in peace, the prospects of success in war are remote. Yet environmental pressures in densely populated North-West Europe have already conspired seriously to degrade the training necessary to exploit to the full the expensive equipment being procured.

What purpose can there be in investing multi-millions in a *Terrain Following Radar* to allow ultra-low level penetration of the enemy defences at night if crews are not allowed to train over their fellow citizens when it is dark? This is no attack on the *citizens* themselves – the author claims full rights under that term – for it is not to everyones liking to have a Tornado, 200 feet over the roof, at two-o'clock in the morning. No matter how familiar with aircraft noise there is no way that it is not going to spoil the night – and the humour.

The answer is to export as much of that sort of flying as possible to parts of the globe where the citizens are not disturbed and many NATO nations currently do so by conducting much of their ultra-low level training in the deserts of Nevada and the wastes of Canada, but there is a price to pay. The confusion factor of large industrial conurbations on a radar screen are quite absent from these two areas and few parts of Europe resemble the desert scrubland of Nevada which is devoid of the masts, pylons and power lines which can make low flying so tricky in Europe.

To train effectively, the aircrews must have the opportunity to use their weapons in peace. When these were iron bombs and machine guns this put no unacceptable strain on the budget. Now, a ground-attack weapon can cost £$\frac{1}{2}$ million and an air-to-air missile can cost £100,000 and, with the new active missiles planned to enter service, will quickly escalate to sums in the region of £250,000. Clearly, training in live missile firing cannot be conducted without a thought for the cost. A squadron pilot will probably fire only one such missile on his tour, two if his aircraft carries two types, and even this varies widely between air forces.

The more complex the weapon systems, the more important it is to conduct live missile firings. A successful firing depends on much more than merely the missile itself. It is the result of a successful interface with aircraft systems and it is these which require the live firing confidence check just as much as the pilot. Indeed, at one stage, a convincing argument was forwarded that the allocation of training missiles should be against the aircraft rather than the crews for this very reason.

Perhaps the environmental pressures have become more pronounced as peace extends and the memory of war becomes more dim. Much greater efforts may have to be made to explain to the citizen *why* his peace is being shattered by noisy aircraft at low level. There are varying ways of tackling the problem; one nation has issued bumper stickers proclaiming that *JET NOISE IS THE NOISE OF FREEDOM* but bumper sticker advocates tend to have wide interests and when stuck alongside *I LOVE NEW YORK* and *JAZZ IS GREAT* suggests that the driver might possibly be hard of hearing.

Where the right dialogue can be undertaken, the result can be a greater understanding of the problem and some better acceptance of the penalties for modern defence. At one station in Scotland the controller picked up the telephone to be assailed for a considerable time by a lady who was, to put it mildly, somewhat annoyed at having her peace shattered by a low flying aircraft. She was allowed to vent her fury before the controller interjected:

> Controller: 'Excuse me, Madam, can you tell me, was it one of ours?'
> Enraged Lady: 'Of course it was one of ours!'
> Controller: 'Thank God!'
> Enraged Lady: (after lengthy pause and in far less enraged tone) 'Young man, you have just made a very good point. Thank you.'

Although the ideal would be for training to be conducted in the area of intended operations, rather than not conduct the training, anywhere is better than nowhere. Despite the obvious disadvantages of Nevada from a terrain viewpoint, some of the most valuable training in the world is available there. This in the United States Air Force *Red Flag* exercise in which squadrons fly a series of sorties simulating the wartime pressures as realistically as is possible in peace. SAM and AAA systems are provided, many closely resembling likely hostile equipment; fighter opposition is provided by squadrons of *aggressor* pilots specially trained to fly the style and tactics of the threat, and who even operate with red stars on the side of their aircraft. Live weapons can be used on the extensive range area and big packages of aircraft can be operated at ultra-low level, in the order of 100 feet. It is the finest training available on the scene today.

The principle behind *Red Flag* rests on the fact, from the record, that the most lethal time in the career of a combat pilot is his first 10 operational sorties. If he can successfully survive those, the theory goes, he starts to develop his technique, his situational awareness and, in the round, his animal survival instincts. Red Flag attempts to give the pilot as close to the experience of those first ten operational sorties as possible and few pilots who have flown on the exercise would say that they are not better men for having done so. Red Flag is a modern manifestation of trying to do something about the vulnerability of inexperience which has been the concern of combat pilots throughout the ages. It returns the argument to the lethality of combat. It has always been lethal and the modern trend is making it even more lethal. It is the duty of a modern commander to prepare his men in peace to the maximum extent possible to enhance their chances of survival in war. Too many commanders avoid the difficulties and the unpopularity of that requirement but the United States Air Force can have confidence in a leadership which recognises the need for and supports training of the Red Flag type, even if, often, it is against vocal opposition.*

*Great strides have been made over the last few years in the use of simulation as an aid to training. It has assumed such importance that it deserves treatment in its own right. That it is not covered in this volume is due only to lack of space and the fear that casual comment could diminish its importance.

THE LEADER

What is *leadership?* If the dearth of sound common-sense books on the subject is a guide, it is a difficult thing to put across. Attempts are made to explain it by treatises on the inner psyche, by Freudian principles, and some would have it that the seeds are sown before the future warrior is out of his crib. All very difficult for anyone other than a psychologist, or even a psychiatrist, to grasp. Yet strangely, everyone knows what leadership is. We are presented with interfaces with *leaders* every day and most people could give examples from their own experience of those who they thought to be good leaders and, equally, could give as many examples of those who they would not be so keen to follow. Leadership qualities can be detected as much in their presence as in their absence. But putting together a consolidated view, as may be the requirement for an organisation trying to train leaders, is a formidably difficult thing to do. Everyone thinks they know what they mean, sometimes quite clearly, but somehow it evades capture on paper or as a training objective.

The test for those who feel that anything can be defined and taught is a simple one. Without using a direct comparison, describe the taste of a strawberry. Other than those allergic to strawberries, most will have tasted them and will know whether they like them or dislike them. They will be familiar with the taste, but can they describe that specific taste which makes the strawberry so different from the apple or the orange or whatever? Everyone knows exactly how strawberries interface with their particular likes and dislikes but few can give a convincing reason why.

So it is with leaders. What makes one man obtain the willing co-operation of others, who would follow him without question, while another is followed out of fear of regulatory powers or, worse, out of curiosity? It certainly does not seem to be physical stature for the great Napoleon was quite short, as were Nelson and Montgomery and, if physical appearance was so important, how was it that the great German nation followed blindly into the abyss a man who bore a close resemblance to Charlie Chaplin?

Perhaps it is not that difficult to answer the last question. Some years ago a film was shown of extracts from Adolf Hitler's speeches. At the completion, one of the small audience exclaimed, 'That was quite magnificent!' Another turned to him asking what had been said, because he did not speak German, 'Oh, neither do I,' said the first, 'it was magnificent because of the way he said it.'

A common thread amongst many successful leaders is the ability to stand before their troops and to inspire them with the spoken word. Montgomery was well known for it and even sniped at by detractors who equated it to a circus act or self-aggrandisement, yet is it not necessary for the troops to see the commander who may, on the morrow, send them to battle?

Slim was an advocate of the same technique and would have been more popular for it if, for some strange reason, the war in the Far East had not swallowed up its leaders more than the war closer to home. And what more successful leader than George S Patton, who was renowned for standing before his troops on every possible occasion giving them the benefit of his philosophy on a variety of topics and, usually, delivered with a vulgarity which brought international acclaim. What a commander, however! His performance with the United States Third Army after Normandy has still to be given the full credit it deserves.

So is this the secret? Stand before the men and inspire them? Care should be taken, for such a policy adopted by the wrong man could do more harm than good and could leave the troops questioning whether such an unimpressive creature, with nothing worth hearing to say, should be entrusted with their lives. But it is not necessarily the secret. As *Bomber* Harris proved at Bomber Command during the 1939–45 war, a quiet, remote man, not greatly blessed with the art of public speaking, could end up as the revered leader of a huge force of intelligent men who, despite the appalling losses suffered during the conflict, followed him without question.

T. E. Lawrence was talking about tactics when he wrote about its intangible nature but he could just as well have been referring to leadership when he wrote:

> Nine-tenths of tactics can be taught from books but the last tenth is like the Kingfisher flashing across the pool, and that is the test of Generals.

Can nine-tenths of leadership be taught from books? The proportion is largely a personal perception but certainly there are things which can be taught which can start a young officer, or even a young manager in business, off on the right track. Some of that teaching has to be the boring mechanics of organisation and administration, for how can a young officer look after his men if he does not know the workings of the organisation in which they both serve? There are ways of talking to those under command which encourge them to tell the reality of the situation rather than parrot what they consider the commander wants to hear and this is an essential element of command. How can a unit be commanded if the commander does not know what is going on within it?

Yet over-familiarity will surely ruin a unit. A man is happier having *the Colonel* or *the Major* order him over the top than *Joe* or *Sam*. In seeking a rapport with the men it is important that respect goes two ways. The military man has not only a desire to be properly and correctly commanded and led, but he also has a *right* to it. No commander does his men any favours by unilaterally removing from them that right by the imposition of over-familiarity.

Essentially, the matter of leadership boils down to personal perception. It is for each man to determine his leadership style and to argue to his own satisfaction those qualities in a leader which he, personally, would be prepared to follow. The four suggested here are merely those which the author, over the years, has either been impressed with in their commission, or appalled by in their omission.

The primary quality in a leader, particularly in a highly technical force such as an air force, is that he *knows his business*. Small errors in the direction of the air war can make such overwhelming differences to survival in the cockpit that the professional competence of air leaders must be beyond reproach. More than a few air forces find that the costs of modern aircraft operations preclude them keeping their senior command ranks current in front line equipment. In an area where technological change is occurring so fast this is a serious deficiency for the opportunities presented by the new equipment will go by default if the senior command chain cannot understand them for the lack of familiarity.

In peace most military forces withdraw into peacetime bureaucratic systems where promotion can depend on factors far from those pertaining in war. Senior commanders in peace can be those who have not necessarily proved their competence at the operational level as well as they might, and this gives them a credibility gap to overcome with front line crews. The cost and effort expended to keep the leadership abreast of the operational task can do nothing but good and will repay the investment manyfold. It is not right to ask of a man a standard of performance which the commander has not, at least at some time in his career, been able to produce. To do so is to resurrect the old Great War suggestion of the *château Generals*. Nothing could be worse for confidence and morale.

> 'Senior officers should fly because it is good for promotion, and the survivors are worth having.'
> *Batchy* Atcherly
> When Chief of the Pakistan Air Force

A leader needs to be a *people's man*. In the modern world this concept is so easily misunderstood because the mind is driven too easily to the perception of the do-gooder, the softy, the excuser of inadequacies. In the military sense the thrust is quite different. It demands a leader who is concerned for his men – *genuinely* concerned for them – not only in the sense of their immediate physical well-being, important as that is, but for their well-being as fighting men who could be called upon to operate on a lethal battlefield. *People men* are not soft commanders; on the contrary, if they are to do their duty to their men and prepare them for battle in such a way that they have the best possible chance of success, and thereby survival, the commander will be a hard task master. But he will never ask of his men anything which he himself would not be prepared to do. If he does so then, of course, there is no reason why he cannot be replaced by a machine in the not too distant future. And should be!

The leader must *believe in the cause*. There is no way of standing before a body of men and encouraging them to give of their all if the leader himself does not believe in the cause for which the effort is being demanded. Not only must he believe in it, he must be prepared to propound it enthusiastically. Western military forces are manned by some well educated and smart young men who will see through sham enthusiasm quickly. If a commander cannot give his wholehearted support to the cause, he should do the honourable thing and request to be relieved. Major issues are being referred to here; it would be no way to run a military force if squadron commanders threw resignation tantrums every time an instruction not to their liking was issued from the higher headquarters, for there will be enough of them. But on matters of principle the stand must be taken, not for the satisfaction of the commander but because of his duty to his men. Too few military forces construct their terms of service to enable the commander to perform this very important duty without the severest personal penalty to himself. Healthier forces would result if this was not the case.

Finally, in this abbreviated list of qualities, comes the most fundamental. The commander must *win*. Whatever the challenge; the Third World War, the inter-squadron skittles, a gunnery competition, the commander must lead his team to success for, ultimately, success breeds success and a team which believes in itself and its ability to succeed is a difficult one to stop even if the odds are stacked against them. Field Marshal Lord Slim, that distinguished commander of men once said:

> 'A Commander has failed in his duty if he has not won victory – for that is his duty. He has no other comparable to it'.

The easiest thing in the world, in peace, is to excuse failure. A thousand reasons can be dredged up to prove outrageous fortune the cause rather than poor planning or bad leadership. Demand for effort and results is traditionally seen to be something moving from the higher headquarters to the field units, yet there is just such a legitimate demand passing in the other direction. Not only should the senior command chain demand results from their juniors; the juniors should positively demand results from their seniors. Only in this way can the essential trust throughout the whole formation be moulded and that other intangible, *the team*, be welded into a war winning whole. It is a matter of *togetherness*, with each having his part to play and being held accountable to all the other players for the results he produces. The good units, squadrons, wings and higher, are the ones which can score highly against these obvious human requirements. The others come second and, as a previous commander of Strategic Air Command said:

'Show me a good loser, and I'll show you a consistent loser.'

He was, of course, right. No man makes his mark either on his men or on history with mediocracy, by coming second.

Who does not know of the victor of Trafalgar, even the name of his ship – Nelson and the *Victory* of course. But, be honest, can you remember who came second . . .?

Self-Test Questions

The questions set out below are intended as an aid to study. The answers are contained in the relevant chapters of the book or may be deduced logically from the information given in those chapters.

CHAPTER 2 – HISTORY

1. Consider the factors which acted against the development of weapons and tactics in the UK during the inter-war years 1918–1939 and seek parallels today.
2. Immelman and Lufberry gave their names to fighter manoeuvres:
    a. Briefly describe them.
    b. Which was basically offensive and which defensive?
    c. Why would they both be suspect on today's battlefield with modern weapons?
3. A study of the great aviation pioneers and the early 'aces' suggests that academic and physical prowess were largely irrelevant to success. Can a common human quality be detected amongst these men?
4. What was the most serious technical deficiency which hindered the development of aeroplanes in the early days?
5. Name the greatest single invention which improved aerial gunnery in the 1914–18 war, outline how it worked, and explain why it had such a beneficial effect.
6. Outline the major tactical formation improvements emerging from the Spanish Civil War, and explain why technical development had made them necessary.
7. Was there a difference between 'air intercept fighters' and 'air superiority fighters' in World War 2? Is there a difference now?
8. What were the merits and de-merits of the Me-262 which made the fast, slashing attack match its characteristics?
9. Contrast Me-262 tactics in World War 2 with MiG-21 tactics in Vietnam, and conclude.
10. Compare the North Korean 'Train' with the Lufberry 'Circle' and trace the logical development.
11. Why was the 'Train' less successful than could reasonably have been expected?
12. In no more than five lines, compare the F-86 Sabre, as flown in Korea, with the MiG-15 and decide which you would have preferred to fly in that conflict.

CHAPTER 3 – PEFORMANCE

1. Sketch a typical V-N diagram.
2. On the V-N diagram, indicate:
    a. Top speed.
    b. Maximum permitted 'G'.

    c. 'Corner-point'.

    d. Stall speed.

3. Either state the formulae for LIFT, or list the factors affecting it.

4. The relationship between Radius of Turn, 'G', Speed, Rate of Turn, and Angle of Bank, is important to aircraft performance calculations. What is it?

5. The Universal Turn Diagram plots speed and Rate of Turn on the 'x' and 'y' axis. Two further performance characteristics can be determined from the chart. What are they?

6. What is a 'doghouse' plot?

7. What is a 'Ps' line?

8. An aircraft flying in a Ps condition of zero pulls the stick back to climb. What other effects will be experienced?

9. What instantaneous climb rate does an aircraft have when on a 'Ps=400' line?

10. Instantaneous Turn Rate and Sustained Turn Rate are predominantly affected by either LIFT or THRUST. Which is affected by which?

11. On which Ps line is the best Sustained Turn Rate to be found?

12. Sketch the 'doghouse' plots to be expected for a World War 2 fighter and for a modern interceptor.

13. Given identical IR missiles with a head-on capability, which aircraft would you prefer to be in; a World War 2 fighter or a modern interceptor? Why?

14. From 13 above, how would you conduct your battle in both cases?

15. Is a sustained 9 'G' usable? If so, under what circumstances?

16. A modern high performance fighter may not necessarily apply full power for performance at the initial stages of an interaction. Explain the circumstances where it would be necessary to throttle-back initially to gain a performance advantage.

CHAPTER 4 – WEAPONS

1. State WIEN'S LAW.

2. Outline some implications of atmospheric absorption in the infra-red band.

3. IR missiles may home on to hot exhaust gases, hot metal in jet pipes or on the leading edges of structures which have been heated by high speed airflow. What IR bands are associated with these sources?

4. Given the answers to 3 above, use Wien's Law to determine the temperature ranges involved.

5. In the proportional navigation guidance in an air-to-air missile, explain the effect of different values of 'k' factor.

6. Consider the differences between aircraft cannon designed for air-to-air and air-to-ground use under the following headings:

    a. Muzzle velocity.

    b. Weight of charge/shot.

    c. Rate of Fire.

    d. Orientation of the gun line.

7. Air-to-air guns have increased their Rate of Fire by a factor of 10 over 70 years. What has been the incentive behind this development?

8. What is the primary operational disadvantage of IR missiles?

9. Head-on missile duels could become increasingly lethal. Explain the relevance of the 'F-pole'.
10. Why will 'active' missiles increase lethality in the missile duel?
11. How is overall missile reliability derived? Give some typical examples of the factors involved.

CHAPTER 5 – RADAR

1. Why is such a large increase in power, or in antennae gain required if the detection range of a radar is to be substantially increased?
2. By reference to the radar formulae, show why radar performance should get better with an increase in height.
3. Major reductions in radar cross-sectional area (RCS) are made possible by good design. Show why a decrease in RCS in the order of one-hundredth results in a detection range reduction in the order of two-thirds.
4. What are the two main design features which contribute to 'stealth'?
5. Passive warning systems can detect an emitting target normally before that target can itself obtain a detection. Why?
6. When active radar emissions from an air intercept radar become too dangerous to use in the modern battlefield, what alternatives are there?
7. Some may find it easier to explain radar principles by parallels with optics. Construct some such parallels.

CHAPTER 6 – BASIC FIGHTER MANOEUVRES

1. Describe a 'lag' turn.
2. Describe a 'lead' turn.
3. Describe a 'scissors'.
4. Repeat questions 1 to 3 – with your hands in your pockets!
5. Explain the circumstances which may call for the execution of a low-speed yo-yo.
6. A 'lag' turn might lead into the need for a high-speed yo-yo. Describe how this may occur.
7. If too great an Angle-off-Tail (AOT) is achieved in a yo-yo manoeuvre there is the danger of a counter. What is that counter?
8. A constant bearing approach results in what?
9. Express 8 above in terms of missile proportional navigational constant (k).
10. In a scissors, a roll reversal can cause less than optimum turn performance. What alternative manoeuvre can be performed?
11. Explain roll-coupling.
12. Outline the characteristics of a design which might be vulnerable to roll-coupling.

CHAPTER 7 – FORMATION MANOEUVRES

1. What is 'cross-cover'?
2. The cross-cover required is governed by the threat. What factors are involved?

3. What was the incentive for the development of the 'Loose Duce'?
4. Describe the 'sandwich' and outline the care required to ensure successful completion.
5. 80 per cent of all kills in modern combat have been obtained by what sort of assailant?
6. Why is it unwise to kill energy in a combat?
7. What is a 'spoofer'?
8. The multi-aircraft combat has been made more lethal by two qualities of the modern agile missile. What are they?

CHAPTER 8 – OPERATIONS

1. The resources necessary to maintain one aircraft on station on Combat Air Patrol varies according to the Turn-Round Time, the Transit Time, and the On-Station Time. According to what relationship?
2. Given a one-hour transit time outbound, a two-hour CAP, and a two-hour turn-round, how many aircraft are required to be possessed if the serviceability rate is 70 per cent?
3. As a prudent air commander, what resources would you maintain to cover the situation in 2 above? Why?
4. Tankers can be used profitably to extend loiter times or to extend the ranges of CAPs. They are not the complete answer because they cannot . . . what?
5. The CAP problem has been greatly magnified by the advent of what sort of offensive weapon system?
6. Explain the 'circumference effect'.
7. How does a low-RCS target exacerbate the circumference effect?
8. Consider some CAP management problems raised by various saturation attack scenarios at varying launch ranges. Calculate the total force sizes required to present an effective defence. Conclude.
9. Consider the matter of aircrew-to-aircraft ratios and suggest a prudent minimum to support 24 hour operations at sortie rates of up to three-sorties-per-aircraft-per-day.
10. How will your conclusions at 9 above be affected by operations under NBC conditions?

CHAPTER 9 – MAN, TRAINING AND LEADERSHIP

1. Name another creature which kills for sport.
2. List some of the qualities which are thought to point to success in flight training.
3. We shall 'genetically engineer' a fighter pilot. Select one quality each from three of the characters mentioned in Chapter Two and say what synergism you would be aiming for.
4. From your own daily scene – business, commerce, the professions, social, sport – identify one of your associates who you would be happy to follow. Select another who you would not consider following under any circumstances. Justify both choices.

5. List the qualities YOU look for in a leader.
6. Justify the ORDER of your list at 5 above.
7. Does a leader have to be a 'nice' man?
8. How strong is 'fear-of-failure' as a de-motivator?

Index